The events of the Holocaust have been well documented. Almost ninety percent of European Jewry was murdered. But for the survivors, the psychological impact of the Holocaust has stretched beyond 1945. An innocence has been eradicated. A view of their fellow man has been indelibly imprinted: "What did the world learn from the Holocaust?" a survivor was asked. "What the world learned from the Holocaust is that you *can* kill six million Jews and no one will care."

The Aftermath offers a perspective of how one who has lived with terror for years is able to avoid paralysis and move forward. It is a book about how people live with gnawing doubts and uncertainty concerning their past actions and inactions, doubts and uncertainties which can cause them to feel ambivalent about their very existence. It is a tale of the anguish they feel because they possess firsthand knowledge of the evil in people, which so unjustly struck and deprived them of what was rightly theirs. For while Holocaust survivors seem, in most ways, to be like you and me, they are also aware of a subterranean world which may afflict them without warning. It is far easier to extinguish human beings than to extinguish their memories.

This is also a book about the incredible resilience of human beings. The survivors you will hear from provide observations of how, after being reduced to less than zero during the formative years of adolescence and young adulthood, men and women were able to revive a self-respect which had been under continuous siege. And because survivors of the Holocaust will soon be gone, this is a unique opportunity to observe a case study of the elasticity of the limits of endurance, and the human need and capacity to reassert a vigorous life. As the mortality of survivors overwhelms them as a group, it may be not only the first but also the final occasion we will have to hear them describe their inner lives.

The Aftermath

The Aftermath

Living with the Holocaust

AARON HASS

CAMBRIDGE
UNIVERSITY PRESS

Published by the Press Syndicate of the University of Cambridge
The Pitt Building, Trumpington Street, Cambridge CB2 IRP
40 West 20th Street, New York, NY 10011-4211, USA
10 Stamford Road, Oakleigh, Melbourne 3166, Australia

First published 1995
Reprinted 1995
First paperback edition 1996

Printed in the United States of America

Library of Congress Cataloging-in-Publication Data is available.

A catalog record for this book is available from the British Library.

ISBN 0-521-47429-9 hardback
ISBN 0-521-57459-5 paperback

For my father, of blessed memory, Nusyn Majer Hasfogel

And for my grandparents, who did not survive,
Aron Hasfogel
Rajzla Hasfogel
Chil Cynamon
Drejzla Cynamon

Contents

Acknowledgments

I am grateful to Professor William Helmreich and Dr. Florabel Kinsler for their support and helpfulness during this project. My thanks to Alex Holzman for his unflagging enthusiasm. Foremost, I extend my respect for the courage and commitment of the Holocaust survivors who exposed their story and their pain so that others would understand.

Introduction

While doing background reading for my previous book about children of Holocaust survivors, I came across the vast literature concerning the postwar psychological adjustment of survivors themselves. The more pronouncements of mental health professionals about survivors I read, the more dumbfounded and exasperated I became. These were not the survivors who surrounded me during my lifetime. Were my perceptions, the perceptions of a clinical psychologist, so mistaken? Were survivors as depressed, as emotionally anesthetized, as unable to love, as dysfunctional as these authors would have us believe?

Indeed, survivors of the Holocaust underwent unimaginable persecution. And while we might assume that individuals who experienced physical and moral blows which exceeded historical boundaries of human cruelty *must* be irreparably damaged to the extent that they could no longer function as the rest of us do, my previous experience told me that this picture of immobilization did not accurately describe the Holocaust survivor. My subsequent investigation confirmed my belief.

This is a book about the incredible resilience of human beings. This is a book about those who survived the Holocaust and reassembled lives which had been completely and violently shattered. The survivors you will hear from provide observations of how, after being reduced to less than zero during the formative years of adolescence and young adulthood, men and women were able to revive a self-respect which had been under continuous siege. And because survivors of the Holocaust will soon be gone, this is a unique opportunity to observe a case study of the elasticity of the limits of endurance, and the human need and capacity to reassert a vigorous life. As the mortality of survivors overwhelms them as a group, this may be not only the first but also the final occasion we will have to hear *them* describe their inner lives.

This is a book about individuals, not about a phenomenon or syndrome. It offers a perspective of how one who has lived with terror for *years* is able to avoid paralysis and move forward. It is a book about how people live with gnawing doubts and uncertainty concerning their past actions and inaction, doubts and uncertainties which can cause them to feel ambivalent about their very existence. It is a tale of the anguish they feel because of their firsthand knowledge of the evil in their fellow man which so unjustly struck and deprived them of what was rightly theirs. For while the Holocaust survivor seems, in most ways, to be like you and me, he is also aware of his subterranean world, which may afflict him without warning. It is far easier to extinguish a man than to extinguish his memories.

Feelings of vulnerability are contagious. Although not directly experiencing the persecution of the Third Reich, children of Holocaust survivors have grown up in its shadow. As one member of the second generation remarked, "The most important event in my life occurred before I was born." Hearing the stories, absorbing the anxiety, anger, and pain of their mothers and fathers, creating fantasies of their parents' humiliation and torture, have instilled a degree of uneasiness in those who never encountered a member of the Schutzstaffel, or SS.

In August 1987, my mother asked my sister and me to accompany her on a journey back to Poland, back to before. We spent one afternoon at Treblinka. After walking throughout the grounds, my mother and sister returned to the awaiting taxi. I lingered at the railroad siding where Jews disembarked at the pathway that would lead them to death. I thought of those days and nights. I wept. And then I experienced what was, for me, the most revelatory and jarring moment of my trip. As I started to leave I felt a sudden tugging at me to remain. I felt an *obligation* to remain, to share the same fate as my brothers and sisters.

(In a 1993 interview, Krystyna Oleksy, deputy director of the Auschwitz Museum, spoke of being contacted recently by many Holocaust survivors who wished to be buried at Birkenau, the killing center of the massive Auschwitz complex. In the end, these survivors feel an obligation to remain as well.)

Introduction

For the first few years subsequent to her liberation from Bergen-Belsen at the age of eighteen, Malka Moskowitz,* whose parents, two brothers, and only sister were murdered, experienced nightmares frequently. Following the birth of her first child in 1948, sleep, as she described it, became "much more restful." Like many survivors, time and the regeneration of her decimated family had salved Malka's wounds. "I didn't dream about those things anymore." The night before our scheduled interview, however, Malka's sleep was punctuated by frightening images. "I was being chased by the Gestapo . . . but this time I had my children and grandchildren with me also. We were running and running. I was crying, but I was also trying to be strong. I was determined they shouldn't get us. We turned around the corner and they were there with guns. They shouted, 'Halt!' I screamed 'No!' and woke up." Malka's ongoing, subconscious feelings of personal vulnerability had now clearly spread to her postwar family.

Hungarian-born Ida Koch, a survivor of Auschwitz and Dachau, had chosen to bury her Holocaust life. In 1946, as rumors spread of the imminent closing of the Czechoslovakian borders by the Russians, she decided to dash for Palestine. "When I went to Israel, I decided I would never look back. I didn't think about that time. I didn't talk about those things. What I'm telling you I never told to my children. Last night I was thinking about the [upcoming] interview. I cried nonstop. Everything came back." The mere prospect of discussion had caused the collapse of defenses which Ida had fortified for decades.

Living in a sprawling suburban home, dressed in a cashmere sweater and gabardine pleated pants, seventy-seven-year-old David Himmelstein projected the confidence of a successful businessman and member of an exclusive golf club as he heartily shook my hand and ushered me to his dining room table for our meeting. However, David's social persona gradually fell away as he began to recount his Holocaust past. It dissolved completely as the narrative reached the point of his arrival at Auschwitz with his daughter. " 'Raus, verflucht Juden,' they were screaming." David stood abruptly and began pacing. "Raus, verflucht Juden." Tears welled up in his eyes. "And then they separated us." The tears were now falling down his ruddy

*In order to protect the privacy of those interviewed, all names of Holocaust survivors have been changed.

cheeks. Pacing, pacing more excitedly. "And they grabbed her away from me and pushed her to the line with the women. 'Daddy, don't leave me!,' she cried." David crumpled in his chair, buried his head in his folded arms and sobbed. "Daddy, don't leave me. Daddy, don't leave me." After a few moments, he looked up, attempted to compose himself, and apologized. "I didn't mean to . . . to cry . . . I usually don't cry in front of other people. . . . Nobody knows how painful it is. Nobody knows how I *really* feel."

Why did these survivors agree to be interviewed? Why did they put themselves through this ordeal? On many a drive home, I agonized: Did I have the right to prod these frayed nerves? During follow-up telephone contact with several survivors, I heard of sleepless nights and the disquieting aftermath of my questions and their answers. A Belgian national, Anna Maline, whose horrific odyssey included Auschwitz, Sachsenhausen, and Theresienstadt, wept often during our five hours together. After a particularly emotional juncture during which she described her arrival at Auschwitz, where she was shaven of all bodily hair and forced to stand naked for the humiliating examination by her captors, I asked, "Would you like to take a break?" "I survived Auschwitz. This is nothing," she responded.

These survivors wanted to be heard. Having kept his Holocaust self hidden all these years, Shimon Newman, who survived by masquerading as a Pole, remarked, "I don't want to die without having told at least someone how it was, how I felt." Shimon Newman wants us to know the full impact the Holocaust had on him, and not simply the events which occurred between 1939 and 1945. "Speaking about this is my way of mourning," Sol Feingold told me. "I dedicate this interview to all who were killed." After arriving as a family in Auschwitz, Sol's mother, father, and pregnant sister were immediately sent to the gas chambers.

Survivors had made promises to those who were murdered. Indeed, for many, staying alive to tell the world what they had witnessed became a vital motivating force during the Holocaust. "This is my obligation," Harry Goldberg intoned. "That's why I'm talking to you. Trust me, I don't need it." While most survivors successfully recreated a more than simply functional life after liberation, and experience an intense desire to "move forward and not look back," this orientation to the future did not imply a wish to forget. On the contrary, speaking with me was further evidence of their intention to remember.

I could not leave without having coffee and a piece of cake, Anna Maline insisted. We finished, and while putting the dishes in her kitchen sink, I thanked her.

"Your interview has been very helpful. I know how difficult it was – "

"You don't understand," she interrupted. "I'm glad somebody wants to listen. Mostly, people don't want to listen. Thank you for wanting to hear. Thank you for wanting to write about it, for being interested."

No one ever asked survivors how they *felt* then. No one asks survivors how they feel now. We may have learned the facts, or even the details, of what transpired, but we do not know about their lasting, emotional effects. (Yet we have the *illusion* of knowing survivors because we have seen Elie Wiesel's pained expression in numerous documentaries.)

The mental health community, writers, and artists have focused their attention on the pathological inheritance of the Holocaust, but they have rarely acknowledged or credited the strengths residing in survivors, which not only have enabled them to pick up the shattered pieces of their lives but also in many cases have resulted in more than adequate postwar functioning. One reason for this failure to note the positive adjustment of many survivors may be the fear of permitting the denial of the trauma's severity. We may feel forced to emphasize survivors' subsequent pain in order not to minimize the reality of previous losses and the pitiless brutality to which they were subjected. Nevertheless, to understand the survivor, to understand the obstinacy of the human spirit not to be permanently squashed, we must also appreciate the successes of those who emerged.

I interviewed fifty-eight Jewish survivors for this work. They came from eleven countries – Poland, Hungary, Czechoslovakia, Rumania, Denmark, Holland, France, Germany, Yugoslavia, Belgium, Austria – and all were caught in the net of the Third Reich for most of the war. They are all presently living in the United States. However, several had first emigrated to Palestine/Israel and chose – after enduring several years of hard labor, inadequate living facilities, and the lack of physical security owing to the ongoing state of hostilities – to make their life an easier one in America. They believed they had already experienced more than their fair share of hardship. Each interview was conducted in the survivor's home and lasted an average of four hours. Except for six, whom I knew superficially through our contact at Holocaust-related functions, the survivors and I were strangers before I got in touch with them. Many, however, had heard of me or my most recent book, *In the Shadow of the Holocaust: The Second Generation*.

Approximately one-third of those I approached refused me. "I want to leave all that buried," they emphasized. One female broke off our interview in midstream as her emotions threatened to overwhelm. Some had never before spoken about their Holocaust past. A few had recorded their testimonies for various archives. None, however, had participated in a nonclinical exploration of the lingering postwar consequences of their previous adversities.

Indeed, for most survivors, it is their Holocaust story which preoccupies them. It is the Holocaust which must be spoken of and remembered: If I have any difficulties now, this is nothing compared to what was. And besides, it already was. I can't do anything about it. You just pick up the pieces and move forward. Of course, not everything is always smooth, but so what? You do what you have to do.

And yet, they weep. Fifty years later.

Although the focus of my interview was on their postwar life, I asked survivors, at the outset, to tell me briefly about their circumstances during the Holocaust. I not only desired a context for my understanding of their adjustment, but I also wanted them to contact those crucial formative years as they attempted to make sense of their life which followed. I understood that I might also find coincidences of certain factors or experiences during the Holocaust and postwar psychological effects.

On several occasions I debated whether to continue this project, distressed to see the pain elicited by the material. As a child of Holocaust survivors, I grew up hearing my parents' often repeated plea designed to control my behavior and limit its potential for causing further anguish: "How could you do this to me after all I've been through?" Perhaps this subconscious taunt periodically disheartened my resolve.

It is singularly disturbing to see older, vigorous men and women cry. We are shaken by the fragility of those who are parental figures, of those who have promised to protect us by the natural strength inherent in parenthood. For these were my parents. There was so much overlap between other survivors' experiences and, more notably, feelings, with those of my own mother and father. They spoke with accents. They gestured alike. They wanted me to eat.

At the same time, I wanted to know and understand more about their past as a way of drawing closer to my own immediate and extended family. The more I knew about what it was like then, the greater would be my capacity to grasp the circumstances of the murder of my grandparents, my aunts, my uncles, and others, and others.

So I wanted to absorb their stories as well as understand their consequences. Because of time constraints during the interview, I always found myself wanting to hear more of what it was like then, and having to control that urge. And there was a part of me which believed (as survivors do) that the stories, the events, are so overwhelmingly important to acknowledge and remember that my focus was misplaced. Despite the numerous personal memoirs about life and death during those years, and paucity of first-person accounts of the aftermath, I still wanted more of the former. It seems as if there is never enough. Perhaps there should be six million stories of six million victims. For those who did not return – they, too, *deserve* to be known. How prisoners were forced to line up in the bitter cold of December at Flossenburg, told to strip naked, and hosed down. More than one hundred at that *Appell* (roll call) froze to death.

"In the ghetto, there was a little child about four years old. And she was a very happy and friendly child. Even the Nazis liked to talk to her. One day she was walking alone and one of the Nazis asked her if she would like a candy. 'Would you close your eyes and open your mouth?' And he shot her in the mouth."

And, as we move further away from the events, because these narratives are so unimaginable, so contrary to our self-perception, more and more voices will assert that they must have been embellished. At the very least, men, women, and children will simply become blurred, abstract numbers. For most, including Jews, the Holocaust is already a piece of distant history. For survivors, the Holocaust was *yesterday* . . . and today.

Introduction

In the spring of 1989 I was invited by the Goethe University of Frankfurt as a Visiting Professor to teach "The Psychohistory of the Holocaust." Understandably, I met resistance from the university-age Germans who attended my lectures about the historical and racial aspects of the Final Solution. However, on a day when I began speaking of the postwar lingering of that period on survivors, I sensed a change in mood, a greater attentiveness, a certain sympathy. The fact that, for hundreds of thousands of individuals, the Holocaust did not end in 1945 was a new concept for these students. This was a contemporary phenomenon, one which coincided with their own carefree lives. (A postscript: Toward the end of my stay, I was approached by a representative of the university administration and asked if I would consider returning the following spring to teach the course again, and perhaps make this an annual event. During that interval, the Berlin Wall, a symbol of punishment for what the Nazis had initiated, was dismembered. When the moment arrived to finalize arrangements, the university suddenly seemed far less interested in presenting such a course, citing budgetary constraints. Reunification had provided further impetus to the German desire to close the book on that period of their history.)

Survivors despair. "I'm glad I can tell what happened, because people don't believe it. . . . People don't want to believe what happened to us," Anna Maline laments. Anna and her comrades dread that the Holocaust will be forgotten or distorted. Anna understands that we want to forget, that we want to move away from reminders of peril. She is also keenly aware that she and others like her will soon pass away and there will be no one with the credibility of the eyewitness to tell us what occurred. But many survivors also feel the personal relief of self disclosure, and a responsibility fulfilled in their efforts to prod our collective conscience.

"I never talk about it. Now, I talked with you. It's like I told the world."

1

A view of survivors

For several decades after its conclusion, little was written about the Holocaust. However, the past twenty years have witnessed an explosion of material. Histories, personal memoirs, fictionalized accounts of life and death under the Third Reich, are plentiful, but far less has been noted concerning the postwar consequences of those traumatic years. During the late 1960s, clinical reports surfaced which described the lingering psychological effects of the Holocaust on survivors. A few survivors, such as Jean Améry, wrote eloquently of their personal estrangement from society, their continuing feeling of being the "other."[1] Fifteen years later, attention was turned to the second generation in order to ascertain what effects had been passed on and how those transmissions mutated and defined themselves. Many researchers asking these questions were children of survivors. In recent years, survivors who were young children during the war have recognized unique reactions because of their particular developmental stage and experiences.

Survivors of the Holocaust, particularly Jewish survivors, are often seen as a unitary phenomenon by both mental health professionals and laypersons. And yet the experiences of individual Jews during World War II varied markedly. Some Jews spent most of the time in hiding, and some eluded capture by posing as Gentiles, with forged papers as proof. Others lived in ghettos and concentration camps and endured slave labor for periods of varying duration, while thousands more were exiled and confined in work camps in the Soviet Union. A handful fought in the forests as partisans. Survivors were not only differentially affected by the diverse circumstances into which they were forced, but by the *details* of those circumstances. For example,

1

while in a concentration camp, was he helped and emotionally supported by another, thus allowing him to retain a faith in humanity?

Most survivors (particularly those who lived in Eastern Europe) experienced the murder of immediate and extended family members. Many lost a spouse or children. But some were lucky enough to have retained a mother, a father, sisters, or brothers. Obviously, survivors' personalities during the prewar years were as disparate as those in any large group of people. Psychologists also recognize that previous life stressors may inoculate the individual against extreme trauma. Observers noted that in the worst of the concentration camps in the east, Jews who arrived from Western countries were likely to become mortally demoralized more quickly than those who had lived for protracted periods amidst the abominable ghettos of Poland.

In 1964, after years of clinical experience in diagnosing and treating concentration camp survivors, William Niederland, a psychiatrist and himself a refugee from Nazi Germany, published a landmark study proclaiming the existence of a "survivor syndrome." He listed a host of symptoms manifest in individuals who had survived Nazi persecution: chronic anxiety, fear of renewed persecution, depression, recurring nightmares, psychosomatic disorders, anhedonia (an inability to experience pleasure), social withdrawal, fatigue, hypochondria, an inability to concentrate, irritability, a hostile and mistrustful attitude toward the world, a profound alteration of personal identity, and, in many cases, hallucinations and depersonalization (an alteration in the perception of the self so that the feeling of one's own reality is temporarily lost.)[2]

Leo Eitinger, a psychiatrist and Holocaust survivor who had extensive clinical contact with many concentration camp survivors in Norway and Israel, observed a similar survivor syndrome:

The most predominant sequel to the concentration camp activity seems to be the deep changes in personality, a mental disability which affects every side of the personality's psychic life, both the intellectual functions, and especially, emotional life and the life of the will, with the many facets of difficulties in adaptation and the complications which this leads to in the victim's life. Chronic anxiety states, often provoked by nightmares and/or sleeplessness at night, by disturbing thought associations and memories during the day, chronic depressions of a vital type, inability to enjoy anything, to laugh with

2

others, to establish new, adequate, interpersonal contacts, the inability to work with pleasure, to fill a position – in short, the inability to live in a normal way – are among the most characteristic symptoms of this condition.[3]

Niederland's and Eitinger's reports focused attention on a group of individuals who, in many ways, had been forgotten. The shocking newsreels of the concentration camps were no longer in view, and the world was preoccupied with the ongoing, inevitable stream of pressing newspaper headlines. But Niederland and Eitinger insisted that persecution had left lasting, perhaps permanent, effects on the survivors, and that the conclusion of the war, the liberation of camp inmates, and the resettlement of refugees had not meant an end to the effects of the Nazi atrocities. The studies by these two men became the point of departure for most psychiatric pronouncements about survivors.

Subsequent articles by other professionals reported a variety of other symptoms and advanced similar explanatory theories. They stated that the intense depression survivors felt led to complete social withdrawal, seclusion, and profound apathy. Survivors were overwhelmed by indelible and grotesque images of death.[4] They isolated themselves because they believed no one could understand or appreciate the horrors they had been through. They had been immersed in a different reality, the world of the *Lager* (camp), a world which would be absolutely incomprehensible to others. A sense of alienation naturally ensued.

Survivors, these writings asserted, would forever have difficulty establishing close relationships. They had lost a basic trust in people because of their own persecution and because they had witnessed the physical and mental deterioration of their parents. Unconsciously, they maintained a fierce anger because their parents had been unable to protect them from such devastation. Furthermore, it was hypothesized, survivors had difficulty "reinvesting in life" and were deeply ambivalent about founding new families.[5] Indeed, a few survivors chose not to have children after the war. They would not allow themselves to become emotionally attached because they feared another precipitous separation.

Some studies reported that the emotional responses of survivors had a pervasively shallow quality. "Psychic numbness" or "psychic

3

closing off" were terms used to describe survivors' inaccessibility to feelings. During the Holocaust, while they were experiencing the overwhelming losses and stresses and the resultant intolerable anger or fear, survivors blocked out all capacity for emotion in the interest of continuously adapting to their changing, hostile environment. Emotional awareness would have brought the potential for demoralization, and it would have distracted from the task at hand – surviving one more day. Although this defense was valuable at the time, its lingering deployment was obviously maladaptive.[6]

Psychosomatic symptoms such as ulcers, hypertension, and premature aging emerged among many survivors who would not allow themselves an emotional catharsis. Some researchers concluded that survivors' massive repression of wartime memories resulted in their generally blunted ability to feel. Contradicting these assessments, other clinicians reported that their survivor patients ruminated excessively about their Holocaust experiences, were preoccupied with mourning, and were generally hyperemotional. Some were subject to fits of violence, as previously suppressed rage, too dangerous to express at the time of persecution, emerged. In psychiatric writings about survivors, contradictory findings abound.

The bleakest psychological snapshot of survivors may have been taken soon after their ordeal, when the imprints of previous blows were most palpable, and when the individual had not yet accepted and adapted to a new life bereft of all those who were lost forever. Later reports of the perennial depression and anger observed in some survivors may have resulted from their failure to engage in "grief work," the necessary mourning of losses. During the war, they had been unable to afford the luxury of that letdown. After the war, they faced the pressures of adapting to a new country, a new language, new customs, and new responsibilities.

However, most survivors suppressed their post-trauma symptoms as they desperately wanted to get on with life once again, "to look forward, not back," as so many of my interviewees reported. They also soon learned that sympathy or compensation would not be forthcoming from others, who appeared uninterested in their Holocaust past.

When asked, "How did you make it through?" most survivors answer, "Luck." For in addition to acknowledging that many stronger and craftier people did not last, those who did experienced countless

4

close calls, made split-second decisions based on little information, and witnessed the death of others who were less fortunate. The attribution of luck may, however, have subtle implications. If one believes one is alive simply or mostly because of luck, one may live with an uneasiness, a fearfulness. Just as one was given life by chance, something just as capricious may snatch it away.

The average human being believes in what psychologists refer to as the "Just World Hypothesis." In order to make sense of the environment and avoid the anxiety producing perception that the world operates on a random basis, we believe that people get what they deserve. I want to believe that bad things happen to bad people and that, because I am basically a good person, misfortune will not befall me as it does to those less deserving. But because most Holocaust survivors do not necessarily attribute survival to their intelligence, their wits, or their unusual fortitude, they are denied this comforting hypothetical illusion. On the contrary: most Holocaust survivors believe, "After what I witnessed and experienced, *anything* can happen to *anyone*." On the contrary: many Holocaust survivors will tell you, "The best – the gentlest, the most sensitive, the most pious – did not survive." It is not surprising, therefore, that most survivors have been unable to rebuild their trust in the workings of the world, or, for that matter, in their fellow human beings.

Most early clinical reports presented a very skewed picture of survivors. They were, for the most part, based on evaluations of patients who deemed themselves sufficiently psychologically disabled to require intervention. (Actually, those who found their way to a psychotherapist often presented physical complaints as opposed to psychological ones as most bothersome.) We know, however, that the overwhelming majority of Holocaust survivors have never sought psychiatric assistance. The most widespread distortions in the composite picture of survivors may have occurred because almost all mental health professionals conducting their psychotherapy operated from a psychoanalytic viewpoint, notorious for its emphasis on and assumptions of psychopathology. These therapists often generalized falsely about the *group* of survivors from single dramatic case studies or impressions derived from contact with very few patients. Theories about human behavior demand generalizations, a selective blindness to individual differences, a leveling to a common

5

denominator, oversimplification. One psychotherapist wrote, "These victims show a submissive, compliant, and always fearful attitude, since they are still afraid of punishment and retaliation from authority figures." While this description may have been valid for a particular patient, it is not true of all or most victims of the Holocaust. A prominent psychiatrist in Los Angeles described the concentration camp inmate's behavior as "sadomasochistic regression." The Jew's masochistic needs, he wrote, *provoked* the sadistic impulse of the SS: a typically neat psychoanalytic pathological complementarity. Another analyst stated:

The acceptance of the slave role may become a permanent characteristic of the survivor, some of whom act as though they have never been liberated. In a few cases, we found a severe inhibition of intellectual function, memory, and interest in anything outside of work and home routines . . . a complete compliance with the picture of the slave laborer permitted to live only if he worked and blindly followed orders, without manifesting any interest or action of his own.[7]

A few recent studies continue to present this dark view of survivors. In an article appearing in 1989, two Israeli scholars, Arie Nadler and Dan Ben-Shushan, compare the results of a battery of personality tests derived from a nonclinical sample (i.e., those not in psychotherapy) of Jewish concentration camp survivors from Poland with a group of similar background who came to Palestine before 1939. Compared to the earlier immigrants, the Holocaust survivors rated themselves less emotionally stable, less emotionally expressive and spontaneous, less assertive, lower in energy level, more depressed, less adequate and worthwhile, more prone to psychosomatic symptoms, more likely to experience insomnia, and more fearful. Two-thirds of the survivors in Nadler and Ben-Shushan's study reported that they could not enjoy life and one-third reported recurring suicidal thoughts.[8]

The Holocaust survivors whom I interviewed presented quite a different profile in many respects, one which, contrary to the descriptions just mentioned, reflects their significant success at coping with a traumatic past. Nadler, Ben-Shushan, and others rarely assess the strengths or the triumphs of survivors over their emotional difficulties. There is little mention of the survivor's flexibility, assertiveness, and tenacity which have allowed her to adapt to a new life. And while the survivor has been photographed through the clinical lens of "survivor syndrome" or post-traumatic stress disorder, her everyday perceptions, thoughts, and feelings have often been lost.

Several recent studies comparing Holocaust survivors with those who came to Palestine before the outbreak of World War II also indicate few psychological differences between the two groups (except perhaps the greater tendency of survivors to invest more energy in their work).[9] Emphasizing his use of a nonclinical sample of 245 survivors who emigrated to the United States, one researcher reported that he, too, found no consistent indication of a "concentration camp syndrome."[10] Indeed, the mental health status of the typical Holocaust survivor is often just as affected by postliberation factors – the extent to which one perceives the Holocaust to have affected one's physical health, marital satisfaction, economic resources, the presence of supportive family and friends, religious affiliation, and the extent of self-disclosure of Holocaust experiences – as by past ones.

Because of the significant diversity in survivors' post-Holocaust adjustment, one would expect that children of survivors, individuals one generation removed from the catastrophe, would therefore evidence an even wider range of Holocaust-related reactions. Yet, just as generalizations have been offered to describe a survivor syndrome, so, too, many investigators have adopted an assumption of the *inevitability* of transmission of pathology from survivors to their children.[11] It is asserted that because Holocaust experiences negatively affected the survivor's capacity for human relations he or she has been unable to be an effective parent, and that this disability has had damaging psychological ramifications for children raised by these adults. "It is reasonable to assume," two researchers observed, "that the price of survival for these people may have been deep rooted disturbances within the families they formed after liberation."[12] A psychologist noted: "Given children of survivors' unique interaction with their parents' Holocaust history, the development of alternative feeling states and an altered view of social life is to be expected. The survivors' Holocaust experiences are evidence of an unprecedented distortion of human social relations. They inevitably incorporated their experiences into their world view, and passed their perspectives to their children."[13] More specifically, it has been suggested that "based on clinical experiences with such patients (children of survivors) our impression is that these individuals present symptomatology and psychiatric features that bear a striking resemblance to the concentration camp survival syndrome described in the international literature."[14]

Indeed, many children of survivors echo problematic themes. They often display an ambivalence when relating to their parents and the shadow of the Holocaust. Depression frequently results from an overidentification with their parents. On the other hand, those who have chosen to extricate themselves from their Holocaust-filled environment are prone to feel guilty about having done so.[15] They see themselves as having abandoned anguished loved ones who are in emotional need. Identification with a survivor parent provides the child with a sense of closeness and understanding. Relinquishing some of the characteristics (for example, depression, anger) displayed by the parent may be perceived by the self as traitorous.

At the other extreme, we find children of survivors who feel that their parents are claustrophobically and myopically obsessed by the Holocaust. They crave a wider view of the world, one not preoccupied with death and persecution, one not constantly reminding them of the ineradicable difference between Jew and Gentile, one not mired in fear and pessimism. (One child of survivors mentioned that she purposely chose to attend an elite WASP college in order to escape her narrowly focused, Jewish survivor world. Another remarked: "I went out of my way not to be like my parents, not to get sucked into those Holocaust-related dynamics. That's how I survived my family.")

Becoming an individual and abandoning the felt obligation to care for survivor parents have been difficult tasks for many children. Parents may have communicated that they could not endure another separation, even the normal developmental disengagement that must occur between parent and adolescent so that the child may develop an identity of his or her own. Disengagement from children may have elicited feelings associated with previous separations and subsequent loss of family members. Survivors may not have had much empathy for their child's struggle because they had no opportunity to learn how to move away naturally, both physically and psychologically, from their own parents and thus did not experience the importance of that process. Finally, in order to justify their existence and alleviate survivor guilt, some survivors may have encouraged dependence in their children. "You are proof of why I had to live." And that proof must always be close at hand to serve as a reminder of their raison d'être.

In fact, we find great variability of response by the second generation to the events which preceded their birth. Within the same family, siblings have often expressed differences in their interest in either the history of the Holocaust or the unique experiences of their parents. Some have been more debilitated by anger, fear, and feelings of deprivation than others.[16]

Obviously, Holocaust survivors had differing personalities and predispositions before 1939. Differences in survivors' wartime environments and in their specific experiences (witnessing a parent or child killed, for example) may also account for variations in their later adjustment. Some researchers have naively quantified the stress quotient assumed to be inherent in various conditions and correlate it with the present symptoms of survivors. Posing as a Gentile would, therefore, be assessed as a less stressful hardship than being in a slave labor camp. Cowering in an attic for a protracted time would be considered a less traumatic occurrence than being exposed to six months of Auschwitz. Ironically, in today's survivor community there is a self-imposed hierarchy of suffering. Those who lived through it in "milder" circumstances are often hesitant to speak of their experiences, deferring to those who were in the "worst" places. This stance also diminishes their ability to derive the sense of strength and heroism at having made it through which other survivors of Stuthof or Ravensbruck access. (There are very few first-person accounts written by those who, fleeing eastward, were incarcerated by the Russians and sent to the work camps of Siberia. Many of these prisoners emerged years later with no knowledge of what had befallen the Jews of Europe.)

But how does one measure fear? Before a rumored roundup of Jews, sixteen-year-old Martha Janusz fled from her home in Chelm, Poland, to Warsaw. Speaking Polish without a trace of Jewish accent and having blond hair emboldened her to register as a Pole and volunteer for work in Germany. During her time in Warsaw and three years in Germany, she lived not only in constant fear of being unmasked but with a dreaded sense of isolation as well. "Every day I looked death in the face . . . . I was so lonely. I thought many times that all the Jews had been annihilated." Armed with a story of her fictional family

9

life in Poland, she attended mass every morning. "Until today," Martha whispered to me, "I carry my rosary in my purse *all* the time."

Even if a Holocaust survivor never had a gun put to her head or received permission to live for another day because she was not singled out during a morning *Appell* at a concentration camp, she had knowledge of others like her who were stamped for annihilation and murdered. She knew that the laws of probability were against her, a Jewess. And she thereby was forced to confront her mortality *continuously*. Moreover, just as the survivor's all too human fundamental assumptions about her invulnerability were shattered, her assumptions about the world's being a just place where the good are rewarded and the bad are punished were also shattered.

Observations suggest that those who actively fought back as partisans emerged from the Holocaust with a greater part of their self-worth intact. They were not paralyzed by feelings of powerlessness. Their wartime activities also allowed for the discharge of a rage which has gone unexpressed for most survivors. Beryl Hyman, however, remembers the need to disguise his Jewishness from the AK, the Polish resistance movement. Indeed, when his true identity was discovered, he was threatened with death. And while Beryl escaped the antisemitic clutches of his countrymen, hundreds, perhaps thousands, of Jews were killed as they attempted to join their "allies" against a common enemy.

Any *potential* effects of particular stressors on a person will always depend on that person's *perception* of the stressors, as well as on his or her coping skills. Defense mechanisms, such as denial, which produce a maladaptive response under normal circumstances may provide the means to survival in a calamitous environment. The probability of emerging alive from Auschwitz was infinitesimal, but Rose Friedland chose to believe otherwise. "I knew there was no way to leave Auschwitz alive. Either you went through the chimney or you were carried out dead. I still did not believe *I* would die." Rose shut out what appeared to be the inevitable. If she had not, she might have answered the rhetorical question, Why continue to suffer when there is no hope of freedom?

Most inmates spent a great deal of their time in fantasy, another escape from the surrounding brutalities of everyday life. Others simply willed themselves not to think about painful subjects. "I promised myself in camp not to think about my wife and daughter because it would kill me." Many, overwhelmed by feelings of desolation, simply gave up. Everyone knew the look, the shuffle of the Musselman. A few, however, were fortunate enough to view the everyday obstacles to survival as *challenges* to be overcome. They were determined to outwit, to outlast their tormentors.

Within each situation, there were mitigating factors other than the intrapsychic coping style of the individual. Having a parent or a sibling at one's side often injected morale and a sense of security. "I always had the comfort of hugging with my mother. This comfort surpasses everything," noted Regina Shomer. As a youngster of fifteen, Regina believed her mother "would always find a way." Not having her father to hold in her arms, Fela Kornblatt manufactured him. "I always felt like my father was watching over me, helping me make decisions, telling me what to do." However, some of the most traumatized survivors were those who, in close proximity to their loved ones, looked on helplessly at their deterioration.

How does one measure the stress, the pain, which Harry Wendel experienced as he was made to sort the clothes of tens of thousands shot at Ponar and came across a dress he recognized as his mother's favorite?

We know that even within kingdoms of the night such as Auschwitz, there were those who endured in more favorable circumstances than others. Being assigned a function which sheltered you from the cold, having a job which provided direct access to a bit more nourishment or enabled you to "organize" and eventually barter goods you could temporarily secret away for future food, were indispensable. The routine was designed to kill you. Simply going along with the program was fatal. And, as survivors repeatedly mentioned, "It's all relative." After choosing a place to meet should they both survive, seventeen-year-old Martin Bornstein bid farewell to his father, who was lying inert on the top tier of his bunk in Birkenau. Martin was transferred to Auschwitz. "It felt a little like heaven. For the first time, I had a bed, a blanket, a little food."

Of course, the stress, the traumas, associated with the Holocaust did not begin in the concentration camps. Initially there were the expulsions from certain occupations and from the educational opportunities necessary for them. Jewish children were first forbidden to attend schools with Gentiles, then their own schools were closed. Material deprivation and the elimination of individuality and privacy as Jews were forced to wear the yellow star and crowded into ghettos followed. Sonya Bernstein described humiliation which struck blatantly. "When the women were being searched for valuables and they didn't believe you and they searched down there . . . the screaming, it was terrible." For Bela Kornbluth, it insidiously gnawed. "We had to get off the sidewalk when a German approached. Can you believe it? . . . Why? Was I not a human being too? Why?"

When . . . the phase of deportation and extermination started in 1942, it found the Jews psychologically deadened, with only minimal objective chance and very little subjective, and even less collective psychological strength to cope actively with the threat of death.[17]

Between the ages of twelve and fifteen, Halina Birenbaum was incarcerated in the Warsaw ghetto, Majdanek, Auschwitz, and Ravensbrück. "The reality of Majdanek weighed me down even more than that pile of bodies under which I almost stifled in the railroad car. I was thirteen. The years of persecution in the ghetto, the loss of my father and my brother, and most painful of all, the loss of my mother, had impaired my nervous system, and at a time when I should have forced myself to be as resistant as possible, I broke down completely. . . .

"We had to fight for everything in Majdanek: for a scrap of floor space in the hut on which to stretch out at night, for a rusty bowl without which we could not obtain the miserable ration of nettle soup which they fed us, of yellow stinking water to drink. But I was not capable of fighting. Fear and horror overcame me at the sight of women prisoners struggling over a scrap of free space on the floor, or hitting one another over the head at the soup kettles, snatching bowls. Hostile, aggressive women, wanting to live at any price. Stunned, aghast, famished, terrified, I watched them from a distance. Had it not been for Hela [her sister-in-law], her boundless devotion and constant care, I would have perished after a few days. Hela had vowed inwardly to my mother that she would take her place, and she kept her vow."[18]

Halina ends her account with her indebtedness to Hela. Many survivors of the camps readily admit that without the opportune advice, emotional support, or physical help of another, they would not be alive today. As Halina's testimony also demonstrates, survivors were debilitated not only by what occurred to them personally, but also by what they witnessed. The whimsical beatings and murders. The cannibalism at Bergen-Belsen. The babies thrown out of the fourth-story windows of the hospital in the Lodz ghetto to splatter on the sidewalk. The fear, the complete loss of faith in humanness, the understanding of the depths and freedom of malevolence. How does one measure those effects?

During the interviews, the most frequently used word by survivors was "innocent." Why did I have to suffer? Why did they have to die? These questions superseded particular circumstances which engulfed individual survivors during the Holocaust. There was no solace to be found in rationalizing one's fate as punishment for a crime or sin committed. With no response forthcoming, survivors' distress was further fueled then, even as it is now.

"How can anyone understand the *fear*? . . . How many times I had to stand naked in front of the SS and model for them. . . . Any blemish on your body could sentence you at Auschwitz. . . . We didn't live five years of Holocaust. We lived a thousand years of degradation, humiliation, and torture.

"Everyone felt the same. Fear, degradation, fear. Ten times fear. How to survive. How not to be hungry. How not to be hit. I had to always be clean. I asked my sister every day, 'Do I look clean?' If you weren't, finito.

"I was a human being. Why did I have to step off the sidewalk if a German was coming? How could they treat me like that? It was so *senseless*."

There are so many factors, apart from the situation in which the survivor found herself, which contributed to the degree of stress she experienced. One of the most painful, and in many instances still psychologically unresolved, moments occurred during the abrupt separation of survivor from a mother, a father, or a child. The sudden loss. The violent detachment. The helplessness. The feeling of being utterly alone.

"I arrived with my mother to Auschwitz. It was night and the lights, and the dogs, and the screaming . . . I was frightened. My mother kept stroking my face, 'Don't worry, we will be okay. Don't worry, we will be okay.' And it only took a few moments and she was gone. I ran after her screaming,

'Mother! Mother!' . . . and she reached out her arms with a bewildered look . . . I can never forget that look."

Ironically, for many survivors the anguished legacy of the Holocaust commingles with an enhanced confidence in one's abilities to prevail in the future. "I survived Auschwitz. I can survive anything" is a theme echoed by those who lived in extremis. Indeed, they fear and brace themselves for the next onslaught. The survivor's informed thoughts assert themselves. The world and its inhabitants, man and woman, have proven their capacity for evil and destruction. But now, I am ready. And this time *I* will win.

Yet, this perception of one's environment must exact a toll. One is always prepared and alert. One reacts swiftly and urgently, too swiftly and too urgently, to threats, imagined or real. For what is at risk is not merely this or that, but everything – just as everything and everyone was lost then.

I did not include in my sample survivors who were young children during the Holocaust. Much evidence suggests that the many psychological consequences with which they grapple differ from those of survivors who were somewhat older at the time. Most of those who emerged derive some pride from their survivorhood. Because of how young they were, child survivors do not have that memory (real or fabricated) of strength and resilience to draw upon. They did not actively contribute to their victory over their persecutors. It is not surprising that we hear less from them.

"Many of the child survivors had a tremendous need to remember . . . they wanted to know more in order to make sense out of it. They spoke of having lost their childhood or having a 'hole' in their past. . . . Inability to remember was fraught with such feelings as emptiness, deadness, or nothingness. . . . Child survivors often complain that they do not belong anywhere, not to the adult survivors and not to their children."[19]

Until recent years, adult survivors had little awareness of the potential for psychological impact on those who were younger during the Holocaust. You were just a child. You didn't understand what was going on. You were relatively safe because the Gentiles you were left with assumed you were one of them. And child survivors remained silent because they remembered little and were treated as though they were not bona fide "survivors." They therefore forfeited their right to ventilate.

As more child survivors have asserted their identities and inclusion in the category of "survivors," they have drawn our attention to themes which have left disturbing impressions.[20] In some cases of those placed in convents or with Gentile families, we found an ambivalent attitude toward a Jewish identity. ("It is frightening to be a Jew. I don't want to be vulnerable and persecuted by stronger Christians. No, I want to be one of them.") These children were understandably confused, and reluctant to surrender a Gentile sense of self which was forged at such a crucial juncture of their lives.

Many child survivors experience extreme frustration because the retrieval of memory is so difficult. Others experience excessive fears of abandonment as the threats of their previous Gentile guardians echo in their subconscious: "You won't be able to stay here anymore if you are not a good girl." As one might expect, those who were orphaned may manifest different concerns than those who survived with at least one parent.

(I vividly recall a conversation several years ago with a survivor who was orphaned during the Holocaust. On his arrival in the United States in 1946, he moved in with his aunt and uncle, who had been living in the Bronx since 1938. "They immediately wanted me to call them mother and father. It made me so angry . . . so hurt . . . I wanted *my own* mommy and daddy," he cried.)

Survivors have lived with the skepticism of others. At best, their interlocutor surmises, Aren't you exaggerating, even a little? This stance also serves to minimize the potential of the survivor's experience for subsequent psychological trauma. In 1954 the West German government enacted legislation designed to make possible reparations to those who suffered during the Holocaust. To qualify for those payments, however, survivors had to undergo extensive medical and psychiatric evaluations, usually by German-born physicians. The burden of proof rested on the survivors, who had to establish a causal connection between their present symptoms and previous persecution at the hands of the Nazis. The West German indemnification office (*Entschädigungsämter*) often denied applicants' claims because of a neatly imposed self-absolution created by the German medical community: the symptoms of survivors were attributed to a faulty *Anlage* (constitution). These doctors proclaimed that survivors would not have developed problems had it not been for their infantile neuroses, which made them excessively vulnerable to stress. William Niederland objected vehemently:

> The etiology of these conditions has all too frequently been attributed to the "Anlage," the constitution, to other events, indigenous factors . . . to something which went on between the survivors and their parents during their first and second year of life. It seems hard to believe that the four or five years in Auschwitz, with total or almost total family loss, the complete degradation to the point of dehumanization, the chronic starvation and deprivation of everything human, are considered incidental factors, so to speak, in fully stated medical opinions for the courts.[21]

Indeed, the early emphasis by Niederland and others on psychopathology as opposed to adaptation may have also been motivated by a desire to sensitize their colleagues to the effects of the trauma. There would probably be a consensus that the generalizations of a survivor syndrome from interviews conducted in the 1950s and 1960s may not apply today as wounds have healed, or, at least, scabs have formed.

Barbara Lowenstein lived in Vilna in 1939 with her parents, two brothers, and younger sister. Sent out of the ghetto by her parents to be hidden by Gentiles in the countryside, she returned after three months, lonely and concerned about her mother and father. Having endured one year in Kaiserwald concentration camp in Riga, she was eventually deported to Stuthof in the spring of 1944. Suffering from typhus and malnutrition, she was taken by her liberators, the English, to a German field hospital. German doctors, wearing white coats over their uniforms, treated her. "I screamed when I saw them. I thought they were going to give me a lethal injection."

Barbara told me about her interview in 1959 with a German psychiatrist who had been asked to evaluate the extent of her disability and consequent entitlement to restitution. "I thought I was in Hitlerland again. He told me I was faking! I was crying during the interview about my parents and he practically ridiculed me. 'I've heard much worse stories,' he said."

After liberation, approximately twenty-five percent of Jewish survivors (140,000) emigrated to the United States, while another fifty-five percent (350,000) embarked for Palestine (later Israel). (Roughly ten percent remained in Europe and ten percent scattered to Canada, Australia, South Africa, and Argentina.) In America, the survivors were met by Jews who soon made it apparent that they did not want to hear about what happened in the concentration camps. Perhaps feeling uneasy at having been exempted from the fate of their brethren, the American Jews immediately offered their own history of scarcities during the Depression and gas rationing during the war. Don't bother telling us about your horrors, we had our own deprivations to bear. Their ignorance of the unprecedented savagery experienced by their cousins did not inhibit the offers of demoralizing analogies.

The accusations of Americans were somtimes explicit and sometimes implicit. Why didn't you run? Why didn't you fight back? Why didn't you do *something*? With hindsight and a lack of understanding of the demoralizing circumstances, the constricted options, the effective ruses of the Nazis, and the unimaginable nature of the fate awaiting European Jews, American Jews at least partially blamed the victims. If we believe others experienced victimization because they did not do what they could have to avoid it, we are able to continue to maintain the illusion that we can protect ourselves from similar misfortune.

Israelis could be equally insensitive. Hanzi Brand spent her first period in Palestine at Kibbutz Givat Haim. Tom Segev, an Israeli journalist and author, wrote of her experience.

Everyone was very nice to her, but they did not want to hear what had happened to her. Instead they spoke of what had happened to them. How the Arabs had attacked the kibbutz. A shell had landed near the chicken coop, they told her over and over again. Even then it seemed to her that they were talking about their war to avoid hearing about hers. They were ashamed of the Holocaust. At one point they suggested that her two sons be sent for psychiatric treatment. She did not send them. One later died, and the second, employed at the Nahal Sorek nuclear plant, was to serve in the Israeli embassy in Bonn. Those people who knew her story always asked her why she and her husband had not done anything against the Nazis early on. And they always, always asked her how she had been saved, until she began to feel that she had to apologize for living. The stories she and her husband told competed with the stories of the Warsaw ghetto uprising, she said, and could not win: They had only fought for their lives, not to be heroes. The country wanted heroes. The Brands could only offer a story of survival. People did not know how hard it had been just to stay alive. They didn't comprehend that; they wanted stories of glory.[22]

American Jews often acted condescendingly to these "greenhorns" and feared their taintedness.

"My husband and I didn't have what you would call a wild romance before we were married. He had been in love with a girl who did not survive, and I with a man who did not come to the United States. I wanted time before we married, I wanted to think for a while, so I went to stay with my relatives in the Midwest while Stefan was getting himself settled in New York. My cousins were American-born Jews: very Middle-Western, kind, generous people, who also shrank from me a little. You understand, the concentration camp experience is nothing that endears you to people. People who came to my cousins' house used to ask me such things as whether I had been able to survive because, perchance, I had slept with an SS man."[23]

Israel afforded survivors an opportunity to develop positive self-images as pioneers building a homeland and refuge for Jews. They were able to identify their own rebirth and rehabilitation with the rebirth and growth of the state. The precarious military situation allowed an outlet for personal anger in action supportive of a national cause, with the subsequent victories over the Arabs providing a boost to self-esteem damaged by past feelings of helplessness and loss. The continuing perilous situation in Israel helped survivors focus their attention on an outside group, and therefore may have prevented their being preoccupied with themselves.

However, as was the case in America, life in Israel did not provide the psychological comfort required by survivors. Thrust into a war zone, these recent immigrants found themselves fighting another enemy bent on their annihilation. Having already outlasted their persecutors, time, and the odds, their existence was once again in jeopardy. And, after military victories, Israelis could only look forward to ongoing harsh, or at best Spartan, living conditions.

Perhaps the fiercest blow to survivors who emigrated to this hazardous territory was the psychological distance imposed by sabras (those born in Palestine). These remnants of the *galut* Jewish communities were not like us, they insisted. *We* do not go like sheep to the slaughter.

Jokes deriding the victims circulated. A popular one began with the question "How many Jews can you fit into an ashtray?" In the 1950s, young Israelies mockingly named survivors *sabon* (soap), referring to the myth that Nazis used the bodies of murdered Jews to produce soap.

Survivors could not speak because they were already condemned. While many Israelis provided assistance to survivors, others blamed them as if they had survived at the expense of their murdered relatives. Far from being perceived as heroes, they were considered reminders of all which the glorious modern Jew must shun. Their history was to be overcome and denied. Even among their own, in a Jewish state, survivors were kept from speaking out. In 1949, David Ben-Gurion referred to survivors as "demoralizing material" who needed to be retrained and imbued with "national discipline." A few years later Moshe Sharett, the Israeli foreign minister, declared that survivors were "undesirable human material."

In June 1989, the film *Cloudburst*, produced by Orna Ben-Dor-Niv and Dafna Kaplanski, first appeared on Israeli television. Israelis heard the author, Yehudit Hendel, who had grown up in a Labor Zionist environment, describe the schism she had imbibed. The references to inferior and superior races are startlingly familiar.

"To put it bluntly, there are almost two races in this country. There was one race of people who thought they were gods. These were the ones who had the honor and privilege of being born in Degania, or in the Borochov neighborhood of Givataim, and I belong, as it were, to those gods. I grew up in a workers' neighborhood near Haifa. And there was, we can certainly say, an inferior race. People we saw as inferior who had some kind of flaw, some kind of hunchback, and these were the people who came after the war. I was taught in school that the ugliest, basest thing is not the Exile, but the Jew who came from there."[24]

Tom Segev, in his brilliant work *The Seventh Million*, wrote of another Israeli's experience:

A few days after he came home from his mission to Hungary, paratrooper Yoel Palgi went to a veterans' club in Tel Aviv. It was June 1945. Everyone received him warmly and with admiration, he later wrote. They all wanted to hear what had happened over there. But no one was interested in accounts of Jewish suffering. They wanted a different story, about the few who had fought like lions. "Everywhere I turned," Palgi wrote, "the question was fired at me: why did the Jews not rebel? Why did they go like lambs to the slaughter? Suddenly I realized that we were ashamed of those who were tortured, shot, burned. There is a kind of general agreement that the Holocaust dead were worthless people. Unconsciously, we have accepted the Nazi view that the Jews were subhuman. . . . History is playing a bitter joke on us: have we not ourselves put the six million on trial?"[25]

Eighty percent of Israelis polled in 1949 said that the concentration of immigrants in the cities endangered the country's economic and social structure; ninety percent believed immigrants should be "directed" to agricultual settlements, and slightly more than fifty percent insisted immigrants should be "forced" to go to settlements.[26] But the kibbutzim were concerned about "the quality of human material" being sent them. They did not want sick people or "social cases," small children or old people.[27] At the same time that kibbutz members believed it was their ideological duty to absorb the new immigrants, they castigated these survivors for their difficulties in adjusting to the kibbutz way of life.[28] In any case, Israeli society, and kibbutzim in particular, emphasized the subordination of individual needs to the common good.

Unfortunately, for some survivors, the collective community of the kibbutz evoked reminders of previous hardships. One of the immigrants sent to Kibbutz Mishmarot explained: "When I sat down at a table in the dining room, waiting for the server to come to my table, I was shaking. I was afraid that there wouldn't be enough food and that my table wouldn't get any."[29]

No one wanted to hear what the survivors had seen and endured. At that time, they were not referred to with the heroically and sympathetically implied appellation "survivor." They were simply refugees.

It was not until the 1960s, spurred by the trial of Adolf Eichmann in Jerusalem, that education about the Holocaust was perceived as desirable by Israeli society. (It took until 1979 for the Holocaust to be introduced as a compulsory subject in Israeli school curricula.) During the Eichmann proceedings, the witnesses whose Holocaust experiences had been silenced for the preceding fifteen years were now asked to render precise accounts and encouraged to disclose even the most horrifying details. Suddenly, the country's leaders realized that this newly acquired consciousness of a common destiny was an invaluable asset in consolidating a national identity and promoting Israel's case abroad.

The primary intent of the Eichmann trial was not punishment. If that were the case, he could have simply been liquidated on Garibaldi Street in Buenos Aires, where he was abducted by the Mossad. Instead, Ben-Gurion's objectives were twofold: (1) to remind the world that the Holocaust obligated support of the State of Israel; and (2) to impress the lessons of the Holocaust, particularly upon the younger generation of Israelis. What was the most fundamental lesson of the Holocaust from Ben-Gurion's perspective? That Israel was the only country which could guarantee the security of the Jews.

Ben-Gurion wanted to remind Jews where they belonged. "Antisemitism is caused by the existence of the Jews in the Exile," he wrote in a letter. "When they are different from their neighbors they awaken fear and derision, and when they try to be like them, and as usual become more Catholic than the Pope, they are repulsed."[30] Ironically, Ben-Gurion's sentiments paralleled one of the justifications for the Holocaust offered by some ultra-Orthodox religious authorities: the Jews brought the Holocaust upon themselves as God's punishment for their increasing assimilation (and lack of adherence to Torah).

The assistant state prosecutor, Gabriel Bach, later recalled other objectives of the show trial: "The prosecution set itself the goal of inducing Israeli youth to identify with the Holocaust's victims. This identification, it was hoped, would replace the arrogance of young Israelis to the survivors."[31]

Events six years later accelerated the humbling process as immediately before the Six-Day War in 1967, Israelis felt as though they were locked in a ghetto under seige. They felt alone and isolated and spoke of the necessity "to prevent another Holocaust." An identification with the Jews who had been annihilated two decades previously was now possible.

For the initial forty years of their postwar life, most survivors escaped the brunt of their past calamities by working, by *doing* not thinking, by *doing* not feeling. However, they and their families have moved to another stage of the life cycle. "The more your children and family life departs, the more your mind turns to the past," remarked Murray Cohen, an artist and survivor of several slave labor camps in

Estonia. Murray's parents, brothers, sister, and wife were shot in Ponar. "Especially when your future is questionable and perhaps unimportant, I find myself back with them, *over there.*"

Advancing years bring a continuous loss of physical ability. Survivors are particularly sensitive to this decline because of their previous terror and feelings of vulnerability. The network of social supports also fades away as spouses or friends die and children move away. Not surprisingly, for aging Holocaust survivors as well as their counterparts in the general population, higher morale is associated with better health, greater financial resources, educational attainment, and the availability of emotionally close relationships.[32]

Naturally, survivors must navigate the same developmental course as others of their generation. According to Erik Erikson, the central task of the aged individual is to achieve integrity by accepting "one's own and only life cycle . . . as something that had to be and that, by necessity, permitted no substitutes."[33] What happened, had to happen.

Survivors have enormous difficulty attaining this goal because, at their very core, what gnaws most obscenely is the *senselessness* of the Holocaust. Survivors cannot be at peace with the Holocaust for this would also be treasonous to the memory of their loved ones. They *must* feel outrage and continue to bear witness, to testify to the *innocence* of those who were murdered, and to the guilt of their tormentors.

2

"Whose fault was it?"

Rose Friedland was nineteen years old when she was deported in the spring of 1944 from her village, which had previously been annexed by Hungary from Czechoslovakia, to a place where they were burning ten thousand Jews every day. "When I came to Auschwitz, my sister was with me. She was only fourteen and it was a miracle she got past Mengele. From the moment we got into the camp, she couldn't eat. Once a week in Auschwitz you received some marmalade made from sugar beets in your hand. She couldn't even eat that. The only thing she ate was the slice of bread she got and I used to get angry with her. Once I yelled at her, 'If you don't eat, you will die!'

"Needless to say, I know in my head I'm not the cause of her death . . . but in my *gut* I've believed that I caused her death. At another point we were separated and I went into the Czech *Lager* where Czech families were brought from Theresienstadt and eliminated and she to the C *Lager*. I tried to run back to her but I was caught by the Kapo, beaten, and thrown back toward the Czech *Lager*. For a while, through the wires, we would meet every day. It was the afternoon before Yom Kippur and that day I got three raw potatoes from somebody and I threw one over the wire to her. She picked up the potato and started to cry. I told her tonight was Yom Kippur and say some prayers . . . [she weeps] . . . I told her to go back to her barracks and we would meet again tomorrow. I was afraid the Germans would see us. The next day, she didn't show up. And she didn't come the following day either . . . [she sobs] . . . I knew it was trouble. I didn't find out until after liberation there was a big action on Yom Kippur.

"I felt guilty for many years that maybe I should have run back and tried to get her with me or stay with her. Maybe I didn't do enough to stay together. Maybe I was too selfish about saving myself. You can excuse yourself and say if I had run back my fate would have been the same as hers. There is no logic to my feelings . . . but those words ring in my ears, If you're not going to eat, you're going to die."

Later in the interview, Rose spoke of her pilgrimage to Auschwitz forty years after. "It was a devastating experience. I took my daughter with me. We went through the museum and I saw those windows filled with hair, and of course it brought back memories of when we were shaved [upon arrival]. And then the room filled with children's shoes. That was the hardest thing. I had been repressing something before I saw the children's shoes . . . I saw children carried by Nazi soldiers to the Pit and dropping them into the Pit. Those were the children who had come with us on the transport. At the time, I didn't want to believe that was what I was seeing. I hid that in my memory until I saw the shoes. Then I decided I wanted to go back to the Pit.

"We came into Birkenau. It was snowing. Where the monument is which talked about all the nationalities which were killed – all the nationalities but Jews. There was a deathly silence. It was a very windy day and in the wind . . . [she sobs] . . . I could hear myself saying, 'If you're not going to eat, you will die.' Something I was trying for years to forget.

"It was like an echo in my ear repeating, and like a crazy person I turned to the Polish guide and I said, 'And where are the children?' And she said, 'What children?' I screamed at her, 'You know what children! I want to go to the children's Pit!' We went to the Pit. I took my gloves off and started to scrape the snow. . . . And tiny fragments of bone were all over. I scraped and scraped. . . . My daughter picked me up and said, 'Mother, it's time to go.' "

"Survivor guilt" is the term used to describe the feelings of those who fortunately emerge from a disaster which mortally engulfs others. On an irrational level, these individuals wince at their privileged escape from death's clutches. From a psychodynamic viewpoint, the Holocaust survivor's guilt may reflect the constraints against the expression of rage toward the perpetrators of his misfortune, toward the Nazis and their collaborators, and toward parents who failed to provide protection from those torturous events. Instead of expressing rage outward, the survivor turns it upon himself. Guilt is the embodiment of anger directed toward the self.

Survivor guilt may also serve to motivate an individual to bear witness to the Holocaust and continue to remember those who were murdered. The call to memory which many survivors answer has the salutary effects of providing education about the Holocaust and ensuring the commemoration of the victims. However, survivor guilt also has the potential to compel an individual to remain mired in his past to the relative exclusion of his present or future. Guilt is the penance one pays for the gift of survival.

For many social scientists, survivor guilt has been an integral aspect of their sketches of the postwar Holocaust survivor.[1] However, I did not find this phenomenon to be quite so widespread as we have been led to believe. Perhaps I would have found a greater incidence of the phenomenon if I had met these survivors soon after the end of the war. It is terribly difficult to maintain an awareness of guilt feelings for such a protracted period, particularly when one is so motivated to move forward with one's life. Approximately one half of those I interviewed articulated an uneasiness about their reprieve. The reasons for this discomfort varied.

The most discomfited survivors I interviewed were those whose children were murdered while they felt powerless to alter their son's or daughter's deterioration and death. These survivors are tormented by their failure and by their loss. At eighty-three, Elisa Korn was the oldest woman I spoke with for this project. A kerchief covered her head because of chemotherapy she was undergoing. After exchanging introductions, Elisa asked if I would like to sit in her backyard as it was such a beautiful summer day. We moved outside, but before I could even arrange my recorder and legal-size pad for notes, she blurted out with bitterness, self-recrimination, and finality, "I had a daughter who was killed. Now you know my story."

Born and raised in Frankfurt, in 1929 Elisa moved to Amsterdam, where she married a Dutchman. Her parents and two sisters emigrated to the United States in 1938. Providing "proof" to the German authorities in 1942 that her grandparents were Aryan and that she was divorced from her Jewish husband, she was spared having to wear the yellow star and able to have the "J" removed from her papers. Nevertheless, over the next three years she periodically moved with her daughter, Lily, to different parts of the city as her neighbors became suspicious of her background. Elisa agreed to serve as a conduit for forged papers to the underground and was arrested after a member of the Resistance was followed to her home. She now berates herself for having gotten involved and thereby jeopardizing her fourteen-year-old girl. "I could have avoided being picked up. I wasn't identified as a Jew. I could have made it one more year. I was stupid. How could I have taken those risks with my daughter's life?"

After the Gestapo smashed in her front door, Elisa's odyssey with her daughter continued in a more terrifying manner. There were additional perceived mortal blunders and feelings of inefficacy – and it was clearly those moments and those scenes which Elisa had compulsively conjured for the past forty-seven years. "When they transferred us from the prison in Amsterdam to the train station to be deported, I think she could have gotten away . . . I should have said, Run! . . . But I didn't . . . I couldn't have gotten away, but maybe she could have." In October 1944, Elisa and Lily were moved from Bergen-Belsen to Ravensbrück. "She [Lily] worked in the winter without gloves or shoes . . . I kept telling her that I would give her the world after it was all over. . . . But she was becoming a ghost before my eyes . . . and I couldn't do anything." Just before liberation, the prisoners were herded onto transports which moved aimlessly across railroad tracks as the Allied armies approached. One morning, the trains finally stopped next to a field and the guards scattered. The prisoners were told there was water a kilometer away. "I left her [Lily] in the field because she couldn't walk anymore. I got to the fountain, put my tin cup down while I drank. When I reached for the cup to fill it with water for my daughter, it was gone, stolen by one of the other girls . . . I couldn't even bring water back to my daughter [she weeps]." After a night of sleep in the fields, Elisa awakened but her daughter did not.

It is the natural order of things for the older to die before the younger, for the adult to die before the child, for the father to die before the son. In questioning their providential fate, several survivors were keenly aware of the unnatural process and outcome of the Shoah. They saw the incontestable innocence of all the children and sometimes measured it against their own. "Why me? And especially with the children?" they torturously asked.

From those I spoke with, I heard repeated stories with the agonizing conclusion of not having done one's utmost to save loved ones.

Oftentimes, survivors discovered the means of atonement for their "failure." Jack Diamond occupied a privileged position in Auschwitz. He was the servant of the *Lager Elteste*. "I had survivor guilt for years. I could never forgive myself . . . I had good connections in Auschwitz . . . but I didn't do enough to save my brother. He was with me from the beginning, but with all the connections I had, I couldn't save him. I had many sleepless nights about him. That was depressing me for years. It's diminished. . . . When I was living in Israel I always imagined what great things he could have done. He could have been a great architect, a great artist. He was so talented. Of all my brothers and sisters, he was the most idealistic, the best of us. The guilt slowly went away because I devoted myself to building the State of Israel. It was hard labor. There was little food. Every day, your life was at risk. So I felt I was doing something for *clal Yisrael*."

The concentration camp provided fertile soil for survivor guilt, for at its most fundamental it was a competitive planet. The overwhelming relief of not being chosen for extinction at the morning selection was coupled with the immediate knowledge of those who were summoned by the Angel of Death. This clash of fortune and misfortune occurred every day as the crematoria demanded their quota.

Seventy-one-year-old Solomon Goldstein was the only survivor from his Orthodox family, who had lived in a small town in southern Poland. After I asked him, "Have you ever felt any survivor guilt?" I was taken aback by the ferocity of his response. His bile spewed forth as he enumerated his sins. "I'm guilty all my life. I'm guilty I didn't save my father, my mother, my sister. I feel guilty, I could have made Aryan papers for them. I'm guilty I tried to talk them into going to Russia, but they wouldn't listen. I'm guilty, I don't want to be richer than my father. I had opportunities to make millions. I always feel guilty. Why should I have more than my parents? Maybe I'm wrong. I'm guilty. I feel guilty all my life."

"In December 1944, when the war started coming to an end, although we didn't know that, or we did not know to what extent – we were taken out of camp and started off to march – the Russians came near and the Germans took us out from camp and they marched us to other camps. It was terrible cold; we had no clothes. Whoever could not walk they shot. We had no food.

"At night they herded us in some farm . . . a barn. Next morning very early they took us out and we had to march again; we marched for days. And during that march, my brother . . . he could not walk anymore and he was taken from me and shot on the road.

"It is difficult to say, talk about feelings. First of all, we were reduced to such a animal level that actually now that I remember those things, I feel more horrible than I felt at the time. We were in such a state that all that mattered is to remain alive. Even about your own brother, one did not think. I don't know how other people felt. . . . It bothers me very much if I was the only one that felt that way, or is that normal in such circumstances to be that way? I feel now sometimes, did I do my best or didn't I do something that I should have done? But at the time I wanted to survive myself, and maybe I did not give my greatest efforts to do certain things, or I missed to do certain things."[2]

"Victor C. was transferred from one labor camp to another, always with his brother. At Funfteichen, a subcamp of Gröss-Rosen, he was working in the Revier, when his brother was sent there because of an illness. From here, he says, there was no exit for the ill, except as a corpse. He himself was offered a better (and safer) job in the camp but couldn't decide whether to stay with his brother or strengthen his own chance to outlive the others. He calls that enigma his albatross, the resultant wound a hurt that he has tried all his life to heal, without success. 'I left him there and I survived [prolonged weeping]. If I forget anything, this I will never forget. I try to justify my act with a practical approach. Can anybody understand it? Can anybody know my pain, my agony . . . that never leaves me?"[3]

Shimon Newman, who had fought with the partisans, had an immediate response to my query about survivor guilt. "I don't have any guilt feelings. I know why I survived. I was lucky and very resourceful." Partisans *acted, resisted,* and that is why they survived, they tell themselves. Guilt feelings are therefore vitiated. If others had been less passive, less naive, perhaps they might have survived as well, some partisans believe. However, Shimon, like Solomon Goldstein, is nonetheless perturbed by his postwar bounty. "But, every time I eat and I see how much I have, I feel guilty . . . because my parents were so hungry [he weeps]." And two hours into the interview, Shimon, who during our initial telephone contact informed me that he never talks about "these things," looks down at his folded hands and tells me, "I wish I had been more persuasive, maybe less selfish. I had in Tomaszów a cousin of about ten. Sometimes I think I wish I had kept him with me and perhaps he would have survived. . . . I met my cousin's father a few years ago and I felt very bad [he weeps]. Perhaps I could have saved him."

(Children of survivors also inhibit themselves from feeling entitled to their abundance, their safety, or even their insecurities. They frequently heard their parents compare the "plenty of now" with "the scarcity of then." They listened to their mother wish that she had had an adolescence. When they spoke of their problems, their father replied, You think *that's* a problem? You don't know what problems are.)

Even when survivors spoke within their reconstituted family of their Holocaust years, they usually omitted disclosure of the fact that they had previous children or a spouse who were murdered. To speak of them might have implied, albeit irrationally, a question of one's total devotion or loyalty to the present family. The quality of "secretiveness," a word which some in the second generation have used to describe the atmosphere in their homes while growing up, can often be traced to this issue. Typically, they did not discover the existence of a predecessor until adolescence or young adulthood. David Himmelstein feels guilty about *replacing* his first- and second-born, who were taken from him. Children are not easily replaced. Furthermore, to *enjoy* his post-Holocaust children (or to enjoy any aspect of life, for that matter) would feel like another betrayal of the two daughters he was unable to protect. "You see . . . you loved so much your children that . . . you're afraid to love so much as you did before . . . not to make jealous the dead children. . . . Like they're saying, You had two children . . . and you lost them in the gas. . . . Don't be too happy."

Not surprisingly, sole surviving members of a family are more likely to experience survivor guilt than those who were left with a parent or sibling. Alone, they feel the void more keenly. The survivor who emerged with a parent or sibling may diffuse onto them his illogical sense of responsibility for the death of others. These surviving family members also did little or nothing to save our loved ones. And ultimately, there was little we could do, he can conclude, as he is faced with others who bore similar obligations. Furthermore, if enough close ones remained alive, one would not feel as though one were an anomaly. There was a logic to Daniel Davidoff's survival. "I cannot have the survivor guilt because my wife and daughter also survived."

29

On a few occasions, I also heard anger from those who were the only remnant of their family. Anger at the injustice of others being luckier than his own mother, father, sister, or brother. Anger at the good fortune of those who survived with other loved ones. This rage erupted during those extreme times as well. Sixteen-year-old Selma Brook and her mother were shipped from Stuthof to Auschwitz at the end of 1943. "You can't understand the humiliation of standing naked in front of the SS. Our heads were shaved and there was a very fast selection. From the entire transport, only three mother–daughter pairs survived, including my mother and me. We were given the blue and white dresses and wooden shoes. After a shower we were put in Barracks Two. The women started screaming and I was terribly frightened. 'Why is *she* alive when my mother was gassed! Why is *she* alive when my daughter was gassed!"

For David Himmelstein, a tragic irony fuels his survivor guilt. After Belgium was occupied, David's first wife was offered the opportunity to be spirited away to her country of birth, England. She refused to leave her family and was eventually murdered. Of course, this pattern was repeated in thousands of homes where individual family members shunned possibilities of escape because of their unwillingness to leave loved ones behind.

"Are you ashamed because you are alive in place of another?" Primo Levi writes. "It is no more than a supposition, indeed the shadow of a suspicion: that each man is his brother's Cain, that each of us . . . has usurped his neighbor's place and lived in his stead. It is a supposition, but it gnaws at us; it has nestled deeply like a woodworm; although unseen from the outside, it gnaws and rasps."[4] Sixty-seven-year-old Barbara Lowenstein, the sole remaining member of her prewar family of six, told me that only one percent of those on her transport to Stuthof survived. She continuously observed "stronger ones than me" expire from disease, beatings, and starvation. "You start taking stock and you know you came from a big family. I don't know how to explain it to you. You think, Why me? Why did *I* survive? I was often miserable about it. You can also explain it in mathematical terms. The Germans had to kill a certain number of Jews. If you survived, you did on account of others. We were lucky, but some would consider it not so lucky. . . . I've suffered from depression . . . I'm told it's because of the Holocaust. . . . Maybe it is, may it isn't. You don't talk about it. . . . What am I going to make other people miserable for?" You can explain it in mathematical terms. Four out of ten Jews living in Western Europe during the Holocaust were murdered. In 1939, there were approximately 3.2 million Jews living in Poland. Nine out of ten perished during the onslaught. Far fewer than one out of ten children emerged. Why me?

The *best* did not survive, many survivors admitted. The pious passively placed their fate in God's hands. The intellectuals placed their faith in the enlightened, rational part of man and the cultured German citizen of Goethe, Heine, and Mendelssohn. What am *I* doing here? I was *less* than him, the survivor frets. "Why did I survive and not my brother and father?" Dora Levinsohn wonders. "They were better people than me. Coming from an Orthodox home, I was the only rebel in the family, and I survived and they didn't."

Finding a meaningful purpose for their postwar life alleviated the guilt of survivors. For many, replenishing their family and the Jewish people served as justification for having beaten the odds. However, when her children did not turn out successfully, the survivor was stripped of her raison d'être, particularly if she blamed herself for the outcome. Esther Fisher's forty-year-old son is a drug addict. Her thirty-eight-year-old daughter has never married, lives with her parents, and for the past six years has been too frightened to venture out of the house alone. "When I couldn't cope with the kids [I had survivor guilt]. I said, Why me? Why did I survive? What for? With all the troubles."

A few of those I interviewed uneasily compare their misfortune to that of other survivors. Not only are they reluctant to speak of their less torturous circumstances, which might elicit a sympathetic response, but in their hearts they feel they have been spared something they *should* have experienced – just as their less fortunate brothers and sisters did. Ethel Janov lived in a small Hungarian village, and her severe persecution did not begin until the spring of 1944 when she and her family were herded into a ghetto. That June, she was deported to Auschwitz with her mother. "I always compare myself to other survivors," Ethel remarked. "If I was talking to your parents from Poland who suffered more, I wouldn't be able to grieve or feel pain . . . I don't feel like I suffered enough. I even always compare my suffering to the suffering of nonsurvivors. I compare it, measure

31

it. His was a ten but mine was only a nine. . . . *I need people to feel for me but I'm also ashamed of that need* [my emphasis].

Later in the interview, Ethel told me that she goes to movies about the Holocaust and reads voraciously in this area. "Why do you do that?" I asked. "It's a physical feeling," she explained. "I go through it again. I need to feel it. When I don't feel it, I feel like I'm numb. . . . There may be an element of masochism. Like I got out of Auschwitz and I want to go back. It's like reconnecting with something very real in me, like my authentic self. I need to feel that part of me is alive." Ethel Janov perceives her *authentic self* to be the self which suffers pain and degradation. Her authentic self is the self which lived in Hell. Afterward has been an overlay, grafted on to cover the pus.

Those who never left there were mortally defined by the death camp. Having been stamped with affliction in Auschwitz, Ethel feels compelled to maintain that identity. She perpetually pricks her wound because she never wants it to heal. Ethel will die, as the others had died, consumed by Auschwitz.

Conversely, Sonya Weiss, who lived in Warsaw in 1939, does not feel survivor guilt because she knows, and is perversely relieved, that she experienced the Holocaust's extremities. Upon arriving with her mother at Majdanek in May 1943, they were immediately separated and her mother was selected for the gas chamber. At the end of 1943, Sonya was moved from Majdanek to Auschwitz, where she remained until January 1945, and then was evacuated to a series of concentration camps in Germany. Significantly, Sonya is proud of how she behaved during those horrifying years. "I was quite a girl. I give myself a lot of credit for being who I was. If I wouldn't be the way I am, I wouldn't have made it. There were ten people sleeping in my bunk in Auschwitz and we all had typhoid fever and I was the only one who survived. How come I survived? In all those terrible circumstances I was the one who gave others hope. I wish I could be that way today. I think I consumed all of my energy during this time. Today, I'm not so strong anymore."

When evaluating their behavior, most survivors told me they felt proud of, or at least at peace with, their actions. ("I didn't sleep with soldiers or anybody else. Why should I feel guilty?" one woman rhetorically asked.) Many of these individuals also believe their survival was a consequence of an inner fortitude and personal courage. They were stronger than others, they tell themselves. "I never felt guilt," sixty-eight-year-old Martin Bornstein remarked. "But in 1948 I was already married. It was Yom Kippur. My wife wanted to go to shul and I didn't want to and we didn't. When we were walking in the street in Astoria [Queens, New York] we ran into some acquaintances. He asked me, How come I'm not in shul? I said, 'How can I go to shul and thank God that I survived when others didn't?' What, was I better than others? . . .

"I survived despite all those who wanted to do away with me. I survived and I'm proud of it. While in Auschwitz I knew I had to risk my life to feed myself and I did it. One of my jobs in Auschwitz was to go through the clothing of those who arrived and of course we had to hand in everything. I and others saved some jewelry and at night I went to get a piece of bread for it. There was a choice – either you became a Musselman or you take chances, get food, and keep yourself alive."

Survivors are keenly aware that they are a tiny fraction of those who escaped their persecutors' sweeping hand of death. To still their discomfort over this propitious turn, they construe a logic or purpose to their timely deliverance. As Daniel Davidoff had told me, "I cannot have the survivor guilt because my wife and daughter also survived." Later in the interview he came back to this theme. "Of twenty-five hundred in my camp, five survived. I told myself I have to survive because God didn't bring me in this world to die like this. Number two: I had to survive to tell the people what they did to us."

At the age of eighteen, Ben Kass left his parents and five younger brothers behind in the Warsaw ghetto and joined the partisans. He told me that, for the most part, he does not experience survivor guilt. "I had an episode like this three or four times. I had a dream about three weeks ago where I saw my mother and my mother asked me why I run away. . . . At least one person from the family is alive to tell the story. If we all would be killed, there would be no one to tell."

And while many have found a "reason" for their survival, Ethel Janov, who is acutely aware of her guilt feelings, still longs for a satisfying justification for her continuing presence. "I always feel like I have to *earn* my life," she emphasizes.

After liberation, the remnants rushed into marriage and parenthood in order to fill the void. After having children, these fathers and mothers would then take a step back, look at their sons and daughters, and articulate an explanation for their individual survival. Paul Handel was the sole survivor of his immediate family of seven. "Why did I survive? We survived not by anything you did differently. It was fate. The guilt was afterward. I had three beautiful brothers, a sister who had a baby. . . . In the beginning, you felt it the most. Then you think, maybe I survived for a purpose. I never thought I would get married, have children, after what I had seen. But I did and maybe that's why I survived."

Olga Himmelfarb found a clear, unselfish reason to persevere. In August 1944, she and her younger sister were deported from Budapest to Auschwitz. "My sister was weak and I took care of her," Olga told me. "The whole time I was in Auschwitz, I thought when I would see my mother and father I would say, 'Look, I brought her back.' "

Some survivors move away from the small, singular moments of felt personal responsibility and turn their wrath on the prime mover of the destruction. "Guilt for what? Whose fault was it?" Mina Fogel demanded. Many are also well aware of the random nature of their chosenness. On September 27, 1942, Eva Brumlick was marched with her handicapped parents (both of whom could neither speak nor hear) through the streets of her native Berlin to the railroad station. They were taken to a concentration camp in Estonia. Eva's brother had committed suicide four years before that day. "I'm just lucky, that's all," Eva emphasized. "Sometimes I think if someone had asked my parents the question, they would say, We'll die and you live . . . [she weeps]. I was many times in selections and wasn't picked. Someone must have been watching over me. . . . Why should I feel it [survivor guilt]? How can you determine who is who? It wasn't my fault. Because I survived was not my doing. I was simply lucky." Eva assuages her guilt by firmly believing that under the circumstances, circumstances in which the great majority of Jews were doomed to death, her parents would have wanted her to occupy one of the favored places instead of themselves.

Helen Schwartz is also certain that her parents wanted her to live. She points out the futility of my question. Helen understands that the Holocaust was unprecedented in nature, and therefore the Jews of Europe could not have anticipated what awaited them. She recognizes that without the foreknowledge of the Final Solution, one's behavior must be seen in a more accepting, less judgmental light. "Even in 1941, 1942 I didn't have any idea what would happen to my parents and sister. Who would have *imagined* what would happen? . . . I know that my parents' last thoughts in the gas chamber were about myself and my sister . . . and they were probably glad we were not with them."

Most of those who did not evidence survivor guilt had contrived a thesis for its lack of personal relevance. Survivor guilt may be a reflexive response to preferential survivorhood, one requiring artificial justification for its suppression. A few survivors, however, simply do not entertain its possibilities as they have numbed themselves to *all* emotion associated with the Holocaust. "I'm not the type who lives in the past," they reiterate in their keen desire to rebuild and live life as fully as possible. Others simply remain perplexed by all of it – the persecution, the wanton cruelty, the undeserved blows, the sudden disappearance of loved ones, and their fortuitous emergence from the darkness.

Little attention has been paid to the reactions of Jews, particularly those from Germany and Austria, who left Europe before the onslaught. We have read about the "brain drain" of scientists, the cultural exodus of those in the creative community, but virtually nothing of the psychological residue of the Jew who invariably left family members eventually caught up in the whirlwind. Although these émigrés are beyond the scope of this project, one former patient may provide clues as to how they have emotionally responded to their fortuitous escape.

At our first therapy session together, Rose Klinger, who was born in Vienna in 1935, told me she had never been able to say to herself, You deserve to live. Rose's father had been deported to Poland when she was four years old. She and her mother then moved in with her grandparents. In 1940, Rose and her mother received affidavits from America which allowed them to emigrate. As a child growing up in her new homeland, she repeated to herself the incantation, "I won't be happy until father and grandmother come." (Her grandfather had died in his bed the night before she left for the United States.) When she was twelve, Rose was informed that her father had been killed during the Holocaust. Throughout her adult life, the richer and more successful she became, the more depression she experienced. When the cloud surrounding her lifts momentarily and she begins to feel pleasure, she acts to ensure failure in some present endeavor. While married to a man twenty-five years her senior, Rose led a promiscuous extramarital lifestyle. All of her lovers have been much older than her as well. Rose searches for her father and all of the substitutes are found wanting. She remains aloof from emotional intimacy for fear of losing or even causing a loss of one whom she might love. Now a grandmother, Rose has found it impossible to enjoy that status. "I feel like I don't deserve to be a happy grandmother." Her unconscious prods her to remember and feel responsible for the grandmother she had left behind.

During the 1930s, the British allowed the Jewish Agency, the recognized representative of the *yishuv,* to distribute the quota of immigration certificates which had been previously decided upon. Many selections were influenced by political considerations outside the awareness of the applicants. For example, Labor Zionists preferred pioneers, those who would work the land. The Betar movement coveted potential recruits for Etzel (the right-wing, militant underground movement in Palestine.) Ultimately, however, it was the immigrant brought to the safety of Palestine who was subject to the psychological consequences of these criteria imposed from afar. For the Jew who received a precious immigration certificate knew that another Jew had not.

I have often been asked by those who left Europe in the late 1930s if they, too, would fall under the rubric of survivor. The question has a pleading quality, the questioner seeking grace. (I have been asked a similar question about these individuals by their children.) The question reflects the need to identify with those who suffered, and the disquieting belief that they did not suffer enough. The question reflects the need to bridge the gap. The question reflects the need to quiet their survivor guilt.

An even more insidious and self-destructive element than guilt has been observed in survivors. Guilt produces sharp pangs, but one can live with it and place it alongside one's prouder achievements. One can balance guilt with restitution. Shame, however, results in a certain withdrawal, a belief that one is not worth consideration. For the survivor who experiences shame, there is a further disbarment from humanity.

One psychoanalyst has written: "They [survivors] have a perpetual need to atone for cowardice or other 'failures.' There is either real personal shame or assumption of collective shame for the failure of Jews to fight the Nazis."[5] Another clinician reported his observation that although survivors cannot recall any particular act for which they feel guilty, they nevertheless experience a vague sense of having committed something for which they should feel ashamed.[6] Primo Levi noted: "When all was over, the awareness emerged that we had not done anything or not enough against the system into which we had been absorbed. . . . Consciously or not, he [the survivor] feels accused and judged, compelled to justify and defend himself."[7] Having experienced such feelings of powerlessness to control the natural order of their life, such humiliation at the hands of another human being, a few survivors, despite outward appearances of success, continue to experience themselves as shamefully inadequate.

Some social scientists have suggested that as a result of the humiliation and utter powerlessness they experienced, survivors developed a hatred of the self. "In the jails and camps of the Third Reich all of us scorned rather than pitied ourselves because of our helplessness and all-encompassing weakness. The temptation to reject ourselves has survived within us."[8] Furthermore, this detestation was exacerbated in those who had introjected the negative images of the Jew propagated by the Nazis.

I did not discern a blatant self-hatred in those I interviewed. Perhaps the relative brevity (four or five hours) of our meeting precluded my glimpsing an element which the survivor, understandably, would not wish to reveal. But I do not believe this was the case. For most survivors, their tenacity during the Holocaust in the face of overwhelming odds and their successful adaptations to a new postwar life have provided a counterbalance to their felt shortcomings during that time. At least on a manifest level, when survivors look back at their behavior, at how they comported themselves during the Holocaust, they are somewhat sanguine. Many remember the aid and comfort they supplied others when there was precious little of either for themselves. They understand the limited control they could exert over the cruel demands of the environment. They remember their *realistic* fear as they were continuously exposed to the fate which awaited them. "First of all, I was very scared. I had to face death day by day. I had to see cruelty for no reason. If he felt like it, a German just let his dog bite us. Or if they wanted, they just took one of us at a *Tzellappell* and shot us. None of us imagined we would ever be free. It was frightening. You always walked past dead bodies. You had to concentrate to always stay straight for hours and hours. If you fell, you knew this would be the end." And they realized that all of one's efforts must be directed at overcoming the seemingly insurmountable obstacles to life. "We were only interested in survival. I don't remember in camp thinking about moral issues, or any other issues for that matter."

Their youthfulness at the time also served to narrow the survivors' focus to the self and its preservation. Indeed, some survivors harbor unconscious anger toward parents who erred in judgment or did not provide the protection the child naturally anticipates. Because of his age, therefore, the child can more easily refuse responsibility for not only his actions, but his failure to shield others as well. Posing as a Gentile, Solomon Goldstein joined the AK, a Polish resistance movement. In 1942, his comrades discovered he was Jewish and threatened him with death. Solomon returned to his family in the Warsaw ghetto. He pleaded with his parents to attempt an escape, to no avail. "Our parents did not believe in killing, in fighting. So we were like sitting ducks," he angrily remarks.

The brilliantly designed deceptions of the Nazis dovetailed with the need for the Jew to retain hope, to avoid consideration of the worst. Jews would survive because of their usefulness as labor for the Third Reich, they believed. "Resettlement" meant fresher air and more bountiful provisions, they were told. And while some Jews embraced the ruse of opportunities for better living conditions in the East and willingly boarded the transports for supposed destinations, most clung to the familiar and hoped for the speedy defeat of their tormentors. Even when rumors of death camp destinations reached the ghettos, they were brushed aside as the hallucinations of men gone mad.

"Looking back, is there anything you wish you had done differently?" I asked. Martin Bornstein was sixteen years old when the Germans occupied his small town of Niemce in southwestern Poland. "In October 1939, many Jews were leaving and going toward Russia. My mother . . . she was a bright woman [he weeps]. . . . She said, 'Let's leave everything and go to Russia.' Then there were all those second thoughts – it will be cold, we don't know anyone, what will we do? Who would have thought such a catastrophe would happen?"

Jack Diamond grew up in a middle-class, modern Orthodox home.

He and his five siblings went to German *Gymnasium* (high school). "I was angry at my parents because they wouldn't leave Germany when we could have. My mother couldn't believe that the world would let Hitler do what he promised . . . I implored my mother to get out. After Kristallnacht, we could have left. But we had a good life in Germany and she wouldn't leave it. Perhaps if I had pushed more . . . My brother left for Palestine and we in the family never forgave him. We decided, we as a family would always stay together."

Paul Handel was fourteen when he was taken with his mother to the Lodz ghetto from their town of Zgierz. On one of the last transports in 1944, they were both deported to Auschwitz. After their arrival, Paul wanted to stay with his mother, but she slapped him on the face and pushed him across to the men's line, to life. "Would I have done something different? No. We didn't know where we were going. We didn't know what Auschwitz was even when we got there. If someone tells you they knew, they don't know what they're talking about!"

A sense of responsibility and a desire to huddle together restrained many from abandoning families and fleeing to safer ground. Despite their intentions, the following survivors were ultimately unable to shield any of their parents from death. They may, however, have spared themselves the pangs of survivor guilt.

"I didn't want to leave my parents. A man came to my house and said he could get me papers to go to Switzerland, but I wouldn't leave them alone. But I am not sorry. I could not live with myself to know that I left my parents."

"I wish I would have run away with my family. We were an extremely close-knit family. When the Germans came into Lodz the whole city was running away. We managed to go with a mob of people in the direction of Warsaw. After about a mile, my father said he was going back with my mother and sisters and we, the boys, should keep going. My brother ran east to the Russian zone, but, after a week, he returned because he felt so guilty about abandoning the family . . . I don't know if I could live with myself if I had saved myself and the rest had perished. I would always worry that perhaps I could have done something."

"I couldn't have done anything differently. I was trapped by circumstances. In 1940, when my sister ran away to Russia, I ran away for a few months too to the other side of the River Bug. But I felt very bad that I left my parents behind so I went back to Warsaw. I was glad I was with my parents. I never would have forgiven myself if I wasn't with my parents until the last minute."

Ripped from the human cloth before, survivors now impose their own segregation from others, convinced that no one can empathize with or comprehend their ordeal. Survivors easily reject you and me as soft and naive. Ironically, this prevents them from making normative comparisons of others, from feeling a part of the whole. I cannot measure myself against you because of my indelible differentness, they believe. No one is like me. Guilt or shame provide further impetus for their psychological withdrawal from us.

How does one overcome guilt, humiliation, shame? How does one shut away a time and a self and assert a radically different identity? How does one splice off a middle section of one's life and maintain a continuity between the before and the after? How does one reassert a dignity?

For the most part, survivors look back and feel at peace with their behavior during the Holocaust. And while they often primarily attribute their survival to luck, they also convince themselves that survival required a particular inner strength. Look what I made it through while millions did not or could not, they reflect. Any feelings of inferiority engendered during their dehumanization are buried by an assertion of superiority. And even after all I experienced, I was able to successfully reestablish a life, have a family, be a productive member of society, they point out. Dignity has been restored.

3

Mourning

Mourning provides relief. When we mourn, we excrete the pain, the sadness, the anger, the guilt. And after our body and mind have been expunged, we can reenter the world afresh, with hope. Survivors, however, have not mourned. They remain locked in their own sphere. Consequently, their bitterness continues to sear their soul.

I asked Paul Handel (the only member of his immediate family of seven to survive) how he had mourned his losses. "You don't mourn them," he reflected. "It's too many to mourn. The only time I mourn is when I go say Yizkhor [the prayer for the dead recited only on certain holidays]. There's just too many to mourn. You mourn when things happen normally. I don't even have a grave to go to to mourn. Even when I have happy occasions, my son's bar mitzvah, you think about these things. I weep sometimes at a Yizkhor . . . but you become dry. There were too many. . . . After the war, I didn't weep either. Would you believe it? When my American relatives asked me what happened to their cousins, I told them and they didn't even cry. This hurt me deeply . . . I cried when I was single, on holidays for sure, before I was married, not in front on my kids or anything like that."

Paul Handel's answer to my question illustrates several factors which contributed to the inhibition of the mourning process for many survivors. There were so many personal losses – parents, brothers, sisters, grandparents, aunts, uncles, cousins, friends, a familiar life, an embracing community, a national homeland – and these deductions occurred almost simultaneously. Where does one begin to grieve? To whom does one direct one's emotions?

When we lose a loved one, we lose a part of ourselves. When so much of the self is removed at once, a disorientation ensues, an emotional paralysis follows. Who am I now? In what direction should I move? How alone am I? Yet, at the same time, the survivor experienced an urgent need to fill the void. To restore a semblance of stability, he began a new family and plunged into his work.

When one attempts to mourn the totality, the personal may be obscured or even lost as it is buried beneath the entire catastrophe. This inadvertence further depersonalizes the loss and hinders a mourning process which should be a more immediate one. There is an identification with the whole, and something singular and near is forfeited. "Every time I go to shul I say Kaddish [a prayer recited after the death of an immediate family member]," Solomon Goldstein remarked. "At shul, people ask me, Who died? I say six million died and no one was left to say Kaddish for them." Rose Friedland put it more succinctly: "I never felt I had the right to just mourn *my* losses. I always felt I had to mourn the six million." For Rose, there is also the matter of permission. Can I mourn only for my own? (Yael Danieli, a psychologist, writes of "the central role of 'we-ness' in the identity of the victims of the Nazi Holocaust, as manifested in survivors' common use of 'we' rather than 'I,' particularly when describing their Holocaust experiences.")[1]

The reaction or lack of reaction by others, including foreign-born family members, unrelated Jews, and the seemingly sympathetic, hindered the survivors' expression of grief. While wanting to avoid the details of the events, while wanting to distance themselves from the trauma, American Jews and Israelis also muted any emotional response they might have offered. They wished to suppress their own feelings of vulnerability. And by seeing the Holocaust survivor as the Other (even though the survivor was a Jew), they could continue to deny their ongoing insecurities. The Holocaust happened to them. It could not and will not happen to us.

Their inexcusable lack of empathy resulted in an environment which was not at all conducive to the expression of feelings by survivors. (At a symposium in Jerusalem during the summer of 1992, I spoke of the rejection of immigrant survivors by Israeli society after the Holocaust. The Israeli moderator took strong exception. "It is wrong to say that Israeli society rejected survivors. *We* took them in!" "Is there no greater rejection than the rejection of an individual's experience and his feelings?" I retorted.) In addition, particularly in

America, survivors wanted to fit in. Having already been mortally persecuted as the Other, the survivor's desire to assimilate, to normalize, was pressing. Having been marked as a Jew, he was also tired of what had been an imposed self-consciousness. While he felt different, he did not want to be perceived as different. And he did not want to engender discomfort in his interlocutors.

At a time when Holocaust survivors were rebuilding their self-esteem, they were coincidentally extremely sensitive to human reactions and rejection. Survivors who immigrated to America encountered a culture which glorifies success, optimism, and happiness, while shunning failure, pessimism, and suffering. To be accepted into that society, survivors were urged to "put all of that behind you." In a sense, survivors were asked to betray their memories. They were also forced to hide their pain.

The final stage of the psychological process of mourning includes the acceptance of the death. Survivors, however, could not acquiesce because the destruction was unjust, senseless. Moreover, the entire mourning process involves a willingness to touch death and experience its ravages. Yet, having miraculously escaped death's clutches, survivors wished to move precipitously away from their previous feelings of vulnerability and the fate of all those who had once stood with them.

In addition, their equilibrium had been shattered. Nothing was as it had been. Anna Maline felt a sense of anticipation as she journeyed to her hometown of Charleroi (Belgium) after liberation. "But when I got there I was depressed. I felt lost. Everything was changed," she remembered.

For the survivor, moving away from death incorporated the keen desire to rejuvenate life. Mourning would have held the survivor back. Her life instinct propelled her forward. William Helmreich, in his wonderful book *Against All Odds*, notes a frequently mentioned remark of survivors: "I always wanted to look forward, not back." He interprets this reference point of the future to the survivor's optimism. Such an attitude helped propel the individual in his new life, but I believe this particular incantation reflects a darker motivation as well. *The survivor was too frightened to dwell on the past.* His chosenness to survive was too arbitrary, and therefore aggravated his ongoing sense of vulnerability. To look back at the destruction, at the loved ones who were consumed, might provoke an avalanche of emotion which would bury the survivor. It was only after decades had transpired that she felt the requisite sense of stability and vigor necessary to touch the past and allow some seepage of feeling.

The vacuum, the absence, was quickly and seemingly replenished, thus further allowing the survivor to skirt the issue of mourning. Children were named after murdered grandparents and siblings. The survivor had new responsibility, life-affirming vessels to nurture. He did not want them tainted by death. The survivor forced himself to focus on adapting to new circumstances and making correct decisions, for example, how quickly to leave one's country of origin (particularly in parts of Eastern and Central Europe under Communist control where antisemitism was rearing its ugly head once again), what to do in Germany, how to remove oneself from Europe, where to emigrate, and so on.

Esther Flamm was married by September 1945, just four months after her liberation. "Did I mourn? I don't know. I got married so soon. I had a child so soon. A new family. My daughter has my mother's name. I had to grow up. I was only a teenager when I got married. Actual mourning? I guess I never did. Once I had a family, that replaced a lot. My children are my life. They are everything."

The unfairness, the *ongoing* injustice of it all, hinders survivors from grieving. One more easily accepts *natural* losses – the death of the old, the passage of time, the separation from children – not arbitrary ones, particularly those perpetrated by one's fellow man as opposed to ones imposed by the unseen hand of the cosmos. Eighty-three-year-old Elisa Korn thinks of her furniture. "One day the Germans sent moving vans to take our things away. On the side of the trucks they painted *Liebesgabe aus Holland* [gifts from Holland]. I sometimes wonder, Who is eating off of my beautiful table? Who is sleeping in my bed?" It is more difficult to mourn while the criminals remain unpunished and the fruits of their iniquity continue to ripen. *Today,* they eat off of my table. *They* live a *normal* life, not the scarred embittered one which is my legacy. Their world continued uninterrupted, unscathed. My world was convulsed and permanently deranged.

Arguably, for females, the most joyous years occur during their adolescence. It is a time of romantic fantasies, naive excitement, and pure hope. Their physical being is in bloom. And as one looks back to those times from the perspective of the older adult, the heartaches of those formative years pale and the sentimental reigns. No matter these distortions, it is indeed a special time. And many survivors keenly feel this privation. They often speak of the romances they never knew, the passion denied them. "I always felt that I lost the best years of my life," Rose Feingold explained. "To this day, I look back and I think I was cheated out of my most beautiful years, my teenage years, my youth . . . I never had a teenage romance. You can buy or replace a dress. But I can never have those years. When I see teen-agers today, I envy them. On top of all, when we were transferred from one camp to another, we were held for a while at a beautiful castle with trees and flowers. I was so much of a romantic. I looked around and I was in paradise, but I was locked up. . . . Many people took off five years from their birthday because they didn't have those years." The haste with which survivors rejuvenated themselves and their family also stems from this particular theft of prime time. There was not a moment more to waste.

For some survivors, the emotional numbing they forced on them-selves in the concentration camps remained a modus operandi after liberation, thus further impeding their ability to grieve. The survivor must not only cope with the numerous losses but the myriad feelings (e.g., guilt, shame, fear, humiliation) derived from his Holocaust expe-riences. Effective grieving requires total emotional responses which are felt and articulated.

"I miss them [my family]," seventy-eight-year-old Dora Levinsohn told me. "But you get turned to stone at some point. I was still in Ravensbrück and a group of people came from Lodz. I knew one of the women and I asked her about my family and she told me about all the members of my family who were dead. I went back to my barrack and I told my sister-in-law the list of my family who were dead and how they died. She asked me why I wasn't crying. I was like a stone. It's still difficult for me to cry about anything personal . . . I still mourn. Holidays are hell for me. Literally hell. The loneliness . . . the memories of what happened . . . how I used to celebrate them . . . my family, the joy, the beauty . . . But I don't cry."

During the initial moments of our interview, I asked Leo Felder, as I had routinely asked the others, "Were your parents alive in 1939?" "I can't talk about them," he abruptly responded. While Leo utilizes his mother's seder plate during Passover, he always quashes any questions or mention by his children or wife of his murdered family. "Through all these years I have been like a stone . . . I try not to think about it. I am not religious. I go to shul Rosh Hashanah and Yom Kippur. When it comes to Yizkhor, I break down . . . [he weeps]. . . . But otherwise, I try not to think about it. On the surface I cope with it very well . . . on the surface." "Why do you go to shul on Rosh Hashanah and Yom Kippur even though you know you will break down?" I ask. "I'm not religious but I want to keep up the tradition . . . I still have respect for my parents . . . [he cries]." At the close of our time together, Leo Felder remarked that he probably would not have agreed to be interviewed if he had known we were going to discuss "these kinds of emotional things."

After the Germans directly occupied Hungary in the spring of 1944, Sol Feingold approached his parents and urged them to attempt an escape. His parents argued that the entire family must remain together, that the Germans needed them for labor, and that the Soviets would soon liberate them anyhow. They were reassured by the Nazis' offer of resettlement. Sol was nineteen when he was thrust into the world of Auschwitz. His parents and pregnant sister were gassed upon arrival. "I remember once lying on my bed as a kid and imagining how I would deal with it if one of my parents would die. I couldn't even imagine it, it was such a horrendous thought. I have to give the Germans credit for turning a normal person into a kind of monster I am. They put us through such terror . . . terror doesn't even describe it . . . that after a few days in Auschwitz, there were no tears. That sensitive child became a monster . . . The Germans removed any of that tenderness. They killed that child. I'm too detached now.

"Constantly remembering is my way of burying my parents and sister. This is my way of being with them all the time. At Yom Hashoah [Day of the Shoah], there may be a reference which brings some small tears, but not the normal tears . . . I'm sitting shiva [the seven days of mourning after the death of a parent or child] all my life."

Remembering implies mourning for many survivors. But as a result, the grieving process is no longer as circumscribed as it should be. Because of their commitment to memory, survivors never achieve closure. Even those who have numbed themselves have not necessarily forsworn remembrances. The typical Holocaust survivor never shouts out. His tears are only rendered painstakingly. Furthermore, in many cases the survivor is mostly left with memories of life, as he was not privy to the details of his loved ones' deaths.

Lacking confrontation with family members' deaths makes it more difficult for the survivor to fully appreciate their finality. He is only left with an absence. Joseph Simon left his family in Lublin and fled eastward ahead of the conquering Nazi divisions. At the border of the Soviet Union he was arrested and accused of smuggling and spying. After weeks of interrogation, he was sent to a prison camp in Siberia. While attempting to buy train tickets for Warsaw at a small-town station outside of Lublin, Joseph's mother was identified as a Jew and denounced to the Nazis by a local Pole. Joseph says Yahrzeit for his mother on the anniversary of that day, October 31, 1941. Even though he is not certain she was killed on October 31, "that was the day she ceased to exist for us," he explained.

Some are panicked at their *failure* of memory. To forget implies betrayal. Barbara Lowenstein frets. "I think about them. I don't know what is mourning. I think about them. There has never been a day after the war that I don't think about the Holocaust. Sometimes I think what they look like. I'm starting to forget, and that is terrible too." The mere passage of time with its concomitant aging process serves to produce an increasing unreality of the events, a creeping bewilderment. Did that really happen? Did I go through that? I was rhetorically asked by several of those I interviewed. Mourning becomes more difficult as memory fails.

A few survivors implicitly shunned the mourning process because of the hope they nurtured of finding loved ones who might have evaded the whirlwind. To have mourned would have necessitated the loss of hope. There were often no eyewitnesses to testify to the death of a relative. Particularly in those cases, the survivor was left with room for doubt. Forty years after the conclusion of the war, survivors still searched for a familiar face at periodic gatherings held in Israel and the United States. And when there would be that occasional, miraculous discovery and reunion, it would fuel the fantasies of others.

The International Tracing Service is housed in a three-building complex in the central German town of Arolsen and has a staff of four hundred. After receiving form no. 1609 from a petitioner, the International Tracing Service will launch a free search through 43 million documents it maintains on victims of Nazi Germany. The records range from tattered prisoner identification cards printed on the backs of cigarette cartons to the dark, bulging concentration camp Death Books. An unexpected bounty of evidence and a new surge of inquiries from the former East Bloc threaten to overwhelm the center. In August 1992, Charles-Claude Biedermann, the Swiss director of the service, which is funded by the German government but administered by the International Red Cross, remarked, "We know of three hundred thousand requests for information waiting in Moscow alone." The Russian queries were triggered by a trove of Third Reich documents which Moscow, in 1989, decided to share for the first time. The International Tracing Service believes that the archives contain 600,000 new names of concentration camp inmates in ledgers that the Russians seized when they liberated camps in the East.

The Arolsen archives are not open to the public and the data are too extensive and complicated to computerize, so requests always begin in the file cabinets where names of the persecuted are recorded on 740 million index cards. A unique filing system was developed both alphabetically and phonetically in order to take into consideration misspellings and the variations which might be found among all the nationalities registered. The Arolsen center receives about seven hundred queries a day, the majority of them from Poland and mostly from people who were deported and forced into labor for Nazi Germany. Now entering retirement, these individuals need proof of their persecution in order to collect special benefits.

Most searches for missing loved ones are initiated by children wanting to find out what happened to their parents. While 490,000 queries lie without answer or resolution, the Tracing Service claims a thirty to fifty percent success rate, counting cases where the death of a missing person can be confirmed and the searcher's query therefore answered.[2]

Martha Janusz was working in a German expropriated factory in Chelm in 1942. Hearing of an action to take place that evening, she fled to Warsaw after her workday without going home and bidding her parents farewell. Martha never saw her father again. She voiced a subtle variant of the denial mechanism. "I haven't mourned . . . I think my father is with me all the time. . . . [she weeps] . . . He got me through. My father was watching over me, helping me make decisions, telling me what to do. I wasn't that smart. There was some higher power getting me through . . . I think it was my father." Martha Janusz retains her father as an amulet. He was and is there for her.

Expressing one's anger fully and finally is another important aspect of the mourning process. But survivors have remained angry through the last four decades. They were angry because others seemed not to care. They were angry because of the rapid rejuvenation of Germany. They were angry because of the ongoing perilous position of Israel. They were angry because of their anticipated repeat of the onslaught. They were angry because their lives were tormented, displaced, broken. And, of course, they were angry because of the senselessness, the unfairness, of the Holocaust.

Jerry Singer lights a memorial candle on the anniversary of his family's arrival at Auschwitz. "My mourning is expressed through hatred," he told me as he chain-smoked through our four hours together. Jerry Singer's ongoing anger is more accessible to him than it is to most other survivors. But to whom can Jerry Singer vent his anger? Another problem.

Survivor guilt can interfere with mourning. I am here and they are not, the survivor muses. If he was more deserving than me, how is it that I can be alive grieving for him? Once again, the "unnatural" order of things inhibits the natural mourning process. "I miss them [my parents]," eight-four-year-old Daniel Davidoff told me. "I remember them all the time. I can forgive *only* for myself, but I can't forget . . . I think a lot about my parents. My father was a very good man, *better than me*" [my emphasis]. A single tear trickled down from the corner of his right eye as he continued, "I wish he would live. In the camp, when I had a little more, I wished he could be with me so I could help him."

Daniel Davidoff couldn't help his father. Others are also tortured by their previous inability to save or succor loved ones. Ben Kass is a tough former partisan who "never took shit from anyone." ("After the war, in Danzig, I had a walking stick and I used to beat the shit out of Germans on the street," he informed me.) Ben told me of how he mourns. "Every day. I think about them every day. I think about when we were together. I cry . . . very often . . . It's hard. . . . It's very hard. . . . They're dead. *There's nothing I can do* [my emphasis]. The only thing I can do is think about them. The older I get, I think about them more often. The older you get, you have more time on your hands and all kinds of things come into your brain." Ben had fled the Warsaw ghetto and found a partisan group which would accept Jews. "I pleaded with my parents to run. My mother only went to the rebbe to ask *shailes* [questions]. She kept asking the rebbe, 'When will the war end?' The rebbe just answered, 'Be strong, it will be okay.' " Previously during the interview, Ben told me of a recent dream in which he saw his mother. She asked him, "Why did you run away?" Ben is perpetually vexed by two questions: "Why me? Why that I am alive?" There was nothing Ben could do then, and all that he can do now is *think* about his parents. Perhaps this will assuage some of the survivor guilt as he remembers those who, he believes, should have been here, perhaps even in his place.

Those whose children were murdered during the Holocaust not only experience the greatest survivor guilt, they also find it most difficult to complete the mourning process. While their depression reflects their gnawing guilt, it also represents their inability to exorcise their grief. It has been said that parents who lose their children to death never fully recover. Again, the unnatural sequence seems to render the natural psychological process of mourning impossible.

A few survivors, angry at their selection because of birthright, fearful of a repetition of the persecution, disillusioned with a faith which did not protect, have turned their backs on their Jewish identity after the Holocaust, some even going so far as to deny their Jewish lineage. Nevertheless, the Holocaust swept away their loved ones simply because they were Jewish, and because of their departure from their people, engagement in the mourning process for these individuals is further encumbered by a refusal to acknowledge their Jewishness. It was their *Jewish* family members who were murdered and must be mourned.

In many instances, survivors are not certain of the exact details or circumstances of a loved one's death. Because of the forced and chosen separations, it was unusual to have been an eyewitness. These limitations of vividness also hinder the mourning process. The deaths become more abstract. "There is nothing left! No tombs, no ashes. I remember my little cousins. They are floating around in the air." Absent gravesites, the monuments and museums dedicated to Holocaust remembrance provide mourning sites and a context. They provide comfort derived from a sense of closeness to the victims. Because of the recent rise of historical revisionists, these sites serve as a treasured document and a refutation to those who would deny the dimensions of the Holocaust.

Annual Yom Hashoah commemorations afford an effective opportunity for individual and collective mourning. The structured, public nature of the event offers safety from the possibility of emotional crumble. The environment is a supportive one, peopled by similar others who truly understand. The ceremony takes place outside the ongoing course of the survivor's life and therefore does not threaten to interfere with his careful adjustment and forward movement. "It is the only time I cry," several survivors told me.

Survivors engage in other rituals as well. They may know the exact date of a death and light a Yahrzeit candle every year. Without definitive knowledge, they may choose an approximate date or a symbolic date (e.g., the liquidation of their ghetto, the arrival at a death camp) to do the same. Some survivors (often with their children) journey back to a hometown or a concentration camp in which they were incarcerated. The smells, sights, tastes, and sounds (imagined or real) of the previously inhabited environs may facilitate a stream of emotions.

Despite being troubled by their religious ambivalence, survivors engage in synagogue activities and observances. As Leo Felder remarked, "I'm not religious, but I want to keep up the tradition . . . I still have respect for my parents." Observing the ritual traditions allows the survivor to pay homage to his parents, and to feel closer to them and his past.

Further losses are heaped upon survivors as they move into the final developmental stage of life.

"Particularly severe losses are sustained in the things one *does* – in all spheres of activity, from sexual, occupational, avocational, and recreational. These losses force a shift from doing to thinking, from planning to reminiscing, from preoccupation with everyday events and long-range planning to reviewing and rethinking one's life."[3]

His increasing debilitation funnels more and more of the survivor's attention to reminiscences. His ongoing decrements – the death of friends, the death of a spouse, the separation from children, physical deteriorations – elicit further feelings associated with deprivations incurred during the Holocaust. *This coincidence provides opportunity for the commingled mourning of past and present losses.*

On June 11, 1942, Saul Garber was left alone in the ghetto of Tarnów after being precipitously ripped from his parents, who were sent to Belzec. The Jewish Council had included his name on the list given to the Nazis of those who were under fourteen, and Saul was spared deportation to concentration camps in Germany for another year. "I've never mourned," Saul admitted. "I have never gone to a temple to say Kaddish. I set up two candles at home on the day I guess they [my parents] died. The whole month is difficult. There is a sadness but I've been unable to cry since liberation. I don't know why I can't cry. . . . Even when I went back to Belzec three years ago and I wanted so badly to cry but couldn't. . . . Perhaps it goes back to the concentration camp when showing your emotions could cost you your life. When I went to Belzec, I was sad, but numb. I scooped up some earth that had bones in it and put it in my pocket. I tried to imagine what my parents felt on the train ride, how they felt when they got there. What were my parents' last thoughts in the gas chamber? . . .

"Both my son and daughter lived at home until they were married. When they got married I felt a similar sadness and pain as when I was separated from my parents. The day after my daughter was married, I took a walk and it was one of the few times in my life I cried."

Psychologically speaking, all losses may resemble one another in their emotional consequences. And while, for the survivor, this axiom may foster a completion of the mourning process, it may also result in the unwarranted elicitation of previous feelings.

Many survivors experience the normal phenomenon of old age as a recapitulation of Holocaust experiences. Thus, they experience their children's having left home and their spouses' and friends' deaths as a reliving of their massive losses during the war. They feel further estranged when their children follow the American ideal of independence. They may experience the sense of abandonment, isolation, and loneliness common among aging people in this country as a repetition of being shunned and dehumanized during and right after the Holocaust.[4]

For survivors of the Holocaust, mourning has proved problematic. Within the Jewish faith, there are prescribed rituals to be engaged in immediately after the death of a nuclear family member. A supportive environment is created which allows the emergence of the requisite feelings associated with loss. After immersing oneself in mourning for one week and completing the most arduous period of the process, the mourner is accompanied out of his house to symbolically reenter the world of the living.

Those who were spared were too exhausted, too frightened, and too disoriented to mourn soon after liberation. They felt compelled to continue to run away from death. They were also denied the support and encouragement to mourn as others were too uncomfortable to acknowledge what had transpired. It has taken several decades, but many survivors are now experiencing the pangs of mourning for their murdered loved ones as they adjust and react to the natural, ongoing losses of old age. Perhaps, at this time, they can be supported in their process by a more enlightened family and community which can finally encourage, understand, and tolerate the sadness and grief of Holocaust survivors.

4

Vulnerabilities

Every Saturday afternoon, Miriam Goldfarb came to pick up her friend Lilah Pinkus, a widow and survivor of Auschwitz, for their weekly card game. Even though the first Scud attack on Tel Aviv from Iraq had occurred during the early hours of that morning, Miriam saw no need for interference with the pleasurable routine of the last ten years. This was their outlet, their time to kibitz, kvetch, gossip, laugh, and forget about the daily travails which accompanied one's advancing years.

As she always did, Miriam slipped her car into Lilah's empty assigned parking space and rode the elevator to the third floor of the apartment building on Rehov Abba Hillel Silver. She knocked on Lilah's door. After several minutes had passed, she knocked once again, more urgently. With no response forthcoming, she pressed her ear to the door and thought she heard a whimpering or weeping and faint words. Miriam hurried to a neighbor who kept a key to Lilah's apartment, returned to Lilah's front door, and opened it. Miriam followed the sounds and glimpsed Lilah in the far corner of the living room, on her knees, rocking back and forth, her head bowed and turned to the perpendicular angle of the wall. As Miriam approached, she heard Lilah murmuring a plea. "Please don't gas me. Please don't gas me." "Lilah, it's me, Miriam." Without noticing, Lilah continued, "Please don't gas me. Please don't gas me." Miriam put her arm around Lilah's shoulder and gently brought her to her feet. "*Sha* [quiet], Lilah. You are alright. *Sha*, Lilah. You are safe." Unable to relinquish her focus, Lilah, slowly moving her head from side to side, continued to implore, "Please don't gas me. Please don't gas me."

On the same street in Ramat Gan, but one block farther north of

Lilah, seventy-year-old, silver haired Fela Grossman, a survivor of Majdanek, lived with her husband, David, who had been liberated from Buchenwald. After a Scud slammed into the apartment building next to the Grossmans, their children pleaded with them to depart for a kibbutz in the relative safety of the center of the country where Fela's first cousin lived. David was frightened but unclear about a course of action. Fela, however, was resolute. "I'm not going anywhere anymore. I won't let Hitlers chase me from my home again." As the siren warnings blared two evenings later, the slightly under five feet tall grandmother of four boys stood at her crisscross-taped window, defiantly shaking her fist in the air. "You'll never get me, you sons of bitches! You didn't get me before and you won't get me now! I don't care what you do!"

Lilah Pinkus's and Fela Grossman's reactions demonstrate the heterogeneity of survivors' responses to their past. In Lilah's case, a new adversity overwhelmed internal resources which had already been severely depleted during the Holocaust. One might interpret Fela's response as an attempt to deny her fear by reacting with bravado. But we must also understand that her gesture indicates a fierce resolve never to be destroyed, and a confidence born of having outlasted previous murderers bent on her destruction.

There is disagreement concerning the psychopathological nature, manifestation, and extent of the Holocaust's effects, but few would argue that they have been completely benign. One striking characteristic of many survivors is their enhanced sense of vulnerability. While human nature begs for an orderly world, one which follows laws of cause and effect and therefore allows for rational explanation and predictability, survivors experienced their persecution as unjustified and, consequently, inexplicable. "Bad things come without our trying," Barbara Lowenstein, the only remaining member of her family, reflected. For Barbara and other survivors, one can never adequately anticipate or prepare for future indignities. Self-protection is ultimately impossible.

Not surprisingly, many survivors expect future danger and ready themselves. After being separated from her mother and siblings at Auschwitz, Mina Fogel persevered through numerous selections while in Section C. Eventually she was sent to Nuremberg as a slave laborer in a factory. "If I'm in an arena with thousands of people or in a theater, I'm always checking where the exits are," she remarked. "I'm still doing my job – of saving myself in the situation."

Ethel Janov grew up in the small town of Miskolc, Hungary. "As a child, being Jewish was never neutral for me. I always felt that I would be hurt or attacked or made fun of." After Auschwitz, her personal sense of jeopardy extended itself to her present family. "I had many fears when my children were growing up. When I would leave them, I would expect not to find them when I got back. When they were in sleep-away camp, I had continuous fantasies of them drowning. When my children were growing up I had a lot of nightmares. . . . In my fifties I developed a hip problem and had to reduce my activities. I couldn't tolerate being at all incapacitated. . . . If I need to run . . . It was very difficult for me to feel helpless again."

We would like to believe that, at the very least, sanctity of life is an absolute. But this potential balm to personal safety has been shattered. Olga Himmelfarb, a survivor of Auschwitz and Ravensbrück, lives a modern Orthodox lifestyle in Los Angeles. She believes, but she is also frightened. "Life is nothing. To kill someone is nothing. Life is not valued like it used to be." Life is not valued like it used to be, like it was before the Holocaust. Humankind passed a Rubicon of evil fifty years ago, a Rubicon from which there is no retreat. A Fury has been unleashed, never to be contained. And as God could not protect us then, He is ultimately powerless today.

Some survivors have attempted to compensate for their feelings of vulnerability. Jack Diamond grew up in a small town in Germany. The only surviving member of his immediate family, Jack embarked for Palestine after liberation and lived on a kibbutz for several years before deciding to leave for America. "The kibbutz necessitated sublimation of individual needs," he explained. "I knew I wanted more for myself."

This self-centeredness was evident before the war. "Even as a youngster, I had a strong personality. I was always tough. Because I was taught in school that Jews were inferior, I decided to show them how tough I can be. I have appropriated some behavior from the camps. I can be very tough and afterwards I am ashamed of what I have done. My experience in the camps made me very strong . . . and very sensitive to the suffering of others. I was a selfish, egotistical person before the war. I never had a social conscience until my experience in the camps.

"I was too rough, too authoritarian with my family over the years . . . I fall into my behavior I learned in the camps . . . I'm too rough, mostly on people who are close to me, not strangers." Jack is rough on those close to him, not strangers. He steels his loved ones for the cruelty which awaits them outside. For Jack and others who emerged from Auschwitz, danger lurks. There is little distinction between the possible and the probable.

Ida Koch also toughened herself for future battle in a world which will inevitably prove rapacious. "I didn't have a childhood. I was fourteen. I feel deprived by all those natural things. Sometimes I'm rough. Sometimes you do mistakes because you go overboard trying to survive. Like you can't have anyone take things from you. I like to give, to give to charity. But if anyone takes anything from me, then I fight them. I made this when I came out of the concentration camp. Nobody gonna take anything away from me."

Survivors of the Holocaust live with perilous uncertainty. Helen Schwartz grew up in Sevlus, Czechoslovakia, which by 1939 had been annexed by Hungary. Helen was deported to Poland in 1941 with her family because they could not produce proof of Hungarian citizenship. In 1944, on a cattle car with her parents bound for Auschwitz, her father, a physician, suggested they all take the cyanide he had saved for such an eventuality. Helen has known how easily home, things, life, can slip away. "I never wanted a big house. I know how little one needs. The material things don't mean much. I know what you need to survive." Helen knows that money, material possessions, or physical barriers only provide the illusion of protection.

"There isn't a day when I don't feel fear," Rose Feingold told me. "I can't stand in line at a cashier. . . . If someone accidentally pushes me . . . I'm always looking over my shoulder. I can't take it if someone walks behind me." Acknowledging the damaging effects on her children of her excessive protectiveness, Rose stared vacantly out her living room window as she spoke. "I'm not living like a real human being. I'm scared of everything. I was scared of the telephone – if it's jail or death or some tragedy." Turning her face back to me, she continued. "Sometimes you think you can't really trust anybody. We were too much careful of our children and we taught them things like that. We always tried to keep them safe too much . . . don't let them do this, don't let them do that . . . I hold on to my family too tight and this is not good. I ruined their life a little because of this. My home and possessions mean nothing. When Hitler came, he took everything away. But I hold on to life, my children . . . I can't control it. I don't want to lose anybody from my family."

Having stood at the entrance to death, perhaps on many occasions, survivors, understandably, feel unusually vulnerable. This "death anxiety" is the source of repeated warnings of impending danger.[1] Relatively innocuous, everyday activities may be perceived as lethal hazards. Children of survivors may react to this apprehension by developing excessive, unwarranted fears of their own. The jeopardy felt by the parent infects the child. Many in the second generation have spoken of the scent of fear which permeated their household.

"Knowing the gruesome details of their experiences must contribute a little pessimism to my nature, a more cynical outlook on life and what my fellow man is capable of than people with more normal family histories would have. They [my parents] taught me not to trust people. Emphasize the dress, the appearance, the external. The way you are is not necessarily okay, so present a false picture of what people want to see.

"I carry a deep sadness in my life. The Holocaust has increased my awareness regarding the dark side in us – because we are mostly machine and animal. There are very few human beings. My mother would say, 'There are a lot of Hitlers out there so you've got to be tough.'

"It is mind boggling, terrifying to realize the destructive nature of man. Some perpetrators of the Holocaust did not set out to murder and destroy. Some murdered unquestionably. The former perpetrators also came to be murderers without remorse. That it can and did happen leaves disturbing implications on my outlook on life. I cannot be so trusting or idealistic. . . .

"For the most part, I have come to realize that you cannot depend on other people. Only a few people will really come through for you when push comes to shove, so you must always look to protect and succor yourself. . . . Life can be a hostile environment, so if you can maintain a confident inner self, you'll be in better shape. I think I am like my father in this way."[2]

After the birth of his first child, Paul Handel, the sole survivor of his extremely religious family in Zgierz, Poland, came home every day at lunchtime from work so he could give him a bath – and perhaps to make sure that he was still alive. "I'm very possessive of my family, to a fault. I love my kids so much. Since my first child, I became overly obsessed with my family. I lost so much, that whatever I have, it's become like a possession. I don't want to let go." After the interview, I had an opportunity to speak with Paul's American-born wife. She informed me that the man she married changed dramatically after their firstborn arrived. "He suddenly developed a terrible temper." This new symbol of compensation resulted in the eruption of Paul's historically dormant feelings of vulnerability, loss, and consequent rage.

Survivors' profoundly mistrustful attitude toward those around them resulted not only from their persecution and betrayal, but from the recognition that pleas from one's fellow man will fall on deaf ears. Elie Wiesel wrote, "At Auschwitz, not only man died, but also the idea of man." One can only count on oneself, the survivor intones.

Those survivors who encountered helpful others, Jew or Gentile, during the Holocaust appear less bitter, less condemning, less pessimistic. In written or oral accounts of human relations in the concentration camps, survivors seem divided in their experiences and perceptions. Some report an entirely selfish, every-man-for-himself mentality. Others readily acknowledge the crucial support of another in maintaining their existence during those times. Not only did this assistance provide physical and emotional nourishment, but it afforded the ability to sustain a belief in man. Often during my interviews, a survivor was more likely to cry when recounting the death of one of his compatriots than when relating the death of a mother or father. The protection of a parent was naturally expected. The succor of a friend was greatly appreciated.

For most survivors, man is perceived to be inherently selfish and murderously aggressive. However, there are certain groups who are most likely to be the targets of these offensive impulses. The Jew has always been and will always be the favored prey. "I distrust humanity," Saul Halpern, a former resident of Berlin and an inmate of Auschwitz and Nordhausen, told me. "I distrust what people can do and will do to other people under certain circumstances. Today, people have no work. That's how it started with Hitler. And then they look for a scapegoat. I'm sure it will be blamed on the Jews. . . . Sometimes I think of a place, an island, where no one could get me and my family."

Believing that their people are under constant siege, many survivors have withdrawn from an identification with humankind and have restricted their focus to the Jewish world. As one child of survivors told me: "My father doesn't trust *anyone* outside of his immediate family. . . . *Everything* in life revolves around the question, Is it good or bad for the Jews?"

Some of the seemingly most depressed survivors I interviewed also voiced the most pessimistic of outlooks. This pessimism often was apparent during the Holocaust ("I believed we wouldn't make it through, the Germans had it in for us and that would be it") and contributes to its lasting effects as the survivor anticipates an ongoing triumph of evil. These survivors serve as examples of how a prewar personality predisposition affected the way they coped with their persecution during the Holocaust. This predisposition may extend its influence to their postwar adjustment as well.

Although a sense of vulnerability is readily accessible, the rage of most survivors has remained suppressed. It seeps out as impatience, irritability, a proclivity for perceiving intended personal affronts. Survivors have been able to control their naked anger and present a mask of conviviality for public consumption. While a few children of survivors have described periodic outpourings of rage, even more have reported a caldron of tension that continually simmers, ready to boil over at real or imagined affronts. The survivor's social façade most often collapses in the safe confines of his home.

"My father is paranoid that his life is about to end. He is almost two-faced. He is wonderful with friends, a real joker. With his family, he flies off the handle at the slightest provocation. You have to walk on eggshells with him."

"My father was always tense. There were so many things that would trigger his anger – war movies, anything having to do with Germany or Nazis. . . . He had little patience with others, including his children. He was quick to judge. Punishment of his children was physical at times. He didn't speak about it, but you knew what he was so angry about – his family, which was completely obliterated during the Holocaust."[3]

For most survivors, the Holocaust was a thousand days of hunger, a thousand daydreams of food (a commodity worth countless gambles with one's life). "Food, I'm different from your average person," Ida Koch told me. "I would never throw away any food. I eat too much. When I was in concentration camp, my only wish was if I ever have a whole bread for myself, I would be the happiest person in the world. I ruin my health with food. I'm not going to deprive myself if I feel like something." Saul Halpern is also influenced by his previous cravings. "I'm afraid of hunger. If I buy bread, I always buy two so I shouldn't be without it." And while it has been forty-five years since Saul's stomach was empty, once again the survivor cautiously anticipates a repetition of history.

We all grieve over the dismemberment of our innocence as we move through life's disappointments. Following personal traumatic events, however, the lifelong process of disillusionment is accelerated and intensified, coming as a sharp blow as opposed to gradually usurping the child's naiveté. Survivors are particularly bitter because their inner purity was completely destroyed at such an early age. "As a child I learned to hate very much," Ida Koch reflected. However, here, too, the prominence and expression of this effect vary depending on the survivor's unique experiences.

Of David Himmelstein's nine siblings, two brothers and two sisters remained alive. Posing as Gentiles, David, his wife, and two children left Antwerp in May 1942 for the hoped-for safety of Vichy France. Eventually, David was interrogated and turned over to the Germans by the French Milice. In September of that year, he and his family were deported from Drancy to Auschwitz. Despite losing his wife and two children to the gas chambers upon arrival, David persevered. He was sent to an auxiliary labor camp of Auschwitz "because I looked healthy and had good shoes." He escaped in December 1942, traversed Europe, and returned to Brussels, where he notified Chief Rabbi Ullman of the death factories in the East. Rabbi Ullman abruptly asked him to leave, incensed with David's fabrications. "I am getting postcards from the camps saying things are not too bad," Rabbi Ullman insisted. David spent the last year under occupation posing as a Gentile, cutting holes into mountains on the French-Belgian border for the V-1 project whose missiles were to be launched against England. David's brothers, fortunately, never encountered a member of the SS. "It's different if you were in a concentration camp," David explained. "My mother was from Vienna and we spoke German in our home. After liberation, I never spoke German again. My two brothers who were not in the camps have different feelings. They will speak German." Simply hearing about atrocities is different from personally experiencing their malevolence. We can be more sanguine, less spiteful of wounds incurred once removed. When we have been in the very midst of another's malicious onslaught, our hatred sears, our memory is unforgiving.

"Can you imagine being in a boxcar for cattle, fighting my way to the window, saying good-bye to my husband and child, being sure I would never see them again?" Dora Levinsohn, a survivor of Ravensbrück and Bergen-Belsen, rhetorically asked me. "The absolute cruelty, the absolute inhumanity I witnessed from the SS women. We didn't have any food or water in the last days at Bergen-Belsen and we had typhoid fever. One of my friends tried to drink some muddy water and an SS woman kicked her and beat her. These things left me numb, not hysterical, numb." For Dora, the emotional consequences of her experiences exceeded the boundaries of what she could process. As an act of self-preservation, we can feel only so much sadness, so much revulsion. Indeed, the emotionally numb survivor has been described and reported by many investigators.

However, the great majority of survivors I encountered did not evidence this characteristic. On the contrary, they felt a range of emotions – sadness, joy, guilt, anger, sympathy – rather intensely. Perhaps enough time has elapsed. Perhaps they feel the perquisite safety and security necessary to experience emotions. Their advancing years may further impel survivors to reminisce and integrate life events and the feelings associated with them.

Some of the apparently least emotional survivors evidenced the ability to remember exact dates, *exact times of the day*, of scenes which occurred fifty years ago. They have adopted an academic's objective approach to their personal Holocaust history. A chronicle has supplanted their tears. "Perhaps I'm too detached, too analytic," Sol Feingold, whose precise memory of dates and times was remarkable, apprised me. "But that's better than to always be in pain." Focusing on the objective circumstances may, the survivor believes, enhance his ability to remember accurately and vividly – a task to which he is devoted. And approaching the "subject" in a more intellectualized manner further aids as a defense mechanism in the suppression of the survivor's feelings.

In addition to a general extinction of feeling, a few survivors withdrew other investments in life. Nothing could be as important as what was lost. It was therefore difficult to generate enthusiasm and value for what remained. David Himmelstein's wife and two children were murdered at Auschwitz. After liberation, he married his sister-in-law. "I was a fanatic photographer before the war. I would get fast upset if someone told me they didn't like a picture I made. After the war I was only interested in working at it but I wasn't interested in being perfect . . . I lost my wife and children so nothing was important anymore. This was like zero. I only work, no more to be an artist, but to only forget what happened. This was nothing. I lost the real thing, what I lost." What could be more valuable, more worthy of effort, than one's child? How does one enthusiastically approach any aspect of life when he knows that what most deserves his ardor has already been taken from him forever?

It is virtually impossible to escape memories of the Holocaust. Because of their physical or psychological association to the past, thousands of stimuli have the potential for eliciting strong feelings in survivors. Sights, smells, sounds, items, situations, people, may evoke sadness or anger as they remind him of a fuller time which has evaporated. "Many times I would come home from work upset. My children would ask, 'Why is Daddy angry?' I wasn't angry, but something hit me that day. Maybe I heard German spoken. Maybe I heard someone talk about the Holocaust and they were wrong." Because of the role they played in the persecution of survivors, authority figures in uniform, and dogs, are the most common symbols likely to arouse anxiety.

Unfortunately, as children, survivors' offspring did not understand the connections that elicited these outbursts by their parents, and often became unduly frightened themselves both by the stimulus and by the parent's reaction, assuming their behavior had caused it since no other readily understandable provocation was apparent. One child of survivors described the following scene:

"I remember stretching up high to hold my mother's hand as we walked to the school to collect my two older sisters, one of whom was in kindergarten, and the other was in second grade. As we rounded the corner, my mother would suddenly grasp my hand almost frenetically, and I would sense terror in her. I could not define this at age three, but I would find out much later what forces were operant. . . . My mother explained to me that as we walked to the school in Gary, Indiana, she would catch sight of the steel mill's smoke stacks and suddenly be seized with the fear that those ugly, gray billows of smoke emanated from crematoria . . . like the ones in which her parents and family were destroyed."[4]

As previously mentioned, because of victories over the powers bent on their destruction, many survivors experience an enhanced ability to cope with any obstacle placed in their path. However, for some survivors, post-Holocaust calamities tax already depleted inner reserves, and may therefore send them hurdling backward to the abyss. Abe Stark was liberated on April 10, 1945, from Buchenwald. He broke down and wept as he told me about that day his skeleton, covered with sores, saw the Americans. "I was twenty-three years old and had spent the best years of my youth in German camps as a slave." In 1969, Abe entered psychotherapy because he was depressed. "Things didn't go right with me. Everything comes together. I had financial problems. One relates to the other. If it wasn't for the Holocaust, I might have been in a different situation. When I came to America, I had no relatives here, it was very difficult." Abe lost his entire business in a devastating earthquake which rocked southern California in February 1971. "Why did this have to happen to me again?" Abe asked. Once again, the innocent is harmed. How much must one endure? How much *can* one endure? were Abe's tired questions.

For many survivors, the night brings danger. As they sleep, defense mechanisms shielding them from memories of a painful past relax. Auschwitz returns. Psychological profiles of Holocaust survivors (as well as other victims of trauma) invariably include a notable incidence of nightmares. In a recently published study, two-thirds of a sample of Holocaust survivors experienced sleep disturbances, a significantly greater number than found in the control group. This investigation also uncovered a positive correlation between the frequency of nightmares and the survivor's duration of confinement in a concentration camp.[5]

In my own work, I have found that the greatest proportion of survivors experienced nightmares most frequently in the years immediately following liberation. As they became more caught up in the rebuilding of their lives and the need to cope with new pressures and responsibilities, wakeful as well as sleep-induced memories often receded into the background, their unconscious. This process was given further impetus by the desire of the survivor not to dwell on the past as that would only impede his present efforts to reconstitute a life for himself and his new family.

While experiencing this pattern of frequency, another group of survivors has noticed the renewed emergence of Holocaust-related dreams in recent years. These individuals also report that their *conscious* thoughts have reverted anew to the events of their traumatic past. This increasing daytime reverie, and the enhanced sense of helplessness which accrues to the aging process, has, understandably, reawakened repressed images and feelings. Now in their seventies and eighties, survivors move inexorably to death's doorstep. That recognition further prods them to review and assess their lives. Incitements in the survivor's present environment also provoke associated past memories. Viewing a Holocaust film, reading of an attack on Israel, speaking about one's experiences, returning from a pilgrimage to a concentration camp, may activate buried fears.

Louis Weintraub, an officer in the Polish cavalry in 1939 and fighter during the Warsaw ghetto uprising, seemed to be one of the toughest survivors I had ever encountered. "When you went through the Polish Army, you were a rough customer," he emphasized. Yet, when I asked about his nightmares, he demurred: "I don't want to talk about it . . . I can't." Because they are too threatened, other survivors are able to remember only fragments of a dream or none of it at all. A few believe they exert volitional control. "My mind is like a machine. I programmed it not to think about it. I had such power. I waked myself up to stop the nightmares."

One-third of the participants I interviewed reported that they have never had Holocaust-related nightmares. Researchers at the sleep research laboratory at Haifa's Technion University have reported that the capacity to recall dream content was significantly lower in well-adjusted survivors than in a control group of those who emigrated to Palestine before 1939. These results imply that the survivor's isolation of interred memories may promote her mental health.

Several survivors reported being periodically awakened by their spouses. "My husband wakes me up and says I holler. I holler for my mother or him or something about guns and chasing," Barbara

Lowenstein told me. Olga Himmelfarb agreed to be interviewed, but her husband, whose parents were shot while he looked on, would not talk about "those things." Olga's sleep is frequently interrupted by her husband. "He screams. . . . Sometimes he hits and kicks me before I can wake him up."

Just as survivors differ in the frequency with which Holocaust-related dreams punctuate their sleep, they also tend to emphasize a varied array of themes. Some material simply reflects previous events. A survivor who was part of the transport *Kommando* at Auschwitz dreams: "I take people off the trains and I see them going to the ovens." Sixty-six-year-old Saul Halpern tells me, "I see myself at selections, naked, going to the gas chambers. I wake up crying, sweating, and then I cannot fall asleep . . . I'm sitting. . . . The most fearful thing in the camp were the selections. . . . If they wrote down your number, that was it. A lot of people got diarrhea at the selection. We had to stand naked in the barracks and just wait, just wait for the death sentence."

Other dreams reflect the terrifying sense of being lost, adrift, alone, disconnected from the safe familiar. Czechoslovakian-born Helen Schwartz informed me that for the first five or six years after the war, she experienced nightly disturbances. "The dreams are the same. I go someplace that I don't recognize and I wonder how I will get back home. . . . Sometimes I feel trapped there." Other survivors commonly dream of being chased, cornered, and, if they awaken later rather than sooner, caught. "There are barbed wires, dogs barking at you. You're trying to hide. You wake up screaming, not letting yourself finish the dream because they were too horrible." Another survivor recounted: "When it's very hot in the room [as it was in the boxcar when they transported her to Ravensbrück] I have nightmares. Germans are following me and catching me. I'm always being chased by the Germans. . . . And that's funny because in real life, I was never chased by them. Or I would be someplace hidden and the Germans catch me."

Some dreams clearly impersonate survivor guilt. Ethel Janov related, "I had a friend in Auschwitz who died there. I have this nightmare where we are racing and she is left behind. In the morning [when I wake up], it feels like I made it at her expense." Survivor guilt impels many to feel an enhanced closeness to the murderous process which consumed loved ones. They search for information which will enable them to understand, as completely as possible, the subjective experience of the last moments, and thereby share in them. When rumors swept through the ghetto that deportees would be sent to work in Germany, Rose Friedland used her contacts to ensure that she would be on the first train which would transport her from the filth and hunger of her everyday life. Two days after departure, her journey ended not in the heart of Germany, but the south of Poland at a place called Auschwitz. "I used to dream of being in the gas chamber. I heard once that people would crawl on top because the air was better and I see myself crawling all the way to the top."

Not surprisingly, the leitmotiv of vulnerability, both past and present, asserts itself during sleep, as it does during the survivor's waking hours.

"The Germans are taking away my children."

"I'm running away from the Nazis. They want to catch me with my old family or with my new family – sometimes the dreams mix them."

"I was with my wife and two of my grandchildren sitting somewhere and waiting to be gassed . . . and I said to my wife . . . and I said to my wife, 'Well, we had a good life until now.' That nightmare went very deep."

Survivors fear losing their reconstituted family just as they lost their original one.

"Anna G. tells of a ten-year-old girl who refused to go to the 'left' (toward death) after the selection. (Earlier she had explained that the members of her transport from Plaszow, having experienced many 'selections' there, had learned to fear their meaning.) Kicking and scratching, the young girl was seized by three SS men who held her down while she screamed to her nearby mother that she shouldn't let them kill her. According to Anna G., one of the SS men approached the mother, who was only in her late twenties, and asked her if she wanted to go with her daughter. 'No,' the mother replied.

"Anna G. admits that at the time in her mind she blamed the mother for not going with the daughter. Then she adds, 'Who am I to blame her?' When her own daughter was born years later, she began to have nightmares, reliving that moment on the ramp. The only difference was that the screaming ten-year-old was replaced by her daughter."[6]

Scenes in dreams may also mirror a survivor's sense of invincibility during the Holocaust and since. A former officer in the Polish Army, Paul Lee was requisitioned from Gröss-Rosen in October 1944 by Oskar Schindler to his camp and factory in Brinnlitz (in the Sudetenland). Recounting his Holocaust years, Paul remarked, "I was so many times close to being shot. I was in many tight spots, but I always knew I would make it. Sometimes I dream that I'm running from something, but I always get away. I always conquer whatever it is."

While survivors experience inordinate vulnerability, or death anxiety, or ongoing fears of losing those dearest to them, what is truly remarkable is the fact that they are not paralyzed by their apprehensions. After reading about conditions endured during the Holocaust, my students often remark, It's amazing that survivors would be able to function at all! How is it possible not to become completely mad after such a personal and collective disaster?

Of course, survivors have not been completely successful at conquering the ghosts, the legacy of the Holocaust. Most have lived a rather full life nevertheless. For the most part, they look and act like you and me. But when they wake up every morning, they have different expectations than we do.

"What did the world learn from the Holocaust?" a survivor was asked.

"What the world learned from the Holocaust is that you *can* kill six million Jews and no one will care."

5

The mask of the survivor

For many survivors, there is little respite from their tortured past. Days are pierced with memories. Nights are poisoned by images which emerge from the unconscious. And yet, when asked, Would you consider yourself normal? the great majority of survivors I interviewed answered emphatically in the affirmative. "Normal, oh yeah. No question about it. You cannot sit in mourning your whole life. It wouldn't help." And while I heard how normal she was, Esther Elfenbaum, whose daughter was murdered at Treblinka, confided that she chose not to have any children after the war because she could not bear the thought of losing another. "For me, life with children was over." After having admitted that "Holidays are hell for me," that "I am a stone when it comes to feelings," that "I am unable to think about the past," Marek Handelman, the only remaining member of his family who outlasted Hitler, is somewhat dumbfounded by my question. "Am I *normal*? Sure, I'm normal."

Survivors must reassure themselves that their enemies did not succeed. To admit irreparable damage, to admit that their tormentors' reach has extended to their new life, would imply that, ultimately, they had lost. And so survivors acknowledge isolated symptoms – difficulties feeling, nightmares, excessive anxieties about the safety of one's children, ongoing fears – but assert their victory. "Am I *normal*? Sure, I'm normal." To be abnormal might also imply that their "disease" may have infected the second generation, the generation of hope, the generation of compensation, the generation of vindication. (When a survivor recently spoke before one of my classes, she was asked by a student, "Do you think that your experiences have in *any* way affected your postwar family?" She replied, "Absolutely not. My husband and I have always been very strong people. Or else we could not have survived in the first place. Our children were always happy and healthy. One is a lawyer, the other is a doctor, and they have both done very well.")

For Rose Feingold, who told me she thinks about the Holocaust every day, being normal is an act of defiance. "Am I normal? Absolutely. But it doesn't shut off my mind. I think back and I'm outraged, but I'm quite normal, thank God. Do you know what it does to a person? I was in one room of girls who were supposed to go to a work camp, and in the next room were mothers with their children who were to be sent to Auschwitz. Some of these mothers ran into our room to save themselves and I heard their children screaming for them. I think of these things but then I don't too much. It would be impossible.

"Tragedies make you strong. That's what I willed myself to do. I was sitting in concentration camp and working on putting together bombs. I was hallucinating, under a spell. I saw what I wanted to see. During the war I wanted to live, to have fulfillment. I wanted to do things. I wanted to learn . . . I wanted to spite Hitler. I wanted to live to show him he didn't break my spirit." To not be normal would be to acknowledge that one's *spirit* had been broken.

Survivors perceive themselves to live a postwar, normal life. They have a home, a family, a business, friends, and so on. But they are also aware that these outward signs of fulfillment belie an inner emptiness, an ineradicable hurt. "Yes, I'm normal. . . . But we survivors are all sick people. We all have broken hearts. There isn't one survivor who doesn't have chipped off a piece of heart."

Aware of the precarious balance of their ongoing adjustment, many survivors guard against intrusions which might send them careening off the course they desperately wish to maintain. While she was incarcerated in Salaspils concentration camp near Riga, the Kommandant, Kurt Krause, ordered Viennese-born and recently married Naomi Leider to have an abortion. After her lengthy odyssey, which included Kaiserwald, Stuthof, and a death march through Germany, Naomi was liberated by the Russians on March 1, 1945. "If you dwell on those things which you can't change, you make yourself miserable. I always had an outlook on life. Look ahead, not back . . . I wanted to *do* always, not to think too much. I did things not to think, not to look.

Mostly at night it comes, when you can't sleep, and then you can't push it away." Keep your gaze forward and your reflections selective, survivors tell themselves. But during sleep, their control diminishes, their defenses weaken.

While in Auschwitz, Solomon Goldstein was assigned to work for four weeks in Canada, where they sorted the clothes and belongings of those who arrived at the death camp. Solomon's assignment afforded him the opportunity to swallow diamonds and gold which he then defecated and traded for food and vodka. "Ninety-nine percent of the time I worked in Canada I was drunk. If I wasn't drunk, probably I would have committed suicide," he explained. Not only am I normal, but I am stronger than others, Solomon believes. "Maybe if I go to a psychologist, he will say I am not normal. But after what I went through as a Holocaust survivor, and after building a life and a family, I think I'm pretty normal. When I look at the American soldiers who came back from the Vietnam War and fifty percent got nuts because we did not give them the recognition that they went to war, I consider myself normal. They didn't see their parents go to the gas chambers." Solomon Goldstein echoes a theme of many survivors: If I was able to do all of this after what I went through, I must be normal. And when Solomon looks at the reactions of others who experienced trauma, he feels superior by comparison, especially since he suffered more than they did, or perhaps more than anyone has ever suffered, he believes.

Daniel Davidoff spent varying periods of time in Auschwitz, Gröss-Rosen, and Flossenberg before he was liberated from Theresienstadt. He is somewhat stoic as he speaks of his Holocaust past. For Daniel, the thread of his autobiography was not completely broken during those years. His life had taken some "funny" turns. "It helped me a lot because my wife and daughter was alive and we came home together. It's like a bad dream. I didn't have any physical damage. And I think life is funny. Because I was dreaming all the time of some food, a piece of cheesecake, and, in America, I can get it and my doctor says, 'Un-huh. It's not good for you.' "

Daniel's daughter, son-in-law, and two grandchildren live in a house next door to his own. His life maintains its continuity through the second and third generations. Having all four close relatives nearby further eases his task of suppressing his fears of annihilation, which extend to them. Some children of survivors who do not live in such close proximity to their parents use the telephone on a daily basis in order to allay the apprehension of a mother or father.

(I am thirty-eight years old and have been invited to lecture in Germany. On my initial night in Frankfurt, the telephone rings in my hotel room before I fall off to sleep. It is my mother, and from her voice, I know she is calling to assure herself that I am still alive.)

Ida Koch, whose twin brothers and mother never emerged from the "twin *Lager*" of Auschwitz, understands the realities, the vicissitudes of life. Her previous losses have provided valuable lessons about how to live normally despite not being completely normal. "I don't think you never could be normal. But I feel more normal than anybody else. I feel so sure of myself. I always have the feeling that if I am here, I have been chosen for something. I'm more normal because I know everything is only for a short time. Other people think it will be this way forever. I never trust that things will last. Nothing is forever. I know I have it today. I'm not sure I'll have it tomorrow." Most of us live with the assumption of tomorrow. Imagine not having the comfort of that assumption. Imagine the fragility and sense of urgency which that absence would provoke.

At times, I perceived that survivors wanted to prove to others that they were not permanently contaminated by the Holocaust, that they were not *less* than others. "I'll show you how normal I am" was the underlying motivation. Furthermore, people don't want to see, to hear, to be reminded, so I will live outwardly as though nothing has happened. They will feel more comfortable and I, then, will be more acceptable. "You live a normal life because there is no choice. I was told by a friend that I walk around like a wounded animal. But either you live a normal life or you kill yourself . . . because there is no place for people who are crying all the time." And just as there was no place in Europe for the Jew, Elisa Korn (and her fourteen-year-old daughter who was murdered), there is no place in America for the real Elisa Korn, the Elisa Korn who must confine her tears to the inside.

Speaking of torture, which he personally experienced, Jean Améry wrote: "In almost all situations in life where there is bodily injury there is also the expectation of help; the former is compensated by the latter. But with the first blow from a policeman's fist, against which there can be no defense and which no helping hand will ward off, a part of our life ends and it can never be revived."[1]

The mask of the survivor

The survivor's belief that he must present a polite, good-humored facade exacerbates the sense of estrangement which he feels from the rest of the "normal" world. Having already been treated as less than human and betrayed by humanity, he is, once again, forbidden from acting in a human fashion, from showing how he really feels. Not only has Améry's and other survivors' trust in man been shattered, but their ability to act naturally and spontaneously has also been abrogated.

"I am very normal," Sarah Binder, a sixty-eight-year-old survivor of Auschwitz, declared. "I believe in myself and I think this is half the cure. It didn't affect me psychologically. It made me stronger . . . and not to believe everything that people are saying . . . and that you have to help yourself. The Holocaust just made me stronger." Sarah had found a silver lining, a reparation for her ordeal. However, there is a subtext, an underside to Sarah Binder's observation, which must sustain a degree of anger and vulnerability: the world is an unfriendly opponent, and you cannot count on your fellow human being.

Many survivors are aware of the *as if* quality of their existence. They act as if their life is a normal one. They are, however, aware that a sense of self has been fundamentally shaken. How *could* one have emerged as a normal human being? is their response to my question. For David Himmelstein, whose two children were murdered during the Holocaust, survivor guilt also interferes with his ability to respond appreciatively to a present, outwardly successful life. "Every day I have memories of what happened to us. My sisters and brothers . . . how they went in . . . how they went to the gas . . . how they suffered. Many times I see the films . . . I see the skeletons and I'm looking different from the way you look. I'm looking at the *details*. . . . It doesn't show how every skeleton suffered so much before he became a skeleton. . . . Others just see the skeletons. . . . They made from you a nothing . . . less than dirt. . . . They killed your family . . . and they made you a slave and you were a nothing. . . . Mentally, they broke you and physically . . . What was there was unbelievable. . . . If you weren't walking to work in the morning with your head far enough down, and if he felt like it, for any reason, he could take a pistol and just shoot you. . . . It comes back and back and back . . . you just can't forget it. . . . You just have to be busy and busy and busy . . . just to forget it. . . . We go to parties . . . and you're sitting and you smile and the smile is not . . . [he weeps] . . . you're afraid to let go . . . you're not allowed to be happy."

"No, no, everything that happened destroyed part of me. I was dying slowly. Piece by piece. And I built a new family. I am not what I would have been if I didn't go through these things. . . . Life was one big hell even after the war. So you make believe that you go on. This is not something that you put behind. And people think that they can get away from it, or you don't talk about it, or you forget your fear when you lay in an attic and you know that the Gestapo is a minute away from you. And rifles against your head. You can't be normal. As a matter of fact, I think that we are not normal because we are so normal."[2]

"I feel my head is filled with garbage: all these images, you know, and sounds, and my nostrils are filled with the stench of burning flesh. And it's . . . you can't excise it, it's like – like there's another skin beneath this skin and that skin is called Auschwitz, and you cannot shed it. . . . And it's a constant accompaniment. And though a lot of the survivors will deny this, they too feel it the way I do, but they won't give expression to it. I mean I will tell you that it's harder in many ways because . . . because we carry this. I am not like you. You have one vision of life and I have two. I – you know – lived on two planets. After all, I was – it seems to me that Hitler chopped off part of the universe and created annihilation zones and torture and slaughter areas. You know, it's like the planet was chopped up into a normal part – so-called normal: our lives are not really normal – and this other planet, and we were herded onto that planet from this one, and herded back again, while having nothing – virtually nothing in common with inhabitants of this planet. And we had to relearn how to live again. Literally, how to hold a fork, how to wash with soap, how to brush your teeth and . . . and we have these . . . these double lives. We can't cancel out. It just won't go away. People will deny it. I mean, probably a greater number will deny it – these memories – than not. But I will tell you, it's terrible . . . I talk to you and I am not only here, but I see Mengele and I see crematorium and I see all of that. And it's too much; it's very hard to get old with such – so ungracefully, because that has anything but grace, those memories, you know. It's very hard."[3]

"After the war, we weren't allowed to fall apart because circumstances didn't let us. . . . We had to educate our children, and we had to guide our children and be nice parents and make parties and everything. But that was all make believe."[4]

The mask of the survivor

Survivors attempt a normal lifestyle to ensure that their children are not engulfed by the posthumous embers of the Holocaust. And ironically, for these offspring who grow up in the shadow of the Shoah, the issue of normality may be more salient than it is for their parents.

"When I was a kid I used to think about which of my parents I'd let the Nazis take to the ovens if I could only save one of them. . . . Usually I saved my mother. Do you think that's normal?"[5]

Just as many survivors spurned an abnormal self-image, they also *insisted* that their ability to enjoy life has not been impaired by their ordeals. Despite feeling angry, guilty, sad, or fearful, these survivors refused to acknowledge further debilitating effects of their past. They want to live a normal life and they are determined to enjoy it. Yet, they are often more accomplished at experiencing joy in response to what they *have* than at attaining any inner contentment. Internally, the struggle to keep so much of themselves from awareness is a never-ending one.

In order to derive pleasure from their ongoing circumstances, some survivors "split" or compartmentalize themselves. The past is kept at bay so that it does not commingle and interfere with the present. Martin Bornstein never talked of his experiences before our interview, and never allowed his tears to flow. He required twenty-five years to pass after liberation before he could respond to his successfully rebuilt life. "After the age of forty, I started to get out of my skin a little. I let myself enjoy life more. I had always been holding back. My wife worked on me. . . . Basically, *I'm trying not to mix up things*. I never told my kids, 'Eat, because I didn't have what to eat!' . . . But I didn't allow myself to be fully happy even though I had all the reasons to be happy." Martin Bornstein will never be "fully happy." There will always be memories, sadness, and feelings of undeserved loss. However, Martin now understands and accepts the need for relief, and does not want always to have the door to his past ajar.

Sol Feingold also endeavors to partition his life. "You owe it to yourself to maintain your sanity and be happy. You experienced so much difficulty, you have a right to be happy. In my life I strive for happiness. . . . The other is kept separate. I am a messenger from Auschwitz and that's just my job. I wouldn't let that make me unhappy."

The aftermath

Sonya Weiss's father and brothers were taken from Warsaw to Treblinka in 1942. At the age of nineteen, Sonya and her mother were deported to Majdanek in 1943. The two were separated upon arrival, and Sonya's mother was immediately gassed. Eventually liberated from Malhof after periods of internment in Auschwitz and Ravensbrück, Sonya has been less successful at creating a division. "I always have an enormous sadness in me. I can go out and enjoy myself but I'm always sad. It never leaves me . . . I'm always a little withdrawn. It's like you're always dragging something behind you. You're never free." It is difficult to assess how much of Sonya's inability to divide herself is volitional. Perhaps she feels a keener sense of survivor guilt, an even stronger obligation to remember.

"All this you lived through, all this you saw, and you go out and work for money, or you go out and drive a car or whatever. . . . How could you? . . . It should be as, you know, some people that turn away from life, because they found it's senseless, it doesn't add up. And I and the kind of people that went through it should know that it doesn't add up. Nothing adds up. It doesn't make any sense. Nothing justifies it. To go on and on after you know what the world is like or what it was."[6]

The orientation of many survivors is never simply to the present. Their perspective always widens to include previous losses. Earlier in the interview, seventy-year-old Rose Feingold told me, "I regret most that I lost my teenage years, my youth. I never had a teenage romance. When I see teenagers today, I envy them." When I asked if her ability to enjoy life had been affected by the Holocaust, she replied: "Of course it affected. You try to enjoy life. But there are always memories. Whenever something nice happens, I think back. My mother didn't live to see me married, didn't live to see this or that. I always think about the millions of children. They took children from their mothers' arms and threw them against the wall with their head . . . I can never enjoy myself fully. At a simcha [a joyous event], I visualize these people as they were in the concentration camp. . . . Whenever the Israeli Army does something good, I think, Get up, Hitler and see this. . . . Any simcha brings back what we lost . . . my little brothers, my father . . ." How could Rose enjoy herself with abandon when she is always so angry?

The mask of the survivor

We want to share joyous moments with those who love us. The delight they feel enhances our own. We especially yearn for that reciprocity with our parents. "Enjoy? Look, how could you compare if you had your mother, your father, your brothers, your sister," Paul Handel exclaimed. "When I got married, it was a happy occasion, but I felt so alone. I never mentioned this to my wife." Paul Handel looks around and sees no familiar faces, only an absence. "It's not one hundred percent like before the Holocaust. It *cannot* be. I'm not a person who can one hundred percent enjoy. I lost so much family, friends. Something is missing. Something is always missing."

For some survivors, joy after Auschwitz is sacrilegious. Joy would imply a betrayal of the memory of all those murdered. Happiness would distort all which had occurred. "I envy people that can get out of themself for one minute sometimes. . . . They can laugh, enjoy. You know you see a movie. Anybody in my situation cannot laugh and enjoy, through inside, you know. Only superficially. There's always in the back of your mind everything. How can you, how can you *enjoy* yourself? It's almost a crime against the people that you lost, that you can live and enjoy yourself."[7]

For Ethel Janov, now a psychotherapist, survivor guilt permeates her being. "I always feel like I have to earn my life," she had earlier told me. "This is one thing I have not been able to overcome, this guilt about enjoying things. I pretend that I'm doing it, but I don't feel good about it. I feel like I'm doing something wrong. . . . We have a lot of celebrations in our family, but it's never because we should have fun. I envy people so much who feel carefree. I'm dying for someone to give me permission."

Survivor guilt smothers David Himmelstein's joy. David's first wife had been born in England and could have escaped across the Channel, but refused to leave her husband behind. A bewildered look crossed his face as David twice repeated, "She could have survived. Instead, I survived." Later, he explained that outward accoutrements do not reflect his inner world. "If I laugh, it's not really what it should be. . . . But it doesn't bother me from being successful or having friends. It affects me only that inside I'm not happy like people think or it should be. You see, my children don't know me. They don't know my laugh is not a real laugh. They don't know someone inside me says you don't have a right to be happy after you lost so many people. I'm a good husband and a good father. I'm a mensch. . . . But something is missing. If I wouldn't be married before and have children, I wouldn't know there is so much more to be happy. I know I was happier. Why? I don't know. My children don't know something is missing."

As a child of Holocaust survivors, I grew up thinking that laughing indicated a certain superficiality. It was not until I reached my thirties that I understood the value and necessity of laughter. I also had to learn not to begrudge it to others. To my surprise, I found this objection to the casualness of life in few of those I interviewed. Because laughter was violently wrested from them, they strive to recapture it.

After arriving in America, Rose Friedland was fully immersed in her career as a fashion designer and never thought of her Holocaust past. She loved the rush she got from the shows, the elegant parties, the attention, the hoopla. After a crisis in her family twelve years ago, she chose to look back, becoming a docent in a local Holocaust museum and a frequent speaker about the Holocaust at school assemblies in the community. "Especially since I started talking about the Holocaust, I definitely believe I don't enjoy things as I might. Certain things seem frivolous now. It's not becoming. I used to love to dance. It's just not becoming to me anymore. Even in things that are enjoyable, I always look for a purpose, for something meaningful." Rose must engage herself in meaningful activities in order to justify why *she* survived. In addition, for Rose, the monstrous times of then seem to bring all else into trifling relief. With the Holocaust as a yardstick against which all else is compared, it is too psychologically incongruous for some survivors to act blithely or without serious purpose.

However, several survivors I spoke with emphasized that they enjoy life more than ever. They are more appreciative of good fortune because they have known the other side. The greater urgency to reap all that life offers, however, also reflected their fears of the ephemeral nature of their newfound bounty. Life and its simple pleasures, once taken for granted, were snatched away so precipitously. That lesson's imprint will never disappear. "I enjoy life," Saul Halpern told me. "Every minute I can, believe me. If you don't do it now, tomorrow you may not be able to do it. One thing I learned in life. If you want something, do it now."

A Jew was not supposed to live. The forces arrayed against him were too powerful. Having defied the odds, Helen Schwartz savors the unexpected extra portion of life following the Holocaust. "The feeling to enjoy things more was deepened. You didn't take it for granted. It was a gift, so you enjoyed it more."

Survivors recoil from an intimation of abnormality. Most insist on their ability to enjoy life. Nevertheless, they are willing to acknowledge underlying difficulties, an inner life which reflects the magnetism of their past. Yet the overwhelming proportion of them have never sought psychotherapy.[8] Survivors, therefore, who coped reasonably well after their traumas would not have come to the attention of those mental health professionals spinning theories about their postwar psychological adjustment.

In the years immediately after liberation, survivors were distracted from their inner life by their need and keen desire to rebuild a life and reconstitute a family. Obstacles – an unfamiliar environment, a foreign language, a lack of funds, an absence of a supportive network – had to be overcome. There was no room for the grieving process, for the ventilation of rage, for the mourning of their loss of innocence.

Many survivors believed in the *necessity* of staying busy, of not thinking about what had transpired. "My psychotherapy was working hard," David Himmelstein remarked. "I opened five studios in one month. I wanted to work, not think, or else you would become crazy perhaps. . . . It's very difficult to forget. You have to do things so you shouldn't think. I'm sitting here with you. I'm so emotional. . . . Instead of going to a psychiatrist, the work was like a psychiatrist for me. I'm still afraid if I am alone to look at a picture of my first wife and children." Others developed mechanisms of denial which were designed to mask the pain and continuing feelings of vulnerability. "I have a habit," Martha Janusz told me. "When I tell stories from those times, I make jokes or say it so I show how I fooled the Germans."

Fewer than ten percent of those I interviewed had ever sought psychotherapeutic assistance. Of those who had availed themselves of professional counseling, half had sought help for problems which were not necessarily Holocaust-related (e.g., marital or child rearing). While these crises may have been indirectly determined by the lingering effects (e.g., impatience, hyperirritability, an unbalanced reaction to present stressors) of the Holocaust, the survivor did not present herself as someone who was seeking guidance as a consequence of her Holocaust history.

Resistance to treatment emanates from many different quarters. Some survivors may fear the transformation of a self-image predicated on a feeling of the uniqueness of one who has survived and conquered death to one who is mentally ill, from one who is unusually strong to one who is damaged. Esther Fisher was perhaps the most depressed survivor I encountered. Her life was severely constricted due to myriad irrational fears. By her own admission, her inadequate parenting had seriously debilitated her children. "And yet I'm proud of myself," she asserted. "That I survived so much during my lifetime." In order to maintain a semblance of self-esteem, in order not to dwell on the crippling aftereffects of the Holocaust, Esther needs to focus on her triumphs.

Because of some survivors' powerful need to forget past humiliations, they react by demonstrating an exaggerated intolerance for human weakness. Only the weak or debilitated need psychological help, they believe. And survivors did not wish to examine closely the compartmentalization of their past for fear of it spilling over uncontrollably onto their present adjustment. While fear and rage and grief lurked in the background, the survivor attempted to keep himself in the foreground, moving ahead to life and farther away from death.

Survivors may also unconsciously fear being blamed by the psychotherapist for particular actions or for their inactions during the war. Authority figures, even in benign settings, arouse anxiety. Survivors had to make many agonizing decisions and engage in activities "because of circumstances" that would create moral dilemmas for them in normal times. Perhaps partly because of this internal conflict and partly because of the disbelief and disinterest they encountered when they tried to recount their stories after the war, most survivors became convinced that no one (including any psychotherapist) who did not live in the midst of the Holocaust could possibly understand the motivation for their situational behavior or the psychological effects of those experiences. In her case, psychotherapy was obviously superfluous, Anna Maline asserted. Psychotherapy would face the hopeless task of eradicating the memories and the anguish. "I don't need it. I went through it. You can't forget it. It's impossible. . . . Nobody can imagine what it was like . . . Auschwitz. People wouldn't even believe it." Anna's remarks reflected another theme of those who eschewed deliberate introspection: it happened. There's nothing to be done now except get on with life.

It was only five years ago that Ethel Janov, herself a psychotherapist, sought professional assistance. Ethel's survivor guilt had been an ongoing theme of our interview. She explained why she had hesitated to seek relief. "It would have been an acknowledgment that I wasn't grateful that I survived. It would have been an acknowledgment that something was wrong, that I was somehow deficient. It would have been like a defeat. And what right did I have to complain when others died?" Others had died, had suffered the ultimate. For Ethel, seeking psychotherapy was tantamount to complaining.

For many survivors, their material and familial attainments indicate an inner strength which, for them, is synonymous with emotional health. They conclude that, apparently, they are doing quite well. A very successful real estate developer explained, "There is no reason [for psychotherapy.] Look how much I achieved. I was working very hard, day and night, because I wanted to give my kids everything what I didn't have."

Other survivors relate ongoing emotional strains to their previous trauma and conclude that, "Under the circumstances, I'm doing okay. What else would you expect?" Their reaction, they assert, is normal and not in need of remedy. Sonya Weiss also admitted a reluctance to disinter the past. "I can't talk about it. It was buried, like something you bury forever. Maybe I need a psychiatrist. I'm sure I do. But I wouldn't consider it . . . I've come a long way. But I'm not so stable as a rock. I'm not so emotionally stable as I would like to be. Life is hard. For us, we have a certain moral stability. All that you went through you think makes you a better person, a stronger person . . . I'm as good as I can be under the circumstances. But life is hard."

Sixty-seven-year-old Carla Granot, the sole surviving member of her family from a small town in Poland, sought treatment soon after arriving in America and moving near her relatives in Detroit. She has periodically returned for help over the past thirty years. At the outset of our five hours together, Carla informed me that "my mother had a sister in the United States before the war and she begged my father to leave before it was too late. But my father thought everything was *traif* in America so we remained in Poland and *we* [my emphasis] got killed." Immediately after liberation, at the age of twenty, Carla married another survivor whom she had known only one month. "I saw many sisters and brothers who found each other after the war, but I was alone in the world. I cried a lot. I searched for cousins and uncles, but everyone was killed. In the [DP] camp, I was like a stranger. No family, no one to talk to. I felt so alone. I felt like a rock in the water . . . alone." Carla explained her motivation for seeking psychotherapy: "I had a lot to cope with my children and my husband. I couldn't understand them and they couldn't understand me. Our family didn't function like a normal family. My husband came out a mentally sick person. He cried a lot about how he was ripped away from his mother and sister in Auschwitz. He begged to go with them. He never got over it. . . . We had a hard life and a difficult marriage. I didn't have any happiness after the war."

For the few survivors who choose psychotherapy, the process may be particularly difficult. Psychotherapy requires a willingness to take risks, be open, and therefore allow vulnerability. This "basic trust," so essential to the success of the undertaking has, in many cases, been previously shattered by wartime psychic losses. Survivors may have an exaggerated concern about losing control, about relinquishing defenses they see as critical to their present stability. Distortions of memory are commonplace. Prewar family life tends to be idealized. Some patients demonstrate an inability to remember past events, particularly those associated with feelings of guilt (and subsequent embarrassment) or humiliation.

Potential pitfalls for psychotherapists include an inability to remain objective in the face of their own feelings of rage or despair upon hearing the horrors they had previously believed existed only in fiction. Conversely, they may be unable fully to appreciate or believe the experiences presented to them, and their skepticism will consequently be communicated to the patient. Worst of all, they may attribute the patient's present symptoms to unresolved childhood conflicts and give scant credence to the impact of Holocaust experiences per se. It was not until 1980 that the American Psychiatric Association coined the diagnosis, post-traumatic stress disorder, thereby fully acknowledging that prolonged symptoms of stress may be purely a result of a trauma itself, and need not be rooted in unconscious frustration and conflicts.

The mask of the survivor

Despite postwar interior strains and environmental obstacles, Holocaust survivors have displayed remarkable adaptive capacities. Upon immigrating to America, most rose rather quickly to middle-class respectability. During the war, survivors embraced a psychological theory of relativity. In the concentration camp, securing a pair of leather shoes to replace one's wooden clogs brought joy. Organizing an extra ration of bread was cause for relief and renewed optimism. The keen awareness of absence produced not only a greater appreciation of simple sustenance, but also resulted in the survivor's not *perceiving* postwar difficulties as particularly stressful. Having outlasted such adversity produced a confidence in his ability to overcome other obstructions. (The exception may lie in his extreme sensitivity to the further loss, whether it be to geographical relocation or death, of immediate family members.) Survivors' coping strategies developed during the Holocaust enhance their ability to actively meet and overcome new challenges. Survivors *do*. They are not impeded by feelings, or daunted by the impossibilities.

Although some survivors are inhibited by the expectation of further catastrophe, most have unconsciously reacted against the terror which might debilitate and therefore prove life-threatening. They deny fear. "The worst has occurred. I conquered it. I can conquer anything," they tell themselves.

While acknowledging the element of luck in their survival, those who emerged also derived self-respect from their life-saving, instinctive decisions, their resourcefulness, their fortitude.

Despite the considerable role that caprice, chaos, and random chance played in survival, survival had its reasons nonetheless, and not a few survivors found those reasons in themselves. . . .

Those who emerged with an increased regard for themselves because they had lived often felt they were alive only because they had risked paths that others had been afraid to take, and so they were confirmed in this pattern of behavior in their later lives; or they believed, at least, that they should be, which often amounted to the same thing. Those who had knowledge of themselves as having made the instant crucial decisions that might have been the difference between life and death held on to that knowledge, and not without pride. Men and women who, when cornered, had plotted and contrived their survival successfully, who had, they saw, reached for it in the thin instant of possibility that presented itself, could not help turning such knowl-

83

edge of themselves over and over in their minds afterwards, as they could not and had no wish to avoid the roots which that knowledge took in them.[9]

In their manner of telling, survivors echoed a theme perhaps not as blatant as pride, but one which infused their past and present – *determination*. "I was not going to give up. I was going to make it through." And now, "I will not let it overcome me. I will manage any stumbling block placed in my way."

Having been separated from and brutalized by humanity, many survivors have retreated to a focused concern only for their immediate family and extended relations, the Jewish People. (Within the Jewish community, Holocaust survivors are the most ardent and single-minded supporters of Israel.) However, several of those I interviewed reported a greater capacity to empathize as a result of their own tribulations. Louis Weintraub, the sole surviving member of a large Chasidic family in Radzemin, Poland, asked me, "Do you know the pain of leaving a child?" Outside of the Warsaw ghetto, in 1942, Louis first fastened a crucifix and then hung a sign around his two-year-old daughter's neck. The sign read: *I am a widow. My husband is in a German prison camp. I beg you have mercy on my child. Jesus Christ will love you.* Louis instructed his daughter to remain on a street corner while he crossed to the other side and hid in the shadows of a building.

He watched as his daughter was led away by a Polish policeman. After liberation, Louis located his child in a convent, and the nuns extorted money from him for her return. "It [the Holocaust] changed me for the better," Louis remarked. "I'm a better human being. I have more understanding and feeling. It had made me more sensitive to suffering, and much more tolerant of others than before."

Earlier in the day, Shimon Newman, who had posed as a Polish Gentile and been active in the resistance, told me, "All through the war years a part of me was numb. There were *reactions* not feelings." I asked him what lasting effects of the Holocaust were apparent. "This *tenderness* that is in me. I didn't think that after all I experienced and lost, that I would break down sometimes. You know, sometimes, I simply cry to myself."

Clearly, most survivors perceive themselves to be different from those who were not trapped in the vortex of the Third Reich. The sense of estrangement which accompanied this unique, indelible imprint was heightened by their experience of betrayal. The human contract which implies a protection of the innocent has been abrogated. "Did the Holocaust have any lasting emotional effects on you?" I asked Sol Finkel. "Very bad [he cries] . . . from the beginning. The world knew what was going on and they didn't give an effort to stop it."

"We perceive life as a precious thing. And then Bessie gives birth to a child and a German takes away the child and kills it. What are we, superhuman, to just brush it aside and say to the world, 'Thank you for liberating us?' And that's all, we wash the hands clean like nothing happened? . . . I can't make peace with that. . . . Maybe other survivors can; I don't know. I myself, if you ask me, I can't. And yet I go on, I'm creative, I contribute, I work, I'm happy that I'm in a country that gives me freedom and everything. . . . But this is not the issue, there's a deeper issue. You cannot brush away the pain, by giving something else. . . . Am I a part of the human community? . . . I don't think so."[10]

If others had cared afterward, if they had, at least, been interested in their unjustifiable persecution, survivors might have clung to a thread of the human quilt. To have their ordeal denied by others would sever any remaining link.

Unless Sarah or someone else asked her straight out, she intended to avoid talking about starvation, the ghetto, Auschwitz, selections, or any other such experience, convinced as she was that people could not accept what was incredible to them. To tell people what they could not or would not believe was to put yourself in a bad position one way or another: either they would resent it or they would feel that you could not be trusted in other things. . . . She was still not inclined to talk much about the past, unless she was asked. Proud, in later years, she could tell a story, albeit not without a small edge in her voice, about how, after they had moved to Houston, a Jewish professor from the university had played cards with her and her husband every week for several years, and never known that they had been survivors or that anything special had ever happened to them, other than the fact that they had come from Europe after the war. They had discussed war, crime, politics, history, and issues of every sort together, but since it had never occurred to the professor or his wife to wonder what she and her husband – who were, after all, Jews – had been doing in Hitler's Europe during the war, she had never told them.[11]

But even if they were believed, survivors knew the frustration of incomprehension by their interlocutor. After all, while in the midst of those circumstances, it was impossible to fathom its unprecedented, obscured reality. At the time, knowledge of their innocence further contributed to the denial of their fate. Ironically, however, this universal belief in a just world might cause others to doubt that their persecution was completely unwarranted. Perhaps, *somehow*, you brought this upon yourselves, is the implicit assumption and accusation.

Survivors emphasize the uniqueness of the Holocaust. They protest attempts to compare their tragedy to the disasters which have befallen others. Their perception of having an inimitable experience further impedes their identification with a less exclusive group. Louis Weintraub expressed the difference between survivors and nonsurvivors. "Let's say they see a story [about the Holocaust.] They see it with other eyes. They can never put themselves in our shoes. They can't understand. I, being myself, when I think back sometimes, doubt that I went through that whole thing. It's not possible. The thing that I went through is not human."

One of the comforts and attractions of close friends is the belief that they understand who you are. With this felt mutuality, therefore, much can and often does remain unspoken, unexplained. Conversely, a belief that the other cannot possibly grasp your essence acts as a repellent. It is not surprising, therefore, that survivors gravitate to other survivors. (A survivor who believes another survivor outlasted "milder" adversities, however, might still feel less than understood by him.) "Maybe I'm more attuned to people who went through the Holocaust," Dora Levinsohn suggested. "I feel closer to people who went through it. I can't talk with nonsurvivors about my experience. They just wouldn't understand . . . I can't stand in line for food, even if it's a delicious buffet table. I'll always see myself in a concentration camp. It's very hard to explain that to my American friends. Even if I tell them, I don't think they'll grasp the meaning of standing in a line of hundreds for a little piece of bread. Not even you, no matter how much you research it. But if I tell my survivor friends, 'I can't stand in line,' I don't have to tell them why. You see, this is the difference."

Most often, our closest friendships are those which begin during childhood. Similar experiences during those formative years provoke a primitive bond, one which implies a mutuality of fundamental experience and an intrinsic knowledge of one another. As we move farther away from our childhood and its environs, we reach back for it with greater longing. Severed from their early history, and having shared in many respects the most formative event of their life – the Holocaust – survivors cling to each other for affirmation and memory. For whether you were born in Poland, Hungary, or Czechoslovakia, the minutiae – the smells, the sounds, the customs, the prayers, the politics – of a common Jewish world assert themselves.

"I was newborn," survivors often said when describing the condition they found themselves in after the liberation. This meant that they were, of course, happy to be alive, that they were ready to take up the life that had been given back to them. But the phrase had a darker meaning, too, as survivors used it. It suggested that those who had been left alive after the Holocaust were not only without a place in the world and without possessions, but also had no past life; the roots and ties of that life – mothers and fathers, the husbands, wives, children and holdings – had been erased entirely. "It was as though I had not come from anywhere."[12]

Survivors further distinguish themselves from others because of the omnipresence of their losses. They notice who naturally stands with others, and remember who was unnaturally wrested from them. Paul Handel, the only surviving member of his family, remarked, "Americans didn't go through five years of hell, didn't see their mother go to the ovens. You go to occasions and you see parents and grandparents. I always ask, Why aren't mine here?" Shimon Newman told me, "I feel a greater kinship with survivors than my nonsurvivor friends. My American Jewish friends I consider them almost superficial because their thinking and their feelings never reached the depths that we went through. I went to a funeral of a friend yesterday and there were the lamentations and grief, but they were complaining that some of the funeral arrangements weren't right. I thought to myself, I don't even know where my parents' grave is [he weeps] . . . I thought to myself, look how lucky you are."

Survivors compare their life experiences to the "superficial" ones of others. And despite their history of devastation, survivors wear that narrative with pride. Born of both past and ongoing rejections, this feeling of being special is often transformed to one of superiority. A further severance from nonsurvivors ensues. Saul Sitowitz and his family remained in the ghetto of Tomaszów Mazowiecki until 1942. While Saul was working outside of the ghetto with his father, his mother and sister were rounded up and taken to Treblinka. At the age of eighteen, Saul arrived in the United States, an orphan. "I think we all are [better than nonsurvivors]. We came here not knowing anybody, without a penny, not knowing the language, somehow was able to bring up a very normal family of four kids and reach an economical plateau must make us something special."

"Are you different from those who did not go through the Holocaust?" I asked Sam Goldberg. "I don't think I'm different. *They* think I'm different. I'm better than them. They look down on me. In Israel, they asked survivors why they didn't fight back. In America, they treated us like greenhorns. I was sent to Corpus Christi, Texas. They came to see my horns. They asked me, 'Have you ever seen a banana?' "

Survivors have a different perspective than nonsurvivors. They are more suspicious, more mistrustful, more vigilant. They have seen the underside and its power.

"I learned more about humanity. They [nonsurvivors] missed a lot, luckily. I learned how unhuman people can be. In the regular world, people are acting according to their environment. But I live differently because I know the other side of the coin."

"First of all, they [nonsurvivors] are more naive. They believe a lot of nonsense. I have more experience. I don't get hurt so much because I don't believe what people tell you."

"I think I can recognize danger much sooner than people who have not gone through the Holocaust. When I see an antisemitic incident in the paper, many people will dismiss it as insignificant. I put a lot of significance on it. That's how it started."

And many survivors are bitter. "If you could lick my heart, it would poison you," Itzhak Zuckerman, a leader of the Warsaw ghetto uprising, has remarked. "I *am* bitter," Hershel Kaplan, the seventy-nine-year-old sole surviving member of his family from Vilna, confessed. "Because I lost . . . and the way I lost, it hurts even more. People die, it's a normal process. The way people die makes a difference to the ones who are alive."

Just as they insisted on their normality, their unimpeded ability to enjoy life, and their emotional strength, a few survivors contended that they were not fundamentally different from nonsurvivors. They had already been singled out once; they refused to be stigmatized and distinguished again. Yet, at the outset of our interview, when I asked Harry Tissor – the only one of his family of five sisters and four brothers to survive – about his parents, his eyes welled up with tears as he demurred, "I can't talk about them."

Martha Janusz emphasized that she has little in common with other survivors. Posing as a Polish Gentile, sixteen-year-old Martha worked throughout most of the war in Germany, where she encountered the kindness of a few Germans. She described the "terrible conditions" in her displaced persons camp at Ulm after liberation. "It was difficult for me. I was practically raised in Germany. Several Germans had been so nice to me. They were so cultured and clean. Here I was in a [displaced persons] camp with people from Hungary, Russia. They were so dirty and rough." While not denying her Jewishness, Martha partly identified with Germans, wanted to be like them. Identifying with the aggressor allows one to absorb his strength. By distancing herself from the survivors she observed in the displaced persons camp, Martha may have further defended herself against feelings of vulnerability aroused by the sight of her Jewish brethren. Unlike the overwhelming majority of survivors, Martha, because of her identification with Germans, was quite sanguine about the reunification of Germany. If Germans are like me, I need not hate them nor fear them, she assumes.

Most American Jews embrace a dual identity of Jew and American. For those who emerged from the Shoah, a self-image emphasizes Jew and survivor. There is therefore a distinction between these two groups made by both survivors and American Jews. Holocaust survivors describe a range of feelings toward Jews who basked in the safety of a continent thousands of miles from the machinery of death. Seventy-eight-year-old Dora Levinsohn is angry. She does not care to hear of the insecurity and lack of political organization of the American Jewish community before World War II. For her, there can be no excuses. "I feel that American Jews didn't do *anything*. They marched in Selma, but they didn't march in Washington while we were being murdered. They adored Roosevelt and forget that he sent away the *St. Louis*. They pretend that they didn't know, but I don't believe it." Dora is also incensed by American Jews' facile comparison of conditions. "I heard many remarks like, 'We didn't have much to eat during the Depression either.' I don't have to tell you how that made me feel." These offensive parallels further contribute to the survivor's alienation from the mainstream of the American Jewish community, for they confirm a complete lack of understanding of the nature of their ordeal. Moreover, complaints of hardship by American Jews demonstrate how spoiled and feeble they are compared to the toughened survivors. "If they don't have their ice cream, they cry," Saul Halpern told me. "American Jews? They're pampered. They tell *me* that during World War II they didn't have their tickets for gasoline."

The survivor's feelings toward American Jews were also affected by his expectations and experiences of assistance after liberation. Some American relatives went to great lengths to locate remaining family in Europe and provide affidavits of support in order to facilitate their emigration. Many survivors were grateful for the aid given to them, both in Europe and after their arrival in the United States, by Jewish organizations such as the Hebrew Immigrant Aid Society. Other survivors expected more, however. In 1942, Esther Flamm's mother and younger brother were ordered to report for deportation from the Riga ghetto. Her father and older brother had already been taken away. With her work permit, Esther could have remained behind, but she insisted on accompanying her mother. Assembled at the *Appellplatz*, Esther's mother realized she had left behind her son's sturdier shoes. Esther ran back to the apartment, but by the time she returned, her mother and brother were gone. She never saw them again. Pictures of murdered family members line the hallway of her home in a suburb of Los Angeles. "They never inquire," Esther remarked indignantly. "To this day, my American friends never said, 'Tell me what you went through.' They don't want to know."

Insulated from the ultimate effects of antisemitism, American Jews are neither sufficiently vigilant nor reactive to its manifestations. You are not as safe as you believe, survivors want to tell American Jews. "I am a survivor and I know what can happen," Rose Friedland, who frequently speaks to school assemblies, emphasized. "When I found out the way they behaved during World War II, I became pretty angry.

Now I'm even angrier. Because they surely know about the Holocaust and they still don't understand. . . . Jewish children must be better informed, for their own sake. I hear Jews talk and they don't understand how serious the situation is."

Holocaust survivors identify closely with their People. Raised in Europe, the home of Jews for nineteen hundred years, they were more steeped in tradition and had developed a greater sense of historical continuity to their ancestors and their fate than had their American cousins. Having been segregated for unprecedented persecution because of their background, survivors have reacted with a furious commitment to their group's survival. For survivors, Israel is the ultimate guarantor of that durability. If there had been a Jewish state in the 1930s, millions might have been saved. Today, Israel remains the only viable refuge for any Jew in danger, wherever he or she may be, survivors believe. And not only does the Israeli military shield those within its borders, it also provides the only reliable cloak of protection for Jews throughout the world. Some Holocaust survivors are exasperated because their perceptions, feelings, and unwavering commitments to Israel are not shared by all American Jews. American Jews are disloyal and naive, they complain. By their failure to unequivocally support Israel, they place all of us at risk. "It's easy for a lot of American Jews to criticize Israel. But we have different fears," Helen Schwartz explained. "We have a different reality. We know how important it is to have Israel. We don't have illusions about Jews being safe and secure."

Holocaust survivors experienced tormented years of being treated as less than their fellow man. It became clear to me that a few survivors I interviewed have felt self-conscious when relating to American-born Jews. These feelings may reflect the insecurity of the immigrant, the awareness of coming from and belonging to a different, and perhaps less "advanced," place. Oftentimes, American Jews have reinforced these apprehensions. Before the darkness descended, Rose Feingold lived the first eighteen years of her life in a small town in Poland. "When I meet American people, I have a little complex. With all my assertiveness, I think they look down on me. I don't know why. I feel inferior to them. In one of my classes, a Jewish woman said, 'You people.' I was furious. It reminded me of the Germans because we were distinguished from them."

Despite apparent, ongoing wounds, it is the resilience of survivors which one finds most striking – their ability to work productively and creatively, their capacity to build a family anew, their desire to enjoy life, their commitment to the continuity of the Jewish people. Few of the survivors I met were noticeably depressed individuals. (Granted, I did not have an opportunity to observe those who refused to be interviewed.) One survivor told me of her sister's repeated psychiatric hospitalizations as a result of debilitating delusions involving Nazis who were coming to take her away. Several prominent Holocaust survivors (Jean Améry, Primo Levi) have succumbed to despair and committed suicide. However, they clearly do not represent the wider survivor community in this regard. When I asked, "Have you ever had thoughts of suicide in your postwar life?" none of those I interviewed answered in the affirmative. On the contrary, the response of a survivor of Auschwitz, Jack Saltzman, echoed the sentiments of many: "I wouldn't give the bastards the satisfaction."

6
The importance of age

Jack Diamond was forced to watch as his brother was hanged in
Auschwitz. Jack told me what it was like to be a teenager in that
universe. "In the camps you became an adult overnight, if you
wanted to or didn't. . . . You had to start thinking like an adult. You
couldn't afford the luxury of being a child. You had to be constantly
on guard not to make a mistake . . . I was like a general planning for a
war . . . not to be noticed, not to be caught. It was an art. Others
much more intelligent than me got too confident, didn't take enough
precautions, and they were killed. In the camp you had to be one of
the masses, not to be noticed in order to survive. . . . There were a lot
of homosexuals in the camp. They were often in positions of power. I
was always aware of avoiding being assaulted. I never was, but many
other boys weren't so lucky.

"The intellectuals were the first to die. . . . They thought about it
all. How could humanity do this? . . . Who wants to live in a world
like this? . . . I just put my head down and didn't ask the larger
questions. I think it was easier being an adolescent, because I wasn't
mature enough to think of the consequences, the larger picture. . . .
My father, he died spiritually before he died physically. . . . He kept
asking, 'Where is God? How is this possible?' I got frightened, I got
scared, but I wasn't internally destroyed. So many adults lost their
will to survive. . . . Sometimes I created an invisible wall shutting out
what was happening . . . as if it wasn't really happening. My father
did see everything that was going on around and it destroyed him."

Recent years have witnessed the increasing recognition of lasting,
debilitating effects of trauma such as child abuse, rape, natural disasters, assault, as well as the systematic persecution inherent in geno-

cide. Conventional wisdom has asserted that the younger the individual during the trauma, the more severe are its aftereffects. The child is at a disadvantage because she has not had the opportunity to develop a fundamental sense of self. Her defense mechanisms are not firmly in place and her methods of coping with stress are immature. However, here again, Holocaust survivors (who were primarily teenagers and young adults during the traumas) defy conventional wisdom in that their youthfulness was clearly advantageous. I am not speaking here of the physical strength and stamina necessary for survival, nor of their captors selecting the very young and older groups for immediate death based on practical considerations (i.e., their relative uselessness as slave labor).

While the youngster lacked the life experience which might provide clues to solutions for overcoming adversity, she was able to adapt rather quickly to her changing circumstances. Less rooted in habit, less tied to the familiar, she could approach new situations with a greater openness to its demands. Ida Koch, who from fourteen to sixteen years of age was incarcerated for various periods of time in Auschwitz, Dachau, and Maldorf, told me, "I became one hundred. I always had to be careful because if they find out I was fourteen, they kill me . . . I didn't have any experience. To begin with, I didn't know about sex either and the Germans took a lot of people for sex. I had to lie and tell everybody I'm eighteen. The first thing they teach you how to lie and how to cheat and how to steal. But I was young . . . I was able to catch on to everything very quickly."

Teenagers did not appreciate the gravity of the situation, the extent of evil forces arrayed against them. They were therefore shielded from their full psychological impact. Adolescents did not agonize over injustice or feel the severance from the human cloth. They were spared theological crises and disappointments. Perhaps, at first, they were less capable of "organizing," but over time they were less likely to be paralyzed by grievous questions and desolating doubts.

"An older person was much more capable of thinking of other things than a fourteen-year-old could. I had in mind only to get as much food for my father and brother-in-law as I could. My father, on the other hand, whenever we were together, he would try to reassure me, to comfort me that everything would be okay *with God's help*. And at that time I didn't even believe that my mother and [pregnant] sister [who had been gassed upon arrival] were already gone. When the adults got together, they always said, they always kidded themselves that 'God will take care of this thing' . . . and God *did not* take care of it. I . . . I just put my head down and tried to survive."

"The person who was twenty-five already had a lot of experience in life. My indoctrination in life was ghetto and camps. I took it as it came. I wasn't smart enough to think much about what was going on. Maybe I was lucky for that. There was a lot of selfishness in the camps. I was naive. When I came to Auschwitz, I put my shoes under my head as a pillow. The next morning, they weren't there anymore. I was naive. I was a child."

Because they did not fully comprehend the power of evil, younger people were generally more optimistic. They succeeded in denying the improbability of survival. Their life was filled with challenges and not daunting obstacles. Even in normal times, young people feel invincible and anticipate an unending life. Rose Friedland, who grew up in the small Czechoslovakian town of Ungvár, maintained her hopefulness throughout. "There was a young couple, he was a doctor, in my hometown who had a little baby. When they found out they had to wear the yellow star, they shot their baby and committed suicide. Maybe they understood more what was going to happen. Even though I sensed danger, I believed I could live through anything. At eighteen, I was still naive. Maybe that twenty-three- or twenty-four-year-old couple were more realistic. Throughout the Holocaust, there was a certain amount of optimism for me, for me personally. I couldn't imagine myself dead.

"My prewar life was very instrumental to my survival. Knowing that that kind of life exists and maybe knowing subconsciously that that kind of life is possible made me go on and not commit suicide. . . . I remember there was a mother and daughter in Auschwitz and the three of us slept on a bunk next to the wall. There were cracks in the wall and you could peek out a little. I used to ask the mother, 'Do you think there are people out there who can see the same stars we see? Does that mean we are as free as they are?' And she used to say to me, 'Sleep, my child, sleep.' . . .

"I was talking with a friend who survived Auschwitz with me. I knew that there was no way to leave Auschwitz alive – either you

95

went through the chimney or you were carried out dead. I still did not believe *I* would die."

Mina Fogel, the sole surviving member of her extremely religious immediate family of nine, lived in a village nestled in the Carpathian Mountains. Separated from her mother, brother, and sisters at Auschwitz, she was placed in Section C and managed to outlast numerous selections for the gas chambers. As a child, she acted impulsively, uninhibited by fear and often oblivious to the potential consequences of her actions. "A child is like a little animal," Mina explained. "An older person wouldn't have the courage to do what I did."

Coping with the increasingly severe, and prolonged, daily hardships of genocidal assault caused many adults eventually to collapse under their weight. Younger people did not feel as overwhelmingly burdened by those adversities. They were not as focused on moment-to-moment subsistence, and therefore not as psychologically affected by its incremental deprivations. Their concerns extended beyond mere endurance. Like all adolescents, they coveted passion and excitement. Their zest for life flickered, but it would not be doused. Esther Fisher found ways to remain in the Lodz ghetto until her nineteenth birthday in 1944. In the preceding three years, she had watched her father and sister die of starvation and disease. "Everybody knew tomorrow was not ours. Only with a miracle, maybe you would live. We made parties. We fell in love. I had those feelings too. . . . It was exciting. . . . But it was hard. . . . You became so strong." Because the surrounding reality told Esther and her peers that there would be no tomorrow, they acted with an even greater intensity and sense of urgency. But a part of Esther also denied reality. When we fall in love, we anticipate, we yearn for a future.

For Anna Mischel, who was the only remaining member of her family by the time she was deported to Majdanek at the age of twenty, youthfulness was also central in expediting her return to a normal world. "We were young. We had a great need to make a life for ourselves. If I were older, I think I would have found the adjustment much more difficult. When you are young, you learn things very quickly and easily." And when you are young, you have an even greater determination not to be dragged down or impeded by a past. Only a relatively small fraction of your life has been poisoned. There is still the time and energy for the antidotes, the elixirs to neutralize the venom and resuscitate an eros.

Upon returning from work, fifteen-year-old Esther Flamm risked her life every day as she smuggled food and letters into the Riga ghetto. She was not deterred despite oftentimes observing others being searched as they entered the ghetto and immediately shot for concealing forbidden goods. "I didn't think what I was doing was heroic in any way," Esther asserted. "I was just young, that's all. It almost seemed like an adventure." Esther's youthfulness aided in the denial of consequences. She did not perceive a risk to her life because she carried the illusion of immortality.

As a member of the underground, Shimon Newman, who posed as a Gentile, relayed forged documents, assisted others in escape, and smuggled guns in and around the Warsaw area. He told me of the satisfaction of a young man's need for excitement and referred to those years as a "peak experience." "I didn't have only bad experiences. My Warsaw years were some of the most meaningful years of my life. I wish my children, not under those circumstances, would have such an opportunity. How many people can say they have saved someone's life? And I had the opportunity more than once! I met some people who I think are the best that there are on earth." Shimon also did not feel betrayed by his Polish countrymen. On the contrary, unlike most survivors, he does not feel angry with Poles. Several had risked their lives while extending a helping hand to him at critical moments. While most Jews' lives were bounded by persecution and hatred, Shimon encountered manifestations of goodness as he fought in a just cause.

The child is familiar with being treated as less than an adult, as less than an equal in relation to one who is full grown. "Because I was younger, I could take more punishment and harassment," explained Solomon Goldstein, who, as an adolescent, worked on the transport *Kommando* in Birkenau. In the face of ongoing torment, Solomon's *pride* was not as severely injured as it might have been if he were ten years older. He was therefore spared subsequent shame as well. For what burdened the adult was the continuous humiliation, the powerlessness one felt in relation to the seeming omnipotence of persecutors who, after all, were only other human beings.

Daniel Davidoff was old for an inmate in Auschwitz. He was thirty-six. He had the advantage of having already ingested more of life's lessons than had younger inmates. But his burden was encumbered by concern for his wife and child. His ego was assaulted by his recognition of his powerlessness to protect his family. The guilt and shame linger. "Because I was one of the older ones I had more experience. I felt fatherly to the younger ones. I felt I have something to give them. But I tried not to think about my wife and daughter . . . but it was difficult [he weeps] . . . I missed them. . . . Maybe I felt that I have to make it, that I have to go home to find them. . . . Listen . . . we were like animals. We were thinking twenty-five hours a day of food. All the time food. I had a dream all the time. If I go home again, I will have a jar of cookies on my desk and I will have it any time I want it."

Of course, sometimes the roles were reversed. The child desperately wanted to shield the parent. In the spring of 1944, Helen Schwartz arrived at Auschwitz with her mother and father. "There were women who had children. They screamed and tore their flesh over what happened to their children. What was tearing at me was that I wanted to stay with my mother, even if it meant going to death. My biggest fear was not to be able to stay with my mother and protect her. She was forty-six, very old for that place, and I had to look after that she wouldn't be selected for death. This carried through my whole life even after the war."

While many of those I interviewed at least partly attributed their survival to their youthfulness, a few were also keenly aware of having been deprived of that romantic and carefree period. Sixty-five-year-old Esther Flamm readily admitted, "I lived through my children my lost teenage years." Many children of survivors have reported the obvious vicarious satisfaction derived by their parents, particularly during this developmental stage.

Several survivors I spoke with confided that they felt sexually insecure throughout their adult life. Adolescence, a time for sexual experimentation (albeit in a muted fashion, given the mores of the environment), was denied them. In the concentration camp, their first sexual "contacts" were often their observations, personal experience, or reports by others of sexual assault at the hands of their captors. These survivors' ongoing sexual insecurities were further exacerbated by their marrying so soon after liberation and, hence, having had little or no sexual experience to draw upon. In many cases, sexual passion was not a prime motivating force in choosing a spouse after the war. Loneliness, a need for the familiar (oftentimes survivors married someone from the same hometown or a distant relative), a desire to rebuild, an eagerness to distance oneself from the immediate past often propelled a survivor into the arms of another.

For survivors, a new life began after liberation. How have they felt during the subsequent fifty years? Has there been an unfolding pattern of adjustment across the decades? In 1945, some survivors were emotionally exhausted, others simply numb. Many were convinced of the previous destruction of family members. However, those who were separated during the early periods of the Final Solution often retained a fantasy of reunion with loved ones. They sometimes returned to their homes in their country of origin and traversed Germany scanning the lists of survivors posted by the Red Cross on the bulletin boards of displaced persons camps. They examined the hollowed faces of other Jews.

In most cases, profound despondency followed their dashed hopes. "I was very sad, very depressed in 1945," Solomon Goldstein, who alone, of his family, had survived, explained. "Every day we were even more depressed. At the beginning you would dream that a brother could come back. . . . And then the reality. I traveled through Germany trying to find somebody alive, but it was hopeless. Then I secluded myself for several months. But I knew I would go crazy. So I had to find a wife right away and move forward with life, to forget about it . . . I'm not regretting this. Otherwise, I would probably be in a nuthouse today. . . . Also I hated the Germans. I couldn't wait to get out of Germany."

Not surprisingly, survivors left without any family were often the most depressed in 1945. "I felt rotten to the core," Louis Weintraub told me. "I was heartbroken. You weren't in this world. Nothing could be good for you. You were sick in your heart." By the age of fourteen, Leo Felder had known Auschwitz, Mauthausen, and Flossenberg. An orphan at war's end, he attached himself to a United States Army unit in Germany. "There was a DP camp nearby called Furth. Every opportunity I had I went there to be among my people . . . I was looking to be among my own. I was lonely. For those days, I had everything I would want as far as food and a roof over my head . . . but there was always something missing. I felt so alone."

99

Freed from the *Kinderblock* at Buchenwald, Jerry Singer described himself as "a very angry young man." In subsequent months, he unleashed his rage whenever possible. "I loved to get into fights. . . . If I heard of a brawl I joined in no matter what the issue." The intensity of Solomon Goldstein's anger was unusual among survivors. Having suppressed their rage during the Holocaust, most survivors continued to do so after liberation. Solomon remembers, "I was very mad. Very mad and upset that I cannot kill and repay the Germans for what they did to our people because the Americans didn't allow us. I'm still mad."

Having been forcibly excluded from the human world for a protracted period, survivors felt themselves at a loss when they were readmitted. Previous familiar anchors – relatives, possessions, home, daily routines, social etiquette, community – had been stripped away. And because they were not yet adults when the war commenced, many of life's lessons had not been learned. They were filled with questions and confronted with suspended answers.

By 1955, Naomi Leider was married, working as a seamstress, going to night school, and happy in America. But in 1945, she felt quite different. "I had no really . . . I didn't know what real life was . . . I was somehow removed from reality. I didn't know how things worked." Ida Koch remembers being "mixed up" during the year following liberation. "I didn't know what happened. Here I was free, but I had no parents, no money, nothing. What do you do when you are free? There was nobody to give us some advice when we came out of the concentration camp. The Americans gave us chewing gum. But I was fifteen. Why didn't they put us to a school or to a home? . . . I was a child . . . You missed your mother, your father. . . . War was over but its never been over. Even after the war, I didn't understand why I couldn't live in my home, why other people had everything what belonged to my family."

Sonya Weiss returned to Warsaw after liberation in hopes of finding her father and brothers even though they had been deported to Treblinka in 1942. Her search having proved fruitless, by October 1945 she was back in Germany. "We were a mess. There were six of us sharing an apartment. One of the men had worked in the gas chamber. . . . I didn't feel good about it that I survived. Life wasn't worth all the effort that I made. . . . We were like people . . . how can I

100

explain to you . . . when a person is hanging in between. . . . You were hanging in between. . . . You didn't belong anywhere. You were a lost soul. We looked terrible. I didn't have any hair. Most of my teeth were gone. I was like a mess. I was fat because I was eating anything I could. I'm glad I don't have a picture from those times."

In the immediate years after liberation, many survivors felt neither dejection nor despair. On the contrary, they were exhilarated. They had been given a reprieve. It is not clear why, after liberation, some survivors reacted with a greater zest while others were more down-trodden. Again, myriad factors may interact – the nature and degree of persecution one had experienced, the presence of other surviving family members, a prewar personality predisposition, a greater ability to deny sadness, a more supportive postwar milieu, a personal meaning ascribed to one's survival, to name a few possibilities.

"I felt new reborn. A miracle happened. I survived. I was very thankful for God for this miracle," Daniel Davidoff told me. Indeed, not only had David been miraculously spared, but his wife, child, and five brothers had also survived. Four months after liberation, twenty-year-old Sally Wasser married a fellow slave labor camp inmate of her brother's and lived in a spacious apartment in Winthen (near Bergen-Belsen). "I felt very good at that time. I was laughing." "Laughing?" I asked Sally. "Why not? The advantage of being that young. . . . We were young, together, and we wanted to enjoy life. There were some people who couldn't get rid of it. Some people are weaker and some are stronger. My husband, who was the only survivor of his family, he was sitting and thinking. Even in Bergen-Belsen and Auschwitz we would sit on the barracks sometimes and sing too. . . . That doesn't mean you forget what happened to you, but *we wanted to live.*

"Every person has inside him a little animal of survival. Let me give you an example. Imagine you are on the electric chair and all your pleas have been exhausted and they are about to pull the switch and suddenly someone comes in and says, Stop, you're free. Imagine the excitement. You don't think. You just run out and live." Don't question your good fortune. Don't be too introspective. And by all means, don't look back. For Sally Wasser, these activities not only indicated weakness, but they would vitiate her instinct for life.

Paul Handel painted a more ambivalent picture of his frame of mind during this time. Survivor guilt preyed on him. "Sometimes I was delighted that I survived. It's a selfish thought perhaps, but that's the truth. Sometimes I was sad, but I didn't talk about it with anyone. We all put on an act during those times. We were thinking about our parents, and brothers, and sisters. You wonder what they thought about in the gas chambers before they died."

Survivors wanted to make up for lost time. They were eager to rebuild and *move forward*. They were driven to leave horror and misery behind. "In the beginning, you live with memories," Solomon Goldstein commented. "Conditions [in the DP camp] were fairly good. We tried to immediately live again. We looked to marry. We tried to forget." In 1946, Esther Fisher married a survivor from her hometown of Lodz. Having lost her family, she needed to reestablish a connection with a loved one, to fill the hole. "All I wanted right away was a baby. This was the only hope for me."

For the period stretching from the late 1940s through the 1970s, survivors were busy. They raised their children, worked diligently, and donated money to Israel. These activities supported their conscious and unconscious efforts to repress their hurt, anger, and guilt. Survivors *did*. They tried not to think or feel. My question to Marek Singer, "How did you *feel* during those years?" elicits a history of the ups and downs of his business ventures. Despite the ongoing struggles with unfamiliar elements in their environment, despite their irrational fears for the safety of their children, despite the sense of the fragility of their new life and good fortune, despite the long hours spent toiling at their trade, most survivors report that those were happy times. They felt alive, productive, hopeful, and relatively safe.

"I was in America," Daniel Davidoff remarked. "I could work. I could fly like a bird." By 1955, Jerry Singer had been married for six years, fathered two children, and already established a successful contracting business in the San Fernando Valley, north of Los Angeles. "I'm having a lot of fun [in 1955]. I'm working very hard. I have fun with my family. I bowl in a temple league. I meet with other survivors for a game of gin rummy. I'm doing well in business. I don't dwell on the Holocaust much. The only time I might refer to the Holocaust is with another survivor and I might jokingly refer to it. The nonsurvivors or Gentiles never had the guts to ask about it."

For some survivors, however, rebuilding a life in a new land did not come easily. Their prewar professional training or degrees were now useless. Having been accustomed to a certain level of intellectual achievement or status, their lack of fluency in English was frustrating and, at times, humiliating. On more than one occasion, these survivors were forced into trades which did not allow the full expression of their abilities. For most survivors, their education was abruptly halted in midstream, never to be continued again.

Saul Garber, the only surviving member of his family from Tarnów, Poland, remembers life during the 1950s as rather bleak. He was seventeen when the war ended and nineteen when, as an orphan, he arrived in the United States. "I had been away from school for so many years. My English was poor, I was completely with Americans, I had financial concerns, and a baby. I had no support system. That time may have been more difficult, there may have been more pressure, than during the Holocaust. I began to develop psychosomatic symptoms." Today, Saul is a dentist and leader of several survivor organizations. Like most survivors, Saul adjusted and succeeded.

Sonya Weiss, whose mother had been taken from her in Majdanek and gassed, married another survivor who had a daughter before the war. The three of them emigrated to Marseilles after a brief stay in Germany following her liberation from Malhof. I asked Sonya how she was feeling in 1955. "It was a hard life adjusting to a new country. We had to make a living. I had a very hard time with Naomi [her stepdaughter]. She was told in the convent that the Jews killed Christ. She didn't want to be Jewish. . . . Normally you have a child and you grow with the child. Here I was a young woman with my own problems. The French treated foreigners like dirt. . . . You had to put together broken lives. I used to go to stores and people would say, 'How come you never smile?' For many years, I couldn't even cry. When they took away my mother I didn't cry and that was it. Now I cry all the time . . . I was much better during my persecution than afterwards. I could take the beatings at the time . . . I used to shop with my children and people would say, 'There is something strange about you.' They were right. I was strange. . . . The best thing that happened was when I started working in my husband's business. I became a completely different person. I was working like three men, not one woman. It kept my mind off all those things." Sonya Weiss works "like three men" because she requires three human forces to suppress her thoughts and feelings. What will happen to her when she ceases her ferocious pace?

While a pattern of the survivor's unfolding adjustment emerges – an initial period of emotional numbing or exhilaration, followed by a time of denial and the repression of disturbing feelings and memories as he focuses on rebuilding a life and family, and culminating in a stage characterized by the integration of past experiences and reactions as she reminisces and speaks more of her locked-away memories – that pattern is always buffeted by the ongoing vicissitudes of life. Business failures, difficulties with conception and miscarriages, serious physical illness or disability, or family crises all influenced the ease with which the survivor was able to regenerate his world.

Perhaps the most dominant leverage determining his psychological well being was the degree of *naches* (joy) he derived from his children. The second generation served as the repository for the ongoing compensatory dreams of their parents. They were to make up for all which had been taken away and destroyed. They expiated survivor guilt by providing a purpose for their mother and father: This is why I survived, the parent iterates. And despite tremendous financial success, two of the most disconcerted survivors I interviewed attributed their ongoing upsetness to the fact that their children had either married outside of the faith or were involved with a Gentile partner. For survivors, this catastrophe implies not only a further victory for Hitler, but also their inability to undo previous losses and provide future reclamation. (The second generation have responded to and incorporated these psychological imperatives. Their rate of intermarriage is far lower than that of the general Jewish population.)[1]

Survivors often speak of the three lives they have led: life before the Holocaust, life during the Holocaust, life after the Holocaust. And while the past commingles with the present for some survivors, the farther away one moves from the Destruction, the more alien it seems. Until recent years, Esther Flamm did not allow herself to think of her ordeal. "If I would have thought about it, it would have affected my children, and I wouldn't let that happen," she told me. And then she went on to describe the hazy lens through which she now views all of that. "I and three girls in the concentration camp were sitting on our bunk and wondering if we could ever have a normal life – not stealing, eating with a fork instead of with your hands like an animal. . . . The further away I get from it, the more my life is so different, the less I think. I have to ask myself, Was that me? Did that really happen to me?" While even Esther questions the possibility of such a disparity between her present normal life and her existence in the concentration camp, we can further understand why "civilians" find it so unimaginable and incomprehensible. Am *I* exaggerating how it was? Esther now asks herself.

I asked survivors, "How do you feel at this point in your life?" Ida Koch reflected the mixture of pessimism and gratefulness of many other victims. "I feel sad because I'm afraid we're going to die out and there won't be any witness that there really was a concentration camp. They're already denying it took place. . . . But basically I'm happy. I live through my children and it makes me so happy how well they are doing."

Those who were spared wanted to live the great portion of life which stretched before them. Indeed, they wanted to make up for time they had lost, and the loved ones who had been jarringly removed from them. If so much of life was not still there to be relished, perhaps survivors would have given up or been less driven to succeed. Fortunately, their relative youthfulness provided the vigor and desire to do so.

7

Intrusions of memory

How survivors have felt about their postwar lives has been influenced by reminders of a life which vanished when the Fascists reigned. "I always think about how it was. I had a nice life. I always said, I need America like I need a hole in the head if there was no Hitler." The survivor was disconnected from a personal and generational history. An identity was dismembered. "Home is the land of one's childhood and youth," Jean Améry wrote. "Whoever has lost it remains lost himself, even if he has learned not to stumble about in the foreign country as if he were drunk, but rather to tread the ground with some fearlessness."[1] For Viennese-born Hans Maier (Améry is an anagram of the alternate form, Mayer) the part of him closely allied with his country was shattered, causing a further profound severance from his roots and ensuing sense of instability. The religious Jew retained a continuity. He still owned the Shema. For Améry, Mann, Heine, and Beethoven were no longer his. After being expelled from the Third Reich, he was aware of "how much home a person needs":

The émigré writers of the German tongue . . . they lived in the illusion that they were the voice of the "true Germany," a voice that could be loudly raised abroad for the Fatherland enchained by National Socialism. Nothing like that for us anonymous ones. No game with the imaginary true Germany, which we had brought along with us, no formal ritual of a German culture preserved in exile for better days. The nameless refugees lived a social existence that was truer to German and international reality. This determined a consciousness that allowed, demanded, forced a more thorough recognition of reality. They knew that they were outcasts and not curators of an invisible museum of German intellectual history.[2]

Having been severed from Lublin or Radom or Chelm does not prevent survivors from thinking of those places, those lives. Imagining those days quiets the need for rationality and normality. Understandably, the survivor who was less successful at rebuilding a new order thought more of a previous routine. The greater the present discontent, the more prone he is to look back over his shoulder and see what had provided delight. For some, despite business success and the creation of a new family, the loss would never be replenished. In 1939, David Himmelstein lived in Antwerp with his wife and two daughters. Racked with survivor guilt, David told me, "I think all the time about those days. I'm thinking I was much happier. I used to sing for hours in my darkroom before the war. I had a beautiful tenor voice . . . I never sang after the Holocaust . . . [he weeps] . . . I remember a speech by Goebbels during the war. He said they would kill all the Jews and if a few survived, they would walk around like zombies. We are not zombies . . . but the happiness was cut out of our lives."

Having reached the final stage, survivors longingly consider their youth as they integrate their life stories. With more free time, with fewer responsibilities, and with their children having left home, they are more keenly aware of who and what else has slipped from their grasp. "I think about it more now. After the war, I had to survive. I had to think about the future. Now I have everything. I tell you something. I miss my parents and my sister and brothers more now. My kids are gone now. When they were little you were more busy with them. They were everything. Now they are not here no more."

Ongoing disconsolateness after liberation was exacerbated for many survivors by their tendency to idealize their prewar life, a life of innocence. We may attribute some of this predisposition to young eyes seeing more simply and young hearts feeling more purely. Children also need to idealize their parents and significant others. If there had been no Holocaust, I could have lived my life in that idyllic world, survivors believe. But, of course, they would not have remained in the uncomplicated world of the child, and would have graduated to the complex, frustrating world of the adult.

A few survivors have a perhaps more realistic understanding of what awaited them in those days. Not surprisingly, they also often came from poor circumstances and lived in rural, provincial areas.

Helen Schwartz grew up in the small town of Sevlus, Czechoslovakia. "If it hadn't been for the war, I never would have had the experiences I did. I've traveled, I've seen so much. Life before the war wasn't much. We exchanged it for a better life. Let's face it. The shtetl, the shtetl . . . things weren't so great then. It was a small village with a dirt road and one movie theater. It was a much harder life. My mother never had the time to wash my hair. We all had to work from an early age. I had nothing then. I didn't even have my own bed." Significantly, Helen and her immediate family survived intact. She did exchange one life for another. Perhaps that enabled her to view her life's change of direction in a more positive light.

Some survivors attempt to avoid recollections of the Holocaust and the years preceding it. "I only think about it when someone says something that triggers a memory. For my own welfare, I have tried to consciously not live in the past. It's not healthy to do that. Life goes forward. You have a family, responsibilities. You have other priorities. You don't want to go backwards, you are going forwards." Yet, survivors socialize mostly with other survivors and conversation invariably harks back to the past. "Do you remember . . . ?" Survivors will tell you, "It always comes back to the same thing." Among their own, references to the Holocaust become almost reflexive. "We would go out to dinner and at the end of the meal, I would ask him, Do you want some *nachschlag* [supplemental food given in the concentration camp when the inmate performed extra work]? Or if we are cold outside and standing on line and we rub against each other just like we did during the *Appell* in winter."

Other researchers report that the vast majority of survivors have vivid and intrusive memories of their Holocaust experiences almost daily.[3] Over the years, many have waged a continuous battle to keep the past at bay. No longer singularly focused on the rebuilding process, survivors find that memories involuntarily intrude with even greater frequency in recent years. Barry Bernstein watched his father die of starvation in the Lodz ghetto. His mother and sisters were gassed at Auschwitz. After his arrival in Montreal in 1948, the Jewish community offered financial support until he could acclimate himself to his new environment. However, Barry insisted on going to work immediately. "I didn't want nothing from nobody," Barry remarks. "I was *numb* all those years [after liberation]. I could only become emotional at certain times, whether it's seeing a movie or reading a book. As I get older I've become more sentimental. . . . It touches me more than it did after the war. . . . Then, I was so busy with my life. I came with nothing. I wanted to put myself on my feet. I got married in 1950 and within two years I had two children. I was busy day and night for my family. I worked like a slave. I was so absorbed with putting myself on my feet that I didn't have time to think about it. When I became self sufficient, then I started to think about other things."

"How often do you think of those Holocaust years?" I ask Ida Koch, who survived Auschwitz and Dachau. Ida now owns and manages numerous properties in the Los Angeles area. We spoke in her mansion on an exclusive, manicured street in Beverly Hills. "Only at night when I'm not busy. I'm a workaholic because I concentrate on nothing else but work. I work seven days from five in the morning till twelve at night. What? Should I retire? To live in the past? This way I am always busy. I don't want to have any free time. People go on a cruise. But what do you do on a cruise? You *think*. . . . Why couldn't my mother be here? Why couldn't my brother be here? . . . I didn't tell anybody about anything all those years. . . . Even before the concentration camp, when you had to wear the star, other kids threw stones at you. I tell you one thing though. You never forget. It is with you twenty-four hours a day but you have to learn how to block it out."

Survivors try to block it out, but there are too many potential links to their personal Holocaust which are encountered in their ongoing world. The associations are idiosyncratic and would not be anticipated by those who had not experienced that other reality. For the survivor, however, because memories of the past are vivid and immediate, because terror left ineradicable feelings of vulnerability, everyday life provides continual reminders of their previous fate.

"Whenever I see a crane [I think of the Holocaust]. I witnessed the hanging of inmates. You know when you hang someone, he falls down and breaks his neck. When I was at Nordhausen, if a machine broke, they said it was sabotage. One day they took prisoners by the dozens and hung them with piano wire onto an iron bar. They had a crane pick up the iron bar and those people just were dangling there for days."

The aftermath

"When I see a line to the movies I see a line to the gas chambers."

"A day doesn't go by without seeing certain things. We lived eight kilometers from Sobibor and we used to smell the burning bones. When I go to the dentist and he drills my tooth, that always brings back memories of Sobibor."

"A few months ago I saw an apple on the street while I was walking in the morning. I remembered when we were on a work detail in Kaufering. We were being marched to work. I saw an apple by the side of the road and quickly ate it. When we got back, the Jewish Kapo called me out of line. I got fifteen lashes."

"The deepest blow was the fact that I lost my parents . . . and *how* I lost them. *That* I can never make peace with. Yesterday I was in the car with my husband and we were behind a bus. The exhaust from the bus was large and I started to faint from it and I started to think how my mother and father felt when the gas was coming. You see you lead a normal life, but it never is . . . it could never be. It's an instant."

"During the [Clarence] Thomas hearing . . . It had nothing to do with the Holocaust, but it reminded me how such seemingly decent people could do such things. . . . It reminded me of the nice people who were killing innocent human beings . . . men, women, and children . . . and living such an outwardly beautiful, gentle life, and pretended they never did anything wrong."

At a point in the interview, seventy-eight-year-old Dora Levinsohn remarked that I reminded her of her son, Mark, a professor of physics at the Berkeley campus of the University of California. My presence caused fragments to erupt. Dora was separated from Mark as she was shipped to Ravensbrück and he was transported to Buchenwald. They were miraculously reunited in Bergen-Belsen immediately before liberation. "I have flashbacks constantly but I don't dwell on them. Right now, I can remember my son saying good-bye to me at the train station with tears coming down his eyes and asking me, 'Mommy, will I ever see you again?' "

Evidence of renewed antisemitism or apprehension concerning the security of Israel are likely to elicit deep vulnerabilities and, sometimes, rage.

"I guess you were born in the United States," Polish-born Rose Feingold remarked.

"No, I was born in Germany," I answered.

"You are a German Jew," she disdainfully concluded.

"No, I . . ."

"You are a *German*?" she asked, panic-stricken.

I explained that I was born in Heidelberg after the war while my parents resided in a displaced persons camp.

"I live side by side with the past," Rose emphasized. "Any little thing – a smell, a person, triggers – and then you are back at home or in the concentration camp. It comes back daily. Politics brings back. Israel brings back. There are more memories now because of the events going on now that you read in the newspapers. The neo-Nazis, the swastikas, the skinheads, the incident in Crown Heights. And I think, *Again*? They're doing it *again*? We were like in a whirl-wind after the war. We wanted to live. We wanted to forget. Some people cut out their concentration camp number. You wanted to prove yourself. Not what they made you out not to be a human. . . . And still you feel helpless . . . that these things are happening now."

Some older survivors clearly *wanted* to keep their past panorama in the forefront of their present life. They had more of a life to remember than younger survivors, a greater investment already apportioned before Hitler's conquest. Survivor guilt also *compelled* them to remember, as their adulthood conferred a greater sense of responsibility for the death of loved ones. Before our interview, eighty-year-old Louis Weintraub had already videotaped his testimony for archives at both UCLA and the Simon Wiesenthal Center. (When approached, most survivors have refused to give their testimony.) He was the sole sur-viving member of his family, which included his mother, father, two brothers, and four sisters. Louis "adopted" a small, Chasidic *shtieble* (synagogue) in his neighborhood. His financial contributions prove critical in keeping the congregation afloat. "This is my *matzeivah* [gravestone] for my parents," he explained.

Jerry Singer, who was only eleven years old in 1939, represented a few survivors who refused to be troubled or risk being impeded by their nightmare years. Jerry purposefully eschews the mantle of the Other. He has consciously moved away from his prewar world. He is a survivor who goes bowling. Jerry drives a German-made automobile, does not belong to any survivor organizations, and did not attend any of the International Gatherings of Holocaust survivors. "From 1945 until today, I don't dwell on those things. When survivors get together and inevitably the conversation turns to the past, I walk away or try to change the subject. I don't work for any Holocaust causes or museums. Just let me write a check and leave me alone."

Many survivors avoid encountering reminders of the Holocaust in their shunning of books and movies about that era. Elisa Korn, whose Holocaust story is a repeated incantation of how she was unable to save her fourteen-year-old daughter, of how she jeopardized her daughter's life by her error in judgment, of how she powerlessly stood by and watched her daughter deteriorate to death, told me, "I was once in a movie when I didn't expect any scenes from the Holocaust and I ran out of the theater because they showed something. It's with me enough without exposing me to that and getting some extra sleepless nights. Once I saw a movie and I thought I was back there. I can't even go to any memorials. I think I would fall apart completely."

Most survivors know little of the general history of the Third Reich and its program for the Jews. If you asked a typical survivor what occurred at the Wannsee Conference, she would not know the answer. Some survivors have a clear understanding of the persecution of Jews that took place in their own country but not of what happened in others. "My Auschwitz world was my barracks," Sol Feingold remarked. "I didn't even think about another barracks." In conversation with another survivor, I mentioned a book concerning the Holocaust that I highly recommended. It was clear that she had been offended in some manner. "I *lived* it. I don't need to read books about it." For this survivor, her experience was sufficient. She had personal, intimate knowledge of the Holocaust. All else, for her, was commentary.

"Do the movies affect me? No. What would affect me more than the truth? It's not nearly as gruesome as it really was. It makes me feel good that people will talk about it," Sarah Binder, a survivor of Auschwitz and Bergen-Belsen, told me. But other survivors are not as sanguine about representations of the Holocaust. They angrily believe that words and images cannot adequately capture the brutality, the smells, the tastes, the *fear*. Daniel Davidoff is exasperated. "I would like it should touch people. Of course, they never show what it was really like. But if they show only ten percent what was there, it's okay. If they showed ninety percent, the people would turn off the television. . . . A lot of things come back to me and I get emotional. I never read a book or saw a movie, they should show the whole thing. It's not like when you feel it in your skin. I never want to watch a Holocaust film because it's not the real thing. . . . Some of the movies, they just don't do justice. People walk out and it's like they just saw a movie. The fear of even a door closing. The fear of those Germans – handsome, clean, walking through camp – you can't put that on film."

Yet, mass media representations of the Holocaust are usually our only contact with that chapter of history. When the television miniseries *Holocaust* appeared in Germany, it stirred a national retrieval of memory. In millions of German homes, children, for the first time, provoked discussion with their parents about that era. The debate between the purists, who insist on complete authenticity (and sometimes doubt its possible attainment), and those who are thankful for representations of the Holocaust which will, at least, stir feelings and promote memory in the audience, is an ongoing one.

Despite some misgivings about the accuracy of portrayal and the inability of the nonsurvivor to comprehend, most survivors are grateful for the creative attempts to memorialize the Shoah. And some survivors are drawn to these images, although they are not quite sure why. Perhaps they need to assure themselves that what they believe occurred actually happened. Perhaps they are driven to psychologically master their experience by reliving it. Perhaps they are hoping to derive some meaning from the chaos. "I don't read books. I'm not interested to read about someone else's experience," Dora Levinsohn explained. "But I go to movies. I see a lot of myself and my experiences. I have nightmares after. But I do it anyhow. I think I'm a masochist. I see myself in many of the pictures. I'm drawn to them. I can't help myself."

Dora, like many survivors, remains so completely immersed in her own Holocaust experience, she has little psychological room for the experiences of others. "I'm not interested to read about someone else's experience." For Dora, her disaster was a complete one in and of itself. Dora reminds us that the Holocaust was personal and not simply a historical cataclysm. *Her* world was destroyed, *her* loved ones were extinguished. What could be worse than what happened to me? Dora rhetorically asks. I know about the Holocaust because *I* lived it, she asserts.

The aftermath

David Himmelstein was separated from his family in May 1942. Two of his brothers and three of his sisters were murdered. David hopes to fill in the gaps of their fate. He wants to know them until their end. "I go to *every* movie. If I wasn't in business I would read every book. Emotionally, I feel bad. My wife always asks, 'Why are you punishing yourself? Why are you reading those books?' I'm always looking for something I'll never find. I want to read that someone worked with my sister, Esther, or was with my brother, Daniel. I read the stories and I want to come across them. Perhaps I'll read something from family or friends. I want to know more and more about what happened to everybody." David wants to retrieve all that he can. By discovering more about the fate of his family, David's memories of them can expand.

Survivor guilt has clearly compelled many survivors to see more and read more. Rose Friedland arrived at Auschwitz with her fourteen-year-old sister, Deborah. Haunted by the belief that she did not do enough to save Deborah, Rose wants at least to share the sensations. "I read day and night. Always. I read books and my hair stands up. I get a headache. I get very upset. I can't sleep at night. I want to know what other people went through. I know how lucky I was. I was only in Auschwitz for three months . . . I feel like I experienced only a small part of it. By reading or seeing I feel like I can experience the rest of it. So I can understand it. It's like an unfinished symphony . . . I want to know more. Where does it end? I want to know *everyone's* story. I would love to interview someone who was in a gas chamber. *How did it feel?* I always think about my sister. *What did she feel in the gas chamber? Did she claw, did she scream?* I want to know every minute of it, everything that happened."

Losing the memory of their prewar environment and their Holocaust years is distressing for survivors. Books and movies aid them in their quest for the integration of their three lives. It also provides confirmation of their strength and a vehicle to reclaim their status. *I survived that.* "While we were suffering, every moment of our life then, we lived for the day to see them lose the war. I relive the victory and see myself as a human being again. When I see movies it's a confirmation of how evil it was, how unprecedented it was."

Solomon Goldstein is a cantankerous old man. Early in our interview, he digressed. For Solomon, my request for an interview implied a curiosity of the unusual, the strange, the disturbed. "Why don't you study the murderers? Why do you only study the Jews. That's what makes me so mad. People teach the Holocaust. What do they know? Study the murderers. Why do you study *me*? I don't have no horns. What? I'm so interesting? Ask the children of the murderers how they feel about what their parents did." Solomon is angry with the world, including many survivors. He is angry with his peers for portraying themselves as more heroic or prescient than they were. The sole surviving member of his Orthodox family, Solomon's point of view is rather unique. "I don't like the people what study the Holocaust. They don't get the right information. Even some *survivors* have made up some of their story. I worked on the transports in Canada [the sorting area of Auschwitz] for four weeks and I didn't *know* they burned the people. They told me that's what happened, and *I could not believe him*. There's a woman goes around telling people she was in Treblinka. How could she have been in Treblinka and alive to tell about it? What, she's trying to be such a hero? Tell the truth, goddamn it. The truth was bad enough."

I have encountered a form of Solomon's anger from a few partisans. They resent those who have adopted the appellation of partisan but did not participate in any actual fighting. Among the survivor population, they are also most likely to be angriest at the passivity of other Jews. Just as there is a "hierarchy of Holocaust experience," there is, for some, a "hierarchy of resistance." Their anger may also reflect an ongoing, unconscious feeling they have toward their parents for not having done more to avoid their own deaths and the deaths of the survivor's brothers and sisters as well. And, on a collective level, if more Jews had risen up, more of their parents and siblings might have remained. Finally, it is the humiliation of passivity from which the partisan wishes to distance himself.

As their years have advanced, survivors have been more open and forthright. Nevertheless, I asked those I interviewed if they had consciously still refrained from speaking of any *particular* aspect of their experience. Most insisted they had not purposely omitted anything. For some, the "theory of relativity" asserted itself. Nothing *they* had endured was too horrible to speak of. "Maybe in a way, [I omitted nothing] because I was lucky. I was never beaten by the SS. I was not tortured by anybody. I saw terrible things happen, but not to me."

Others clearly wanted any audience to hear an inclusive rendering of those days, particularly if they perceived that listener to be genuinely interested.

While having told their children a great deal, a few survivors, who coincidentally happened to be partisans, excluded the gorier details or incidences of the punishment they personally inflicted on the enemy. These resistance fighters may have wanted to spare their offspring the shock (and fear) of imagining their father occupying such a role in this gruesome scene. They may have been concerned that their actions, conceived in extraordinary circumstances, would taint the idealized picture they wished to present to their sons and daughters. They wished to avoid the potential for blurring the distinction between the forces of good and the forces of evil, the difference between justified actions and actions which were inexcusable.

Solomon Goldstein is forever overwhelmed by survivor guilt, which renders him incapable of viewing his behavior in a noble light. He has never confided to anyone that he had killed a German. He, too, does not wish to give the wrong impression, but for other reasons. "I wasn't a hero, I was a coward. When I smuggled something into the ghetto, I was shitting in my pants. I don't want people to think I was a hero because I killed a German. I had to in order to survive. I was a coward, I didn't save my parents. My father told me to throw away a gun, I did. You can't understand how confused everything was. I was a *coward*." Solomon believes he failed in his gravest responsibility, that of saving his parents.

From those survivors who hesitantly spoke of that which had been locked away, two themes trickled out. One motif involved the betrayal of Jews by other Jews. In order to prevent feared German reprisals in the ghettos, Jewish police sometimes arrested those attempting to organize resistance. There were other mortal treacheries as well.

"Have you ever purposefully not talked about any of your Holocaust experiences?" I asked a survivor of the Warsaw ghetto uprising.

"Things from the Warsaw ghetto."

"Would you talk to me a little about it?"

"No [he begins to cry]. . . . It was what Jews did to each other . . . I won't leave a stain . . . I love the Jewish people . . . I don't want the new generation to have a bad feeling in their mouth [he cries]. There were Jews who jeopardized other lives. Some people are weaker. He

116

thought by denouncing, he would save himself or get some food. . . . But I can't judge others. . . . They showed the Gestapo where the bunkers were in the ghetto. Bunkers had one to two hundred people. The bunkers were made so smartly. They wouldn't have discovered hundreds of people if not for them."

Controversy has surrounded the variety of roles which Jews occupied during the Final Solution. Members of the Judenrat (Jewish Councils), Jewish Kapos in the concentration camps, and those who served on the Jewish police forces in the ghettos have evoked a range of feelings, reactions, and interpretations from historians. Survivors' responses to these individuals have been bifurcated. Some fiercely condemn the men who occupied those roles as traitors, as being worse than their Aryan tormentors. There are several reports of Jewish Kapos murdered by Jewish inmates after liberation. Others are more measured in their response, refusing to judge individuals for behavior engaged in under great psychological duress.

Survivors feel exceedingly embarrassed by the sexual assaults they experienced, and have refused to speak of them. One male I interviewed admitted being coerced into homosexual contact while he was an adolescent in Auschwitz. Several females I interviewed spoke for the first time of their experiences with rape and sexual humiliation. Sixty-seven-year-old Carla Granot was freed by the Russians at Gerlitz. "They [the Russians] behaved like animals trying to catch the women and rape the women. The Russians said, 'With the Germans you went to sleep and with us you don't?' A few days after liberation, me and three girls who were sisters were going into German homes to get clothes to wear or anything else we could. Two Russians found us. They locked the doors and pointed a gun at us and told us to do what they wanted. They had already killed a lot of German girls. That was a horrible experience. Here you thought you were free and now the Russians were doing these things to you. I was able to run away completely naked out of the house, but two of the sisters were raped."

Esther Flamm had also narrowly escaped being raped on two different occasions. She had never mentioned those episodes nor "the time we had to go in the shower in concentration camp and the SS men were standing around and pointing out the girls' breasts and laughing which ones were nicer than others." Occurring at an impressionable age, these sexual violations left a disturbing imprint. "I could live a long time without sex," Esther mentioned. "My husband has always told me he wished I would initiate sex, but I never have."

Whether it be concerning their entire Holocaust experience or selected moments, some survivors have not spoken because they have felt it was useless. Words could not articulate the full measure of their ordeal. They are also convinced that the unmarked can never imagine or understand.

"When I came out of the shower at Auschwitz before they cut off my hair, there were SS officers watching us walk by. A friend tapped me on the shoulder and told me that a German was waving to me to come over. I later found out it was Mengele. How do I explain that I was never in a slip in front of my father? And here this German officer was telling me to come over while I was naked.

"I walked over and he put his whip under my chin and lifted it up. Mengele asked me, 'Why are you here?' I answered, 'Jude!' He asked, 'And your parents?' I said, 'Jude.' 'And your grandparents?' 'Jude,' I said. I then saw the line of my girls moving on to have their head shaved and I ran to them because I didn't want to be left behind. I never talked about the experience with Mengele because *I could never explain how that felt*. I could never explain how it felt when I saw my father in the camp through the barbed wires."

Despite the ineradicable hurt, survivors have moved on. They have been able to maintain a delicate balance between remembering the past and living in the present. To aid in this task, a few have adopted a strategy of assimilation and have avoided contact with survivors and other prompts of their ordeal. When I asked survivors, "How do you explain your ability to have lived a relatively normal life after all you witnessed and endured?" most simply saw no other choice in the matter, for themselves and for their children. They often resorted to tricks of the mind. "You'll never be able to live a normal life," Ida Koch emphasized. "But you *pretend*. A lot has to do with imagination. I always *think* I'm happy and I make my husband and children happy. You block out whatever happened. You don't want to look back. You just pretend. But when you are alone or at night you think about it. You *have* to live a normal life to protect your children . . . I live two lives. One for the outside, for my children. And I live my own life which is more depressing. When I'm by myself, I stop pretending. If you talk with anyone, they will say I'm the happiest person. But I myself know how I feel. I am always two persons. Every survivor is like that." And when Ida returned to her hometown in Hungary with her thirty-two-year-old daughter and thirty-four-year-old son, she still did not allow her children to see the tormented Ida, the Ida who weeps. "I had to be a little cheerful for them," she told me.

If you act normally, you may begin to believe you are normal; and if you believe you are normal, perhaps you will feel somewhat normal. "There are masking devices. You do what you have to do. You put up a good front. You come here, it's another country, another culture. People don't want to hear complaints. You get used to everything. You get used to the camps too, so this is easier." Compared to what I had to cope with, why shouldn't I be able to be relatively normal now?

Just as they explained their Holocaust survival to themselves, a few of those I interviewed attributed their ability to press forward to their fortitude and tenacity. "Because I'm stronger than anyone else. I'm a strong Jew never to be downpressed. I'm a Jew who is here to say, 'Never again.' " Many survivors looked for explanation to their family background, which provided an unshakable foundation. "You tell me. You tell me how is it possible for a person to witness the ultimate bad and remain good and decent and moral. I think when a person is brought up to be basically good, they remain good." Finally, two of those I spoke with were simply thankful for the life which had remained to be lived. Their perspective begins with the Holocaust and does not widen to include their prewar life. "I've had *more* than I ever expected I would have," Saul Sitowitz responded. Orphaned by the Shoah, Saul is financially successful and blessed with three children and six grandchildren.

As they reach the last stage of life, survivors reminisce more about their past. Feeling more vulnerable because of their increasing frailty and approaching mortality, survivors remind themselves of previous perils and of those who have slipped away. As the pressure to successfully rebuild their lives loses its compelling quality, the careful balance between moving forward and holding paralyzing memories in abeyance shifts. The Holocaust, once again, threatens to overwhelm.

8

Survivor families

Families were murdered, families were reborn.

Survivors miraculously outlived their oppressors and sired replacements for their lost loved ones. Sarah Schneider's husband, Morris, had lost his wife and child in Auschwitz. He proposed to Sarah after only four days of acquaintanceship in January 1946. Sarah was pregnant by February. Guilt, anger, and sadness were vitiated by the innocence of a newborn. A child represented a clean slate, one not poisoned by horror. And perhaps the arrival of this fresh daughter allowed the parent to symbolically recapture some of her own lost innocence.

Two years after liberation, Dora Levinsohn marveled at the continuation of herself and her family name. "I wasn't euphoric when my baby was born. I was fascinated that it was my baby. It took me a while to realize it was *my* baby." Indeed, Dora was not alone. In the years immediately after the conclusion of World War II, the displaced persons camps experienced the highest birthrate of any Jewish community in the world.[1]

Survivors married one another, often precipitously. "There was at least one wedding every day at Bergen-Belsen," Sarah Binder told me. "People paired themselves, because if you have nobody, out of loneliness, we got together." Approximately eighty percent of survivors chose another survivor for a mate.[2] Circumstances contributed to this high figure. Huddled in or near displaced persons camps, survivors were in close proximity to one another. The urge to live asserted itself almost immediately among the mostly young adult population. Dances were arranged by the Allied civil administration and Jewish organizations. Abbreviated courtships moved quickly.

The Holocaust years were bracketed and life moved forward once again, with a fervor.

For some, practical considerations fueled connections. He already has an apartment, a job. He is strong. I can depend on him, she mused. Sole surviving members of a family, particularly if they were female, latched on hastily. Polish-born Carla Granot was the only member of her immediate family of six who still stood in 1945. "I came into the DP camp like a stranger. No family, no one to talk to. I felt so alone. I felt like a rock in the water . . . alone. I cried a lot. I got married and pregnant. But I wasn't ready to make commitments. It was only because I was so lonely. And he saved my life from the Russians after I was liberated. Under normal circumstances we would never have married . . . I would have liked to come to the United States by myself, to start a new life. But it started a different way."

Oftentimes, relationships developed between survivors who came from the same city or area, and who longed for familiarity and psychological continuity. Prewar social class barriers evaporated and religious–secular distinctions disappeared as the physical tie to the past ascended in importance. People who would never have considered each other "marriage material," people who, by virtue of their divergent home life, background, and values, would never have even come in contact, clung to each other and decided to move away from the ashes together. All ties with the past had been severed. But one could still touch and speak with someone from back there and back then, from before. One's life, one's self, had not been completely obliterated.

There was also a sense of safety which accompanied familiarity. Many survivors who were still single when they retreated from Europe after the war met and married Europeans who had emigrated to Palestine or North America during the 1930s. But in some cases, the absence of a shared Holocaust overshadowed this commonality of previous geography and created an estrangement. Elisa Korn married a German refugee who had arrived in the United States in 1937. "I have not told him anything about my experience," she declared. "Why not?" I inquired. "He never asked me."

Survivors who became spouses to one another served an additional function as well. Not only could they understand what their partner had lost, but they might also comprehend the traumas and deprivations experienced during the nightmare years. Those who were not there cannot possibly fathom what it was like, what it did to a person, survivors believe.

For survivors, experience in a normal world, in normal relationships, was often lacking. The optimism which allows for more idealistic choices was missing as well. Saul Sitowitz was only ten years old when the Germans invaded his Polish village and turned his life upside down. Three years after liberation, Saul married a woman who had fled Austria to the United States in 1939. "My choice of a spouse was affected by the inexperience of the person I was at the time. I basically went from childhood to manhood without any adolescence in between. I was twenty when I got married. We were compatible. I was lonely. I have no regrets. It was a question of comfort. The terminology of love at that time was not something in my vocabulary." For Saul and many other survivors, the omission of a routine young adulthood also produced insecurities about sexual performance. "I don't know if I did the best job, passionate wise. I was ignorant," Saul admitted.

Some survivors who immigrated to the United States preferred to marry American-born Jews. Marrying someone without that indelible imprint may have reflected an overwhelming need to leave Europe and what it now represented completely behind. The survivor's rebirth in a new country would hopefully be assisted by the avoidance of the shadows of the past. Marrying an American might also provide an escape from the *greener* community, another painful reminder. Sometimes these unions worked beautifully and quickened the sense of normality the survivor sought.

Oftentimes, however, the survivor was destined to live a life in which she did not feel understood. Anticipating a response which was less than comforting, she may have censored herself. Arriving alone in the United States in 1948, Mina Fogel did not wish to burden her American relatives. So, at seventeen, she married an American fifteen years her senior. "It was a very poor marriage. He didn't understand me. He didn't understand why I became upset at certain things. He also always assumed that I had been violated by the Nazis."

Understanding the context of loneliness – the loss of parents, the uprooting from everything which was familiar, the disorientation, and the recently experienced prolonged period of mortal fear – perhaps it is not surprising that some female survivors clearly married father figures, individuals considerably older than themselves. Romance was not in their vocabulary. Feeling safe and secure was paramount.

Only a few survivors married outside of the Jewish faith. Some of these men and women located to American cities with small or nonexistent Jewish populations. A handful of survivors chose to remain behind in their country of origin and marry a Gentile who perhaps hid them during the war. (In one dramatic instance, a Polish woman living in Warsaw marries a man whom she believes is Catholic, but who, in fact, is disguising his Jewish identity from the Nazis. When her husband reveals his true origin at the conclusion of the war, she begins to drink heavily and, within six months, commits suicide.)

Holocaust survivors cleave to one another. American born Jews are more likely to be divorced than survivors and are also more apt never to have married.[3] Approximately eleven percent of survivors are divorced as compared to eighteen percent for American-raised Jews of their generation.[4] Obviously, this does not necessarily imply that survivor–survivor marriages were more satisfying than the marriages of American Jews. The sociologist William Helmreich attributes this greater reluctance to dissolve a marriage to the Old World values of the European-born survivor. You marry once. Marriage is not dependent on romance. It is a partnership, for life. Perhaps some survivors also felt too frightened, too weakened, to contemplate another beginning.

The ongoing marital dissatisfaction many survivors chose to endure contributed to their overinvestment in their children. Already traumatized by the sudden and unnatural loss of so many loved ones, survivors' fears for their children's welfare often created overly dependent relationships, ones in which the child experienced guilt or ambivalence about rebellion and separation. Realizing early on that they had chosen a mate not out of passion or even love, many females, in particular, looked to their children for gratification and, oftentimes, vicarious excitement. Their child's adolescence was an opportunity to experience their own.

Survivor–survivor marriages evidenced only half the divorce rate of survivor–American-born marriages,[5] but the deep, common bond of a shared life-defining catastrophe was not necessarily sufficient to produce marital happiness. Some survivors emerged in 1945 more psychologically wounded than others. When this disparity impinged on the marriage, resentments sometimes flared.

"I wish he wouldn't talk about it so much. It upsets everybody."

"He was so hurt, he can't show his feelings."

"She doesn't have patience."

"He has a terrible temper."

"She falls apart whenever there is trouble."

But even when a spouse voiced discontent or annoyance, it was clear there was a fundamental, underlying respect as well, and a reverence for what the other had been through. The Holocaust provided justification, and therefore engendered sympathy. "After what he experienced, what can you expect?" In survivor–survivor marriages which seemed to be the most gratifying, there was a palpable admiration for the strength, the tenacity, the humaneness, despite all the other had endured. There was a loving, mutual protectiveness, and a profound bond.

Despite the seeming profusion of eyewitness accounts, relatively few survivors have spoken extensively of their experiences either with strangers or those much closer to them. "I couldn't open up to nobody," Saul Halpern declared. "Sometimes I don't believe myself what I went through." Saul Halpern's acknowledgment reflects the resignation of many survivors. How could others understand or accept what I went through, when it is still incomprehensible to me?

A notable number of survivors have related relevant incidences or facts. But it has only been within the past fifteen years that significant numbers have come forward to tape their testimony for posterity, to publish their memoirs, to speak to various groups, to open up with their children and grandchildren. To this day, only one-third of those I interviewed indicated that they had thoroughly discussed their Holocaust travails with their spouses. Even with their survivor mates, most admitted, "I never went into *details*."

"I married Simon in 1950," Ethel Janov, a survivor of Auschwitz, began. "I came from a religious home. I probably would have married someone who came from a 'good' family. I probably would not have come across Simon in my lifetime. His family was Zionist and mine wasn't. After the Holocaust, I was looking for someone who was peaceful, someone like my father.

"I don't ever remember sitting down with him and talking about it. . . . He has a very hard time with all this. He left his home without ever saying good-bye to his parents. He can't talk about this . . . I don't think he ever asked me and I won't talk about it unless someone asks. Anyway, the details aren't important. There were categories – you were in concentration camps or you were in hiding. He was in hiding and helping others to hide and never expressed his experience as being horrible. I think he experienced the Holocaust as a game, as exciting, as adventurous. Having helped others, he felt good about what he had done during the Holocaust. The pain over his losses was never dealt with."

Spouses, too, observed the "hierarchy of suffering." If one suffered in "milder" circumstances, one was silent and deferred to the spouse who suffered greater adversity. Oftentimes a survivor assumed that because of the qualitatively different (and assumed less stressful) circumstances of their spouse's ordeal, the extent of her trauma would not be fully appreciated.

Belgian-born, seventy-year-old Anna Maline endured Auschwitz, Sachsenhausen, and Theresienstadt. Her husband eluded capture by first posing as a Gentile and then joining the resistance in Belgium. "He didn't go through camp," Anna explained. "If I would marry a man who went through camp, he would have more feeling, more compassion. It's different. It's a big difference, I guess." Anna has told her husband very little of her ordeal. Yet, she confided to me, "I wish he would have asked more."

Survivors, like all of us, wish to be known, wish to be sympathized with. Several of those I interviewed regretted their partner's lack of inquisitiveness. "He wasn't interested," Selma Brook ruefully remarked. "He had so much pain of his own. He thought his experiences were so terrible compared to others." Some survivors, regardless of the extent to which they were traumatized, simply would not allow the past to be addressed in their households. As a result, their partners felt the frustration of having to keep it all bottled up inside as well. I asked Leo Felder why he was so adamant in his refusal to speak with his wife. "Aaron, what is there to know?" he rhetorically replied. The implications were clear. It's the past. It's too incomprehensible. How can one measure the effects of that experience anyway?

In many survivor–survivor marriages, one feels more compelled to speak than the other. Both David Himmelstein's and Fela Himmelstein's first marriages were murdered by the Nazis. "I married my sister-in-law," David explained. "I couldn't live with another wife. . . . She understands that I miss my wife. . . . If it wasn't her sister, she wouldn't accept it. She always says, 'When we die, you will go to your wife and I will go to my husband.' Fela doesn't like it when I talk about the Holocaust. She always says, 'Do you have to talk about it *again*?' But maybe it's because she was never in a concentration camp." Perhaps Fela feels guilty about not having suffered as much as others. Perhaps reminders of the worst provoke too much fear. Perhaps she is tired of having to understand her husband's pain. Perhaps Fela is already filled with the anger and fatigue of her own losses.

Saul Sitowitz married a distant cousin, a refugee from Berlin who arrived in the United States during the spring of 1939. While Saul acknowledged that "my wife never fully understood me," he also admitted that his reluctance to speak about his Holocaust memories was deliberate. "She didn't inquire and I didn't say. People have to accept me for who I am regardless of what I went through. I never wanted anyone's pity."

To inhibit ongoing thoughts or feelings is associated with physiological work. . . . If active inhibitory processes are maintained over an extended period of time, they serve as a long-term cumulative stressor that increases the probability of stress related diseases. . . . A particularly insidious form of inhibition occurs when individuals have experienced a traumatic event that they are unable to discuss with others.[6]

Actually sharing a similar disaster or simply revealing one's previous agony to a spouse can forge a deeper bond. As ongoing, painful reminders emerge, they are more likely to be disclosed, thus further reinforcing a closeness. Conversely, keeping the trauma to oneself must create distance. One can never feel known, understood. And one's spouse will be left to confront the fact that a broken-off piece of her partner has been locked away from her, never to be revealed.

This mixture of closeness, distance, and empathy (or its absence) is also apparent when we examine the relationship of survivors to the second generation. William Helmreich notes that "the average survivor's decision to have children was often preceded by a series of contradictory and ambivalent feelings. On the one hand, they were afraid to have children because of apprehension that their off-spring might suffer the same fate that befell the survivors them-selves. Quite a few admitted having given their children Gentile first names for this reason."[7] Indeed, many survivors may have been ambivalent about bringing a new family into a world which had demonstrated its murderous antipathy to the Jew, but they forged ahead with a vengeance. Nevertheless, they prepared their children for an uncertain future.

"My name is Joseph," a child of survivors told me. "It's an interna-tional name given to me so if I have to flee, it is easily translatable. Growing up, I was repeatedly told to be a doctor so that if I have to escape a place, I can use those skills anywhere. My life has been a preparation for the potential need to uproot myself at a moment's notice. . . . Every day I heard about the Holocaust and I've been getting ready for it to happen again."

Survivors moved forward, rebuilt their lives, and looked to their children for solace and compensation.[8] Usually named after mur-dered relatives, the second generation suggested the ever-present potential for harm as well as the precarious status of those who es-caped the jaws of death. Magically, they implied the prospect of filling the void left by others. Survivors wanted to guarantee the safety of these vulnerable vessels. Their need to control their child and his environment might also have reflected other undercurrents.

Feeling guilty for not having done more to save parents, siblings, or friends, the survivor may have taken a more active stance in his new life in order to undo that failure and diminish past feelings of impo-tence. In addition, those who were passive during the Holocaust perished. Passivity and death, therefore, were inextricably inter-twined. "If I can only keep my child out of harm's way . . ." And, perhaps, on a more unconscious level: "My parents were unable to protect me. I must be sure to safeguard my children."

Having stood at the entrance to death, perhaps on many occasions, survivors continue to feel unusually vulnerable. This "death anxiety" is the source of repeated warnings of impending danger.[9] Relatively innocuous, everyday activities may be perceived as lethal hazards. Children of survivors may react to this apprehension by developing excessive, unwarranted fears of their own. The vulnerability felt by the parent infects the child.

Deborah Wolf, an attorney and a thirty-one-year-old child of Holocaust survivors, revealed the potential of parental fear to color reactions to their offspring.

We were overly protected. My mother would say, "Because we've lost so much, you are so valuable to me." My parents were totally nonreligious, but, when I was seven, they decided it was time for me to go to Hebrew School. But there was an intense discussion about whether or not to raise their children as Jews. They didn't want us to be vulnerable, visible. They didn't want us to go through what they did.

They always needed to know where I was, when I'd be home, who I was with, and so on. I had to do a lot of calling while I was growing up. Even when I was in college and would go back to visit them on vacation, if I was at a friend's and it was 10:30 P.M., the phone would ring, and we would all know it was my mother! They also did not encourage sports or outside activities. They were afraid I would get hurt. There was always this "fear" which pervaded a lot of activity. If I drove with a half tank of gas they would be afraid I'd run out and get stuck on the road. Exploring the environment or the outside world was discouraged.

In so many instances while I was growing up, I saw them being more worried, more prohibiting, more careful than nonsurvivor parents. They wanted to protect me from any harm, any danger, any bad influences. As a result, I was not allowed to do things at times that other kids were doing them, or to go places. They didn't allow me to take new steps or do things independently until everyone else had been doing the same thing for a long time – for example, wearing a bra, wearing makeup and high heels, dating, going out at night with girlfriends, going away to camp, living away during college. They were always a bit more cautious, a little more scared to let go.

My parents held on tighter than other kids' parents. They had to know where I was all the time. I remember going to Jewish camp and I had to call as soon as I arrived. I thought to myself, "The other kids don't have to call, why do I?"

They always seemed to fear something else going wrong in their lives. They were also very giving. They will spend any amount of money for us but none on themselves, as if they are not worth it.

I was overprotected and spoiled with love. They tried to remove any chance of suffering. Compared to Jewish nonsurvivor parents, my parents were always home for us. They devoted their lives to us – far too much. They still do, and we don't even live in the same city.

They – my parents – held on very tight. To this day, they have a difficult time separating. My parents are still terrified of losing my sister and me.

128

Perhaps the most frequent observation in the psychiatric literature concerning Holocaust survivors has been the overprotectiveness which characterizes many survivor–child relationships. Survivors warn, shield, and exhort their children for safety's sake in an attempt to assert that they can have some control over the life and death of those close to them. Indeed, in a previous study of the second generation, when I asked participants, "How do you believe your parents' experiences during the Holocaust affected the way they raised you as a child?" by far the most common and spontaneous response concerned this trait. It was also the most often mentioned discerned difference between the upbringing they experienced and that of their Jewish friends from nonsurvivor households. Having suffered so many earlier losses and experienced such a dangerous, life-threatening universe, survivors often had inordinate fear that harm would come to their children. The second generation grew up amidst a pervasive scent of vulnerability.

Survivors may have communicated to their children that they could not endure another separation, even the normal developmental disengagement that must occur between parent and adolescent so that the child may develop an identity of her own. Disengagement from children may have elicited feelings associated with previous separations and subsequent loss of family members. Survivors may not have had much empathy for their child's struggle to individuate because they were denied the opportunity to learn how to move away *naturally*, both physically and psychologically, from their own parents and thus did not experience the importance of that process. Furthermore, to justify their existence and alleviate survivor guilt, some survivors may have encouraged dependence in their children.

The often enmeshed lives of survivors and their children were counterpoised by positive qualities as well. While many survivors were overly protective, attempting to bind their family together in order to reduce their anxiety, their children grew up with an enhanced sense of closeness to their immediate and extended relatives. Similarly, while many children of survivors were burdened with the task of compensating for losses endured during the Holocaust, they also grew up with an appreciation of the importance of familial continuity and their place in that process. A few children of survivors may feel weak in comparing themselves to their heroic parents, but most have identified with and adopted the survivor's resilient characteristics.

Survivors and their children often experienced role reversals. Many in the second generation acted as caretakers to their parents.[10] In one study comparing children of survivors with their Jewish peers raised by American parents, the authors noted: "In the course of our study, we were impressed by how frequently 'American' subjects, when asked, 'Have you ever found yourself acting like a parent to your parents?' would say, 'Can you explain what you mean by that?' This never happened with a Holocaust subject; they knew immediately what we meant."[11]

To some extent, this role reversal reflects a pattern we might expect to find in any immigrant household. Children "front" for the parents because they often learn the new language and customs more rapidly. They are called upon to write a letter, answer the telephone, speak with the stranger who rings the doorbell. However, the protectiveness toward parents described by many in the second generation includes dimensions specifically related to the Holocaust.

Children of survivors are aware of sheltering their fragile parents from emotional distress. They are more likely than their American-reared contemporaries to inhibit their desires as they calculate the effect their behavior might have on their mother or father. Perhaps they have heard, "You will finish the job the Nazis started!" when their activities precipitated parental anxiety.

"My mother is very tense, prone to anxiety. She worries excessively. She has certain habits; for example, she still takes rolls from restaurants – this is the last meal mentality. She may be too close to her children. There's a kind of hovering. I don't think she'll ever be truly happy because she'll always turn around, remember, and see what happened. I don't think we could ever give her enough in terms of personal achievements that would make it go away. She might overreact to a particular stress or loss and I know it's not just this but also because of what happened. That's why we won't tell her anything bad. You can't have a realistic relationship with her. Bad news has to be diluted enough before we would tell her about it. She can deal with death very well and be strong. She must have seen so much of it and that must be why."[12]

Perceiving their parents to be overly taxed and permanently traumatized by their losses during the Holocaust, children of survivors often refrained from relating their emotional difficulties, including the usual, normal developmental trials which occurred in their lives. Survivor parents contributed to this conspiracy of silence. Some were preoccupied with their own mourning and failed to hear or see the telltale signs of disquiet. And most survivors had an exaggerated need to perceive their children as happy and problem-free so that they could serve as the requisite compensatory symbol for all that was lost. Their children knew this and played along – though not without resentment.

"Because my mother endured what she did, I have always felt protective of her. We were always careful not to let her know if anything bad happened to us. My mother was like the youngest child in the family. We felt we had to make her happy in order to make up for all her losses. She lived so vicariously through us. Everything we were living, we also lived for her. It was a shared life. I don't know that she raised us with that intent, but I think that was the result. . . . My mother was always prone to overreact to a particular stress or loss, and I know it wasn't just that event but also because of her past.[13]

Survivors often had difficulty empathizing with their children because they were preoccupied with their horrific memories, because they were grieving, because they so needed their children to be stain free, and because no pain experienced by their children could match their own ("You think that's a problem? You don't know what real problems are!"). In many different contexts survivors contrasted the child's good fortune to their own deprivations. There were often comparisons between the plenty of now and the scarcity of then.

Understandably, these allusions created obstacles to feelings of entitlement in children of survivors, entitlement not only to a physically more comfortable life, but entitlement to express anger, to express opposition to parental expectations, to separate from the first generation. "How could you do this to me after all I suffered?" was the implication. "For this I survived Auschwitz?" was the accusation.

Many survivors have very little awareness or understanding of these obstacles placed before their children. When this is pointed out to them, some may acknowledge their overprotectiveness, for example, and reply with a shrug, "After what I went through, what do you expect?" But most will portray their motives in a selfless, nobler light. "My children are everything." "I worked hard to give my children everything I didn't have." And even while admonishing their children not to cry "because it doesn't do any good," they urge them to be strong because the world is dangerous (especially for a Jew) and people, even your "friends," can be cruelly selfish.

After personally experiencing the savage impulses of their fellow man, it is somewhat remarkable that survivors chose to procreate and thereby implicitly expose other loved ones to potential dangers. In 1947, twenty-four-year-old Gitta Milstein, a survivor of several concentration camps, became pregnant while living in a displaced persons camp in the southwestern part of Germany. Gitta and her husband, Max, awaited visas which were being arranged by her cousins in Philadelphia. "I didn't know how long the visas would take. Many people were being disappointed at not getting it as soon as they hoped. I was still a young girl . . . I was frightened. I had no parents, no one to give me advices . . . I just couldn't have a child on German soil. So I had an abortion." In 1952, Gitta, safely esconced in a Jewish neighborhood of Philadelphia, gave birth to a daughter.

A few survivors, particularly those who already had lost sons and daughters to the fires, chose not to parent again. They wanted no reminders of the past. And anyway, the world was too perilous a place to warrant inviting more accessible, innocent victims. Dora Levinsohn, who survived with a child she had borne before the war, was also afraid that her luck might run out. "After the war I didn't want any more children. The unknown after Bergen-Belsen frightened me. I had several abortions when we were in Germany [after the war]. . . . You see, to save a child during the war took too much out of us. This was such a gift . . . I couldn't have more."

David Himmelstein did replenish his family. But he has gnawing doubts about his loyalties. "I never spoke about this. . . . You think so much about how happy you were with your old children . . . I worry that I'm not so happy with the new children. . . . *Like it's missing something* . . . I don't know . . . [tears trickle down his cheek] . . . like it's missing something. When it's different, it's a problem." For David, his murdered children can never be *replaced*. They occupy a special place because they came first. They occupy a special place because they were innocent victims. They occupy a special place because I failed them, David believes. Therefore, what right do I have to replace them? By what right should they be replaced? Is past, murderous injustice to be compounded by the injustice of the present? Do my present children have the right to live when my previous ones did not? Can I ultimately protect them, anyway?

Despite their parents' ambivalence, overprotectiveness, and cynicism, most in the second generation have flourished. Inculcated with a sense of being special, a miraculous remnant, most have achieved a great deal, both personally and professionally. And notwithstanding their parents' portrait of an untrustworthy humanity for whom the Jew will always provide a convenient scapegoat, most children of survivors display a greater identification with and commitment to the Jewish people than their American Jewish peers. They are less likely to marry outside of the faith. They are more likely to have visited Israel.[14] Perhaps the Yiddish language which surrounded most of the second generation served as a primal progenitor of Jewish identity.

Children of survivors have accepted the stamp of Jew and have embraced it with a mixture of pride and anxiety. For some, the endurance of the Jews, despite unrelenting persecution, has imbued them with a sense of superiority as they identify with their resilient people. The belief that the Gentile world will never accept them has undoubtedly further prompted the second generation to embrace their ethnic heritage. Finally, because of their unique background, many children of Holocaust survivors feel a poignant sense of responsibility to those who were murdered. They must ensure the continuity of the Jewish people.

The premonitory lessons which survivors took from the Holocaust were explicitly and implicitly imparted to their children. "You can't trust others" was perhaps the most often heard harangue. Beverly Diskin, a thirty-one-year-old elementary school teacher, spoke of what she had been told by her mother and father.

Knowing the gruesome details of their experiences must contribute a little pessimism to my nature, a more cynical outlook on life and what my fellow man is capable of than people with more normal family histories would have. They [my parents] taught me not to trust people. Emphasize the dress, the appearance, the external. The way you are is not necessarily okay, so present a false picture of what people want to see.

133

The aftermath

I carry a deep sadness in my life. The Holocaust has increased my awareness regarding the dark side in us – because we are mostly machine and animal. There are very few human beings. My mother would say, "There are a lot of Hitlers out there so you've got to be tough."

It is mind-boggling, terrifying to realize the destructive nature of man. Some perpetrators of the Holocaust did not set out to murder and destroy. Some murdered unquestionably. The former perpetrators also came to be murderers without remorse. That it can and did happen leaves disturbing implications on my outlook on life. I cannot be so trusting or idealistic. . . .

For the most part, I have come to realize that you cannot depend on other people. Only a few people will really come through for you when push comes to shove, so you must always look to protect and succor yourself. . . . Life can be a hostile environment, so if you can maintain a confident inner self, you'll be in better shape. I think I am like my father in this way.

Despite not knowing details of their parents' trauma, the second generation, from an early age, understood that something terrible had happened to devastate their family. Perhaps the most obvious symptom of that catastrophe was the absence of grandparents. A stream of pointed parental pronouncements such as "I've suffered enough already" reinforced the sense of darkness. Many children of survivors have commented that there was a continuous undercurrent of "You have no idea what I have already gone through."

Single-minded in their desire to move forward and distance themselves from the destruction, most survivors did not speak at length about their experiences until perhaps thirty years afterward. For survivors, there has always been the tension between their urge to remember vividly the details of the trauma and the feelings of guilt, humiliation, and powerlessness which would motivate a repression of those memories. If the survivor dwelt on his near-death experiences, past anxieties resulting from his precarious hold in this world might be excavated. In addition, the Holocaust was not in the public consciousness. The groundwork of receptivity had not been laid. There were no popular books, no movies. There were no widespread public memorials which might spur discussion. There was no such thing as a Holocaust museum. There was no inquisitive audience exhorting the survivor to disclose.

During the past two decades, a few survivors have chosen to speak about their Holocaust experiences in open forums. But this phenomenon does not reflect the norms for discussion within the typical survivor family. Most survivors' revelations to their children have been fragmentary, at best. It is the rare survivor who has sat a child down and imparted to her a complete account of what happened to him and his family. Rather, the same selective events, impressions, or encounters were related repeatedly, so that in fact very little of that period of the parent's life was truly told.

Survivors' disinclination to relate experiences to their children reflected a desire to avoid imposing an unnecessary burden or inflicting unwarranted pain. Survivors, above all, wished to foster a normal family life once again. "I cried, but *never* in front of my kids," Ida Koch emphasized. "I didn't want to involve my kids. They used to ask me questions. I used to change the subject. I didn't want to think about it or hurt them. I didn't want they should know, they should feel. I cried, but never in front of my kids. Ask them. They will tell you I was always happy and laughing. But it was all not true."

Saul Halpern didn't want to frighten his children. But he wanted them to be prepared. "When my children were small and they would ask what is the number on my arm, I would tell them it's my telephone number. When they got older and heard things at school I had to tell them a little. But you don't want to scare your children with gas chambers. I have known two survivor couples who drove their kids to madness by constantly dwelling on the subject. I don't want to dwell on those things. I want my children to be generally aware of what happened so they can see the signs of when it happens again."

The pain of rejection, the perceived disinterest of American Jews, and the desire for acceptance further extinguished the survivor's impulse to report. The lessons learned from their early encounters in the New World were sometimes applied within their own families as well. Esther Fisher told me of how she was made to feel uncomfortably self-conscious. "They don't want to hear it. The children resent you at the beginning. . . . You don't know how to talk and people make fun of you."

But the survivor's reticence was determined by other factors as well. He may have anticipated an accusatory inquisitor ("How *did* you survive?") who would prick his ambivalence about having outlasted the others. Reliving those times might prompt memories and images that could elicit survivor guilt. He may have feared the indictment of exaggeration. He may also have felt at a loss to describe the destruction accurately and fully. Primo Levi asked, "Have we – we who have returned – been able to understand and make others understand our experience? What we commonly mean by 'understand' coincides with 'simplify.'"[15]

Oftentimes, the child had to ask about the parents' Holocaust experiences in order to receive any information. Other discoveries occurred indirectly. A child came across a memento of a parent's past. She overheard a conversation between mother and father or between friends of the family who shared Holocaust tribulations with her parents. Unable to confront the issue directly, a parent may have proffered a book and encouraged the child to read it. "This is my life." It is clear that some survivors wanted their children to know at least selective elements of their Holocaust nightmare. Forty-one-year-old Steven Frankel, an actor, director, and child of survivors, told me how he had eavesdropped.

"I can't remember the first time that I heard about the Holocaust. I have always known about it and always knew stories about my parents' experiences and details about the deaths of my members of my family. My parents were in a DP camp in Türkheim, Germany, after the war and many of the people they knew there emigrated to the United States at about the time they did, so our house was often filled with these other survivors, and talk around the kitchen table was always loud and pained and angry about the war and the camps and the people who never made it. There were poker games I remember on Saturday nights that were always filled with survivors and their children and we all, from our first days, were fed stories of the camps. I think I was eighteen before I discovered that there were Jews who hadn't been in a concentration camp."

Some survivors have talked openly and explicitly about their Holocaust years. What motivates them to do so? For many caught in the whirlwind, there was a sense of loyalty to those who were destroyed, and the desire to bear witness was a crucial incentive to go on through their darkest Holocaust ordeals. They may have believed they would serve the function of gadfly to the conscience of the world in the postwar period. For a few survivors, educating the public remains their raison d'être. Even those survivors who have never spoken openly of what they saw and experienced during the Holocaust urge their children, "Never forget that it happened."

The argument has been made that if Israel had existed during World War II, the destruction of the Jews would not have occurred. Until 1941, Jews might have emigrated from Europe and taken sanctuary in their own homeland. Indeed, Israel is presently seen as a bulwark against threats to Jews in any part of the world. Yet, even with the existence of a militarily capable Israel, most survivors still believe in the possibility of another attempted mass assault on the Jewish people. They have, therefore, often told their children of their experiences in order to prepare them for a possible future onslaught from an enemy fueled by centuries of antisemitism. "I don't want my children to be caught off guard," sixty-five-year-old, silver-haired Selma Brook told me. "When the war broke out and I was a kid in Bialystok, I didn't know anything about history or the world. I want them to understand when danger is so they can run in time."

Often, survivors who, for various reasons, had been reluctant to speak directly of the past with their children finally did so during a developmental milestone or crisis in either the parent's or the child's life. "Their experience came out over many years," a member of the second generation explained. "It was hidden from me but not actively. I would overhear them talking about experiences although I'm sure my parents knew I was nearby. They never spoke about the Holocaust while I was in the room. The facts didn't come out openly until eight years ago from my father. What precipitated it was my separation from my wife. At that time my father told me his wife and two-year-old son (who I am named after) were killed. Shortly after, my mother told me she had lost her first husband as well. They told me to console me and assure me that life would continue."

Holocaust survivors are excruciatingly sensitive about issues of intermarriage, for it represents a symbolic extension of the purposeful eradication of the Jewish people. Having barely escaped the completion of the Final Solution, survivors are angry that Jews may do it to themselves. Anna Maline chose to finally speak with her son about her eyewitness memories only after he announced his intention to marry a Gentile. "We never spoke," Anna regretfully acknowledged. "He knew because I had a number. I didn't want him to be sad. Perhaps that was a mistake. . . ." Perhaps if she had spoken earlier,

Anna Maline believes, her son would understand the implications of his decision.

Those survivors who, over the years, did refer to their past a great deal tended to repeat the same stories. They seemed to have mastered their feelings concerning those events and willingly related them to their children. Reiterating particular scenes may have also helped cordon off more painful memories as a certain focus is maintained. Some survivors went further in their attempt to encapsulate the horror years. They chose to speak only of their pleasant (and often idealized) prewar lives.

The survivor's typical pattern of fragmentary disclosure has another source besides his psychological mastery of select material. His listeners, including his children, *did not ask for more.* When a survivor is asked to elaborate by an interviewer during videotaped testimony, he is usually quite capable of doing so. An interested, probing interlocutor can also revivify memories which had been repressed. Often during one of my interviews, subjects for this book would recall more and more material as we progressed. My inquisitiveness, my desire to know, implied permission to remember.

Those survivors who were partisans are the most likely to speak with their children about their experiences during the war years. They are proud of their active stance. They often exult in their previous ability to wreak havoc and exact retribution on their enemy. Not surprisingly, children of partisans have more knowledge of their parents' lives during the Holocaust than do children of concentration camp survivors. In addition, because of their pride in their parents, children of partisans have more positive attitudes toward victims of the Holocaust in general than do children of concentration camp inmates.[16]

Even while sporadically referring to previous deprivation, there were subjects of which survivors rarely spoke. They did not speak of the personal torture, abuse, or humiliations they may have experienced. They did not wish to relive the pain or shame, and they wanted to avoid frightening their children with their vulnerability. Survivors were also reluctant to stir the too painful memory of a murdered spouse or child and any guilt associated with that loss. To have acknowledged those taken from them might have precipitated fears for their present children and the concomitant feelings of powerlessness to protect them. To talk of a previous child or spouse might have implied additionally, albeit irrationally, a question of one's total devotion or loyalty to the present family. The quality of "secretiveness" some children of survivors use to describe the atmosphere in their home while growing up can often be traced to this issue. As one child of survivors remembers:

"I thought I knew a lot about their experiences. But only recently, I found out my father had a family before the war. They kept it a secret from me. I found out from my cousin who casually mentioned it in passing. He assumed I knew. When I asked my father why he didn't tell me, he said my mother didn't want to think about it and out of respect for her he didn't tell us. It was very shocking for me to find out he had a wife and son. My mother tells me that the last few years he talks about his lost son a lot. The older my parents get, the more they talk about it. They want people to know about it before they die. . . . It's made me wonder what else they have kept from me. He walked around with guilt his entire life because of his inability to save his wife and child. When he talked about the Holocaust he always talked about his strength and his leadership qualities which he exhibited during his three years in Auschwitz."

The reticence of some survivors to speak partially occurred in reaction to a child's anxiety or seeming disinterest (which may have also reflected anxiety). It is not unusual for a survivor to have chosen to disclose his Holocaust experiences to one of his children more than another. Furthermore, in many survivor households, we may find one child extremely active in gathering information about the Holocaust and another avoiding the topic completely.

Some in the second generation asked other survivors about the Holocaust while refraining from directly approaching their own parents. By assuming a similarity of survivor experience, these children could satisfy a need to know about their parents while dodging the prospect of seeing their parents suffer further anguish in being asked to relive the past. And by once removing themselves from their own families, they could also more easily quell the fear of their own powerlessness in the face of such adversity. ("If that could happen to my parents, what could happen to me?")

Many of the second generation exhibit a need to identify with their parents' suffering in order to understand more fully and to feel closer to them. Understandably, however, questions designed to satisfy these needs often had to await the mastery of unpleasant feelings associated with their parents' past experience and present behavior. Thus, children of survivors often refrained from approaching their parents for information until adulthood, when their fears and anger were more effectively controlled.

Offspring of survivors have reacted in a great diversity of ways to the disclosures of their parents. One clinician believed that the more the parent divulged of his or her Holocaust experiences, the more likely the child would become depressed and feel guilty about his relative good fortune.[17] Children may also feel guilty becaue of an irrational belief either that they were responsible for their parents' suffering during the war or that they have failed to compensate their parents for their losses.[18] (One child of survivors recounted a frequent daydream. She would be walking on a busy street near her home or riding on a bus when she would find her grandfather and bring him home to her mother, who missed him so much.) Attempting to stave off guilt, some children have reacted with anger and annoyance at their parents' information.

It is not unusual for children of survivors to remember only heroic, triumphant aspects of their parents' experiences. Frequently, survivors elected to emphasize those deeds. It is not uncommon for children of survivors to perceive their parents as heroes. Knowing of their parents' success in repeated life-threatening situations may also engender a feeling of invulnerability to future danger.[19] On the other hand, those survivors who ascribed their escape from death to luck may contribute to a child's sense of fragility, as the gift of survival not only is randomly bestowed but also relies on factors one cannot control.

Whether survivors refrained from speaking to their children about their past or released scattered information over the years in short bursts, most of those in the second generation have wide gaps in their knowledge of their parents' experiences. Fantasies of their parents' Holocaust life, therefore, frequently emerge. Many children of survivors "have created a myth about the Holocaust or their parents' Holocaust experiences based on their own fantasies, particularly in families where parents had been silent about their personal experiences."[20]

Hannah Bergman, a twenty-seven-year-old business consultant, related the following: "Because I don't know much about my parents' experiences I used to have frequent nightmares about them. For example, in one recurring dream, the Germans were making soap and lampshades out of human flesh. My father walked on a selection line being inspected to see if he would be subjected to that. I only learned later in life that my father never went through any selections."

Such inventions often influenced children's perception of the survivor parents, and as a consequence may have affected their attempts to cope with their parents' Holocaust background. For example, those who imagined their parents to have been meek and passive may have felt ashamed or angry with them. In addition, their own feelings of vulnerability may have been exaggerated. By contrast, children who perceived their parents to have taken a more active or even heroic stand were not only likely to respect them more but were also apt to feel confident in the face of adversity.

Perhaps the most common concern of children of survivors, and one that fueled the most dreaded vision of a parent's ordeal, was the actions or behaviors the parent may have performed in order to escape death.[21] The answer to this question often played a central role in determining the child's view of that parent. Frequently, it was the child's imagination that produced the explanation.

Those in the second generation vary widely in their general familiarity with the history of the Holocaust. One investigator reported that children of survivors do not have more factual knowledge about the Holocaust than their American Jewish peers from nonsurvivor homes.[22] My observations confirm this finding. Nevertheless, many in the second generation *believe* they know about the Holocaust simply because they have perceived its aftereffects on their parents. As already noted, many Holocaust survivors know little of the general history of the Third Reich and its program for the Jews.

A minority of survivors talked of their Holocaust years with their young children. For various reasons, however, many more opened that door later. A keener sense of mortality impelled them to discussion. With greater distance from the Holocaust, their exposed nerves recovered their myelin sheath. Having adapted to and prospered in a new environment, their energies could be more safely directed to recollection. And, many decades after the destruction, the world seemed more willing to listen. Some parents have accompanied their children and grandchildren back to their prewar hometown or camps where they were incarcerated.

Children of survivors regret that their parents had been so self-absorbed and so unable to demonstrate empathy. They wish there had been more room for *their* feelings. They are angry because their problems were trivialized when they were compared with those of their parents. However, survivors, too, craved understanding. Many wish their children had been more interested in their past. They needed to speak and longed for the moment when a child would *ask* so they would not feel the guilt of burdening.

"It hurts me, they never asked," Carla Granot, the sole surviving member of her family, remarked. "I feel sometimes I didn't do a good job with my children. They're not interested. They haven't even watched a tape my husband and I made of our experiences." Ethel Janov echoed Carla's sadness and bitterness. "I would have liked them to be more interested in my Holocaust experiences. I suppose that's why I talked with other people's children. Now I would like my children to sit down like you are sitting here and ask me all about it. I would like them to carry on the history, the memory . . . and I don't think they will."

Many children of survivors display an ambivalence when relating to their parents' experiences and the Holocaust in general. On the one hand, they identify with their mother's and father's traumas. And when they do so, their sympathy allows a closer relationship. But other feelings – anxiety, guilt, anger, vulnerability – engendered by the catastrophe which befell their family and people act as a repellent. They wish to avoid the sadness of their parents and all that it symbolizes in order not to be engulfed by its concomitant sense of powerlessness.

With respect to their children's interest in the Holocaust, survivors are ambivalent as well. They fear the Holocaust's lingering capacity to infect their sons and daughters with fear and sadness. At the same time, knowledge may prove critical, and survivors want their children to be strong and prepared for the inevitable hatred of others. It is also clear that while most survivors have been reluctant to speak directly of their ordeal to their children, they nevertheless have a keen desire to be known by them. All human beings crave empathy and understanding.

9

"Was God watching this?"

"There are five Yizkors [the prayer for the dead]. I never miss one," Sarah Schneider told me. "My brother who lives in Israel doesn't believe at all, but I call him before every Yizkor and tell him to go because my parents believed. So he does me a favor.

"I hate to say it. It's a big sin. To confront God? How dare I? But I can't help it . . . when I read the translation, the tears roll down my cheeks. . . . My parents believed so much. On Yom Kippur, they asked for God's forgiveness, for His help. My God, if you knew how they believed God would help them. . . . My dog is better protected by me than God protected His people.

"When I arrived at Auschwitz, a mother was holding her baby and she was told to give the baby to her mother and she would survive. The grandmother tried to take the baby, but the mother wouldn't let go. . . . And they argued and an SS man came over, took the baby, and threw it against the wall, and the baby's head smashed open in front of the mother. Was God watching this?"

Before World War II, most of the Jews of Europe (particularly Eastern Europe) were religiously observant. Even the typical, secular Jew who did not follow the dictates of Jewish law was nevertheless psychologically tied to a sense of peoplehood through his identification with Jewish tradition and Jewish culture. For the religious and the secular, being Jewish meant belonging to something of value, something which compelled a connection. For the religious Jew, of course, this specialness emanated from the unique relationship between God and the Israelites. We had entered into a covenant with Him: in exchange for our witness to His supremacy, we would receive His divine protection.

143

There has always been a tradition of Jews putting our faith in the miraculous. He brought us out of Egypt. He parted the Red Sea. He saw us safely to the Promised Land. The God of the Holocaust survivor's prewar family was a God who intervened. He was an all-seeing, all-knowing God who punished individuals for their sins and rewarded individuals for their good deeds. He was the Parent who judged fairly, who loved His children, who promised His shield. And for countless Holocaust survivors, He was the Parent who abandoned them.

For many theologians, the Holocaust produced a crisis of faith. There was a rush, therefore, to articulate a plausible theodicy (a vindication of divine justice in allowing evil to exist). In their assessment of the victims, Holocaust survivors repeatedly invoke the adjective "innocent." So many *innocent* people. The *innocent* children. Wasn't God supposed to protect the innocent and strike down the guilty?

On the night of conception, according to one Talmudic legend, God decides over a drop of semen whether a child will be poor or rich, stupid or intelligent, handsome or ugly, male or female. The only quality not determined by God is the child's moral character. The angel escorts the nascent soul through Paradise, where the rewards of the righteous are displayed, and through Gehenna, where the wicked are lashed with scourges of fire.[1]

God gave man the freedom to choose. The price of free choice is evil. The Holocaust was perpetrated by man, not God, many insist. The great majority of Holocaust survivors, including those who are most devout, eschew the notion that the Holocaust was God's will.[2] Men killed men. "During the Holocaust, I wasn't thinking where He is," Dora Levinsohn, whose husband and child survived, remarked. "I was too busy with day-to-day survival. I worked twelve or sixteen hours a day and only thought about my food at the end of the day. But after the Holocaust, I thought about God. Every man can choose. Hitler did it, not God."

David Birnbaum explains further that evil is a by-product of God's creation of good. For there cannot be good without evil. In short, God did not create evil itself but, rather, God created the potential for evil. And the potential for evil grows proportionally as humanity ascends in knowledge and freedom. The greater the human freedom, the less the obvious divine providential care, so that God appears to become increasingly hidden.[3] God must absent Himself for man to be.

God sees man act immorally but hides himself, a dynamic referred to as *Hester Panim* (Concealment of the Countenance). God hides himself as punishment for abandoning His ways.

> Then my anger will burn against them and I will forsake them. I will hide my face from them and they shall be devoured, and many evils and troubles shall befall them, so that they will say on that day: "Are not these evils come upon us, because our God is not among us?" And I will surely hide my face on that day for all the evils which they shall have perpetrated. (Deuteronomy 31:17–18)

Perhaps God did not turn His face away simply in response to human sin; perhaps the sins themselves obscured God's vision. He would love, but He is thwarted by the failings of His chosen partners in love. Fundamental to Jewish theology is the idea that the Almighty created an imperfect world awaiting perfection. If we are to be full partners with God in perfecting the world's shortcomings, God must, of necessity, hide Himself. When Job confronts God and demands to know the reason for his apparently meaningless suffering (in effect questioning the hiddenness of the Divine), God responds from the Whirlwind: "Gird now your loins like a man: I will ask *you* and you must answer Me. Will you nullify My laws; will you make Me the evil one in order that you appear righteous? Is not your arm [as powerful as] God's, and can you not thunder with a voice [as strong as] His?"

God reminds Job of human responsibility, and insists that instead of condemning the Divine, he, Job, must activate his own human potential as a partner with God in protecting the world. It might have been easier for God to do it alone, but that is not the axiom upon which the world was created. God can step in at any time, but He, using supreme inner strength, remains hidden so that we can bring about our own redemption.

While survivors have been repelled by any offered causality between the transgressions of the Jewish people and the Holocaust as a manifestation of the wrath of God, some rabbis, many of them Chasidic, have proposed such a link. These teachers imply that Hitler was God's instrument.

> But if you do not obey Me and do not observe all these commandments, if you reject My laws and spurn My norms, so that you do not observe all My

commandments and you break My covenant, I in turn will do this to you: I will wreak misery upon you – consumption and fever, which cause the eyes to pine and the body to languish; you shall sow your seed to no purpose, for your enemies shall eat it. I will set My face against you: you shall be routed by your enemies, and your foes shall dominate you. And if you remain hostile toward Me and refuse to obey Me, I will go on smiting you sevenfold for your sins. I will loose wild beasts against you, and they shall bereave you of your children and wipe out your cattle. They shall decimate you, and your roads shall be deserted. And if these things fail to discipline you for Me, and you remain hostile to Me, I too will remain hostile to you: I in turn will smite you sevenfold for your sins. I will bring a sword against you to wreak vengeance for the covenant; and if you withdraw into your cities, I will send pestilence among you, and you shall be delivered into enemy hands. And you I will scatter among the nations; and I will unsheath the sword against you. You shall not be able to stand your ground before your enemies, but shall perish among the nations; and the land of your enemies shall consume you. Those of you who survive shall be heartsick over their iniquity in the land of your enemies; more, they shall be heartsick over the iniquities of their fathers; and they shall confess their iniquity and the iniquity of their fathers, in that they trespassed against Me, yea, were hostile to Me. (Leviticus 26)

Jews, these rabbis asserted, have always been punished for their tendency to assimilate and for their forswearing of the Torah and divine commandments. Writing in the late nineteenth century, Rabbi Joseph Soloveitchik reminded Jews that there is a distance which must be observed that separates Israel from other nations. When Israel comes too near, God has the Gentiles push them back, and the deeper the attempted penetration, the more furious the repulsion. The Chofetz Chaim placed his hopes for humanity in Torah observance. When Torah is lost, the evil inclination emerges, he believed. To restore the memory of identity, God surrounds Israel with enemies. The *umipenei hata'einu* ("because of our sins we were punished") premise has been the prophetic approach to explaining calamities befalling the Jews for thousands of years. Did God use the Nazis as He used Assyria of old, as "the rod of his anger" (Isaiah 10:5)?[4] The Piazesner Rebbe, whose son, daughter-in-law, and mother were killed in a German bombing of Warsaw, attributed their deaths to his *own* sins.[5]

David Himmelstein told me of his encounter with the self-flagellation of believers. "One day the German guard told these three religious Jews with beards to bring their *tefillin* with them to work. He told them to kneel down, put on their *tefillin*, and pray to their God to help them. They were laughing and hitting them. I saw them a few days later, and I asked them, 'This what they did with you there, Can you believe in God? They took my children and your children and put them in gas.' They told me, 'Yes we believe. We sinned. Jewishness is becoming less and less. Jews are marrying Gentiles. And that's why he's punishing us here.' 'But, why did they kill the children, who never did anything?' 'Ah, that's the biggest punishment for us.' I walked away."

From the perspective of certain rabbis, such as Rabbi Yoel Teitelbaum of Satmar, the "idolatry" of the modern Zionist movement was to blame. The establishment of another Israel must be God-driven and not provoked by man. The venerated yeshiva dean Rabbi Yitzchak Hutner has argued that the Mufti was not an avowed enemy of the Jews until pressure for a Jewish state was applied. Zionism, therefore, *induced* a collaboration between the Christian West and Moslem East to destroy the Jews. (Rabbi Yissachar Shlomo Teichthal, a Hasid of the Munkacher Rebbe, broke with his teacher over the role of Zionism in Jewish fate. In his *Em Habanim Semechah* [A Happy Mother of Children], written in Budapest in 1943, before the formal German occupation, Rabbi Teichthal passionately urged Jews to leave the Diaspora and rebuild Eretz Yisrael as a necessary prelude to the Geulah Shelemah [Final Redemption]. The author accused leaders of Orthodox Jewry who opposed settlement in Palestine during the decades preceding World War II of having unwittingly contributed to mass murder. Rabbi Kook echoed Rabbi Teichthal in adopting a neo-Orthodox position which advised Jews to adapt to their modern surroundings and modify their relationship to God. The Jewish nation, he believed, must take control of its fate and *initiate* a return to national life in its homeland.)

From a Chasidic perspective, all which emanates from God is hesed (goodness, kindness), though its understanding may be hidden (*nistar*) from man's finite perspective. Suffering must, therefore, be accepted with love (*kabbalah be'ahavah*) and personal sacrifice (*mesirat nefesh*) on the basis of faith (*emunah*) and unquestioning trust (*bitahon*) in God's ultimate justice. In this light, the Holocaust is a supreme test of faith, a modern *akedah* (sacrifice of Isaac.)

But despite the aphorism first attributed to the Chafetz Chaim – "For those with faith there are no questions, and for those without faith, there are no answers" – Jews struggled for an explanation which would ease their suffering. As they filed to their death, some ardent believers sang the words to a song based on Maimonides's twelfth Principle of Faith.

> I believe with a perfect faith
> In the coming of the messiah
> In the coming of the messiah
> Do I believe
> And although he may tarry
> Yet do I believe

Facing certain death, Rabbi Ben Zion Halberstam, the Bobover Rebbe, was urged to flee by his followers. Instead of escape, Rabbi Halberstam embraced the concept of Hevle Mashiah, the period of suffering which heralds the messianic era. "Why hide?" he responded. "Shall one hide from the Hevle Mashiah?"[6] And, in Treblinka, Rabbi Yisrael Shapira, the Grodzisker Rebbe, told his disciples: "We should not question God's actions. If it is indeed destined that we shall serve as a sacrifice for Hevle Mashiah during this period of redemption, and thus be consumed in the flames – how fortunate then that we have been privileged for this purpose!"[7]

For Chasidim, suffering is a form of Hesed Nistar (God's hidden kindness). Suffering presents man with the opportunity to draw close to God. When the Belzer Rebbe's firstborn son was burned alive in a synagogue set afire by the Nazis, he expressed his loss in terms of a sacrifice to God: "It is indeed a kindness of the Almighty that I also offered a personal sacrifice." As an aspect of Hevle Mashiah, suffering also serves to impel the return to Eretz Yisrael.[8]

For some ultra-Orthodox, martyrdom was a comforting thought because it gave meaning to their tribulations. The calamity drew redemption and its promised reward closer. It was also through Jewish martyrdom that all nations would recognize the one, true God. However, recent voices have vehemently objected to this formulation in their repudiation of the use of the term "Holocaust."[9] Holocaust, of Greek origin, means a ritual "whole [burnt-] offering," what the Tanach refers to as 'ola. But the destruction of the six million was not an *'ola* of Jews offered to God as Patriarch Isaac offered himself. Jews were *condemned* to a death which they did not choose.

Survivors, except for some of the most steadfast believers, remove the six million from the realm of the religious. Survivors revere the six million because of the victims' innocence, because they did nothing to warrant their torture and murder. Otherwise, they were ordinary men and women, not martyrs.

I knew personally hundreds of the dead from my own town and others I met during those years. They were like people everywhere, some good, some scoundrels, some a little of both. There was the dishonest butcher of our town, a crass, shamefully wicked man who suffered very greatly and lost his life and his family in the gas chambers. And there was a neighbor's immoral wife who, with no concern for what others might think, had her clutches out for every man she saw, who disgraced her fine family repeatedly. These and others were hardly righteous and pure and they didn't die for the sanctification of God's holy name. Neither did the many other low and unprincipled scoundrels who preyed on others in the camps, most of whom died and some of whom lived. One I see all the time on the street even though I try to avoid him and he tries to avoid me. Usually the more unprincipled and corrupt they were, the greater their chance for survival. They didn't volunteer their lives for the sake of God's name like the Jews of Spain and other places for example. Some would have committed any despicable act to remain alive even though others would suffer and die because of them. No, very few saints were among the Six Million.[10]

Rejecting the Jewish tradition of faith being placed in the miraculous, contemporary thinkers have approached the conundrum of evil and God with amended definitions of the Divine. Perhaps God has created a grand design for the universe, but nevertheless does not *participate* in history. Perhaps God is all good but not all-powerful. To speak of God absenting Himself is more palatable than "God is dead." (Acceptable to some, perhaps, but agonizing for others to believe that He *could* have intervened had He wished.)

In August 1961, the American theologian Richard Rubenstein participated in a public panel discussion with the dean of the Evangelical Church of East and West Berlin, Heinrich Grueber, during which the Protestant clergyman asserted that God had used the Nazis as the instrument of His will. Appalled at the assertion, Rubenstein felt compelled to reject the notion of Divine will or Divine concern. The human condition reflected no transcendental purpose, he insisted.

For Rubenstein, God, the Covenant, and Chosenness were killed at Auschwitz. A God who either permitted or was powerless to stop the extermination of His people is unworthy of their belief and life. Doctrines of covenant and election are training for powerlessness. After the Holocaust, a transcendent referent for morality had become obsolete. We live in an age, wrote Rubenstein, which is "functionally Godless."[11] More recently, however, Rubenstein has retreated somewhat. "When I wrote *After Auschwitz*, I stressed both the punitive and exclusivist aspects of the doctrine of covenant and election. Over the years I have come to appreciate the other side of the picture: humanity's profound need for something like the covenant or its functional equivalent."[12] Thus, all the more reason for continued ritual and communal existence. Rubenstein understands that men and women need to create meaning for their existence.

For the most part, Orthodox Jewry has neither asked questions nor sought answers for the recent murder of millions of their brothers and sisters. For some, it is simply too disquieting a question, too unnerving a challenge. The foundation of their faith may have already been cracked. It could not withstand more pressure. Others offer the traditional bromide: finite man cannot understand infinite God's ways.

There has always been a tension between divine promise and divine judgment, a tension between the God who brings salvation (e.g., Exodus) and the God who chastens (e.g., the destruction of the Temple). Most Torah scholars deny the uniqueness of the Holocaust. They object to a special nomenclature and use the term "Churban." As the sensitive and compassionate Eliezer Berkovits has noted: Auschwitz is unique in the magnitude of its horror, but not in the dilemma it presents to religious faith. The predicament, therefore, of the post-Holocaust theologian is no more troublesome than the ones encountered by Jewish leaders after the years 70 (the destruction of the Second Temple) or 1492 (the Spanish Inquisition).[13] Optimism is maintained by viewing the Holocaust as a continuation of the pattern of Jewish catastrophe followed by regeneration. *Am Yisrael Chai!* The Jewish people live!

The philosopher and rabbi Emil Fackenheim was there. He refuses to borrow answers from theodicy. For Fackenheim, the task is "not to explain God, but how to live with Him." Fackenheim's new 614th commandment (in addition to the traditional 613) is the sacred obligation for a Jew to remain a Jew and not grant his enemies a posthumous victory. The messianic age will reveal the solution to insolvable theological dilemmas.[14]

Most Holocaust survivors are far removed from formal theological discourse. And because human beings (and especially survivors) feel vulnerable, because they need an amulet, many continue to believe. Despite often attributing "luck" to their survival, it would be too frightening to live in a world where chance reigns or where the forces of evil predominate. Survivors have been so undermined, they cannot bear to lose the support of their faith as well.

"Where was God? . . . I have to believe in something. If you don't believe in anything, you are an animal."

"I happen to be a believer through my background. . . . But what I witnessed of pious people in the concentration camp who asked the question, Where is God? . . . I believe there is a Supreme Being. I believe some miracles happened to me and there must have been a Supreme Being then. But where was God when the really pious and decent people went up the chimney? . . . Basically, I believe. If we don't believe, civilization will be finished. My belief might be stronger if I hadn't seen those atrocities with my own eyes. What did a baby do to deserve his head smashed against a wall? Where was He at that time?"

"We ask ourselves a lot of questions. . . . But yet you can't understand a lot of things in the world. Some good things came out of the ashes. . . . You can't give up everything. . . . You want your family to believe because your heritage is all combined and if you lose that, you lose everything."

Approximately one-half of those survivors who were believers before the war remained believers throughout the Holocaust and until today. Those who were ultra-Orthodox before the war were the least shaken in their beliefs by subsequent events.[15] Saul Halpern sent his children to Hebrew School, attends synagogue regularly, and observes all Jewish holidays. He has stared at man who acts as though there is no God. The prospect of that world arouses mortal fear. "I don't know. If there is a God and we are the Chosen People, why did he let so many little children be killed? . . . I know so many people who are not so nice who survived. Before the war, we were afraid if you did something bad, God sees. He punishes. Now I don't know what He sees. But you still want to believe in something." Saul's God may be a less personal one, *But still you want to believe in something*.

The randomness of survival demands order. Our life is too precious to resign it to ongoing caprice. The anxiety of our perilous existence must be quieted. For Ida Koch, there was a Divine logic to her survival. "First of all I figure out if there was a God, why did He first kill all the *good* people – the children, the old people, the religious people? Later I thought, maybe God wanted to kill them first to save them the pain. I didn't believe for a while, but I saw certain things happen to me so I thought God saved me for certain reasons." *The need to believe that you were chosen to be saved by God also alleviates survivor guilt.* Perhaps He spared me for a purpose.

To believe in chance is to deny protection. Naomi Leider, a modern Orthodox Jew, would rather believe in God. "I believe even more . . . especially what I went through and lived through. When you get shot and are alive, you must believe in God. It was definitely the hand of God who saved me." In the face of the probability of disaster, we strike bargains with God. Any glimmer of rescue brings us closer to Him. And when we reach the other side, we repay our debt with our confidence in Him. The following concentration camp inmate, a non-believer before the war, also sensed God's presence in his survival.

You must remember what I went through and what I saw: monstrous things with my own eyes in the camps and out, infants being dashed to death and other young people starved. And yet I escaped and lived. I had to interpret that fact for myself.

Others say, How could you be religious and keep the commandments after what God did to you and all the Jews and how He let the Nazis murder us like flies?

I can only speak for myself and try to understand what happened to me personally. Time and time again I survived the appel, the selection. I'd pray to God and He would hear me. And I made vows that if I would survive this selection I'd eat only kosher after I was set free. And when the next came I'd say if I will survive this selection I will keep the Sabbath 100 percent. And if I'd fool them into thinking me healthy and strong when I was weak and nearly dropping, and should have been selected for death, I'd vow to do more, be a still better, more observant Jew.

I never went back on my word. And in this way I became a religious Jew, keeping the commandments and living a Jewish life. And my wife, when she was alive, would even go to mikveh and preserve the purity of family life.

During the long death march, when so many others fell aside, and I kept promising so many vows to God, I had resolved to be a very pious Jew. And I am that today, as you can see.[16]

Selma Brook subsisted on faith. "If I didn't believe in something above that things would change and get better, I wouldn't have had a reason to survive. Whether there is a God, He has never spoken to me, I have never spoken to Him. But during the worst times, without some faith in a higher power, I don't think I could have survived."

Although most of their past was wrested from them, many survivors have retained a sense of continuity through their traditional activities. With their pleasant past associations, such observances have aided in keeping survivors near to their lost family and concurrently engendering a feeling of loyalty and respect for the murdered. "Going to synagogue brings back good memories of home," Saul Sitowitz, who no longer believes, explained.

"How has your belief in God been affected by the Holocaust? I asked Rose Feingold. "I won't answer you. My upbringing tells me one thing and my experience tells me another. Because I live with my parents' memory, I live as they would have wanted me to. Perhaps if they had lived, I would have deviated." Rose's devotion to her father and mother enjoins her from turning away from a God whom they worshipped. Preserving God further enables Rose to preserve her love for her parents.

If the objective of evil was to erase Jewry from the face of the earth, remaining observantly Jewish is a statement of spite. Remaining Jewish is also an irrational affirmation that the six million neither lived nor died in vain.

Before the Holocaust I was a simple observant Jew. Today I'm an observant Jew but very complex, not at all simple. Due to the Holocaust, I can now say that every single religious practice I keep – and I keep most – is because of what I have undergone and witnessed and experienced during those terrible years. I observe the mitzvot now because of the Holocaust, specifically because of the Holocaust. I have now a clear reason in my mind and very deep motives for practicing Judaism – whereas before it was not as clear. Besides everything else, it's my revenge against Hitler and the Nazis . . . it is spitting on their graves. My way of getting even is by practicing my religion with fervor and enthusiasm. Serving God and the Jewish people and carrying on my father's, my grandfather's and ancestors' traditions.[17]

Not surprisingly, many survivors are confused, uncertain of their past beliefs, which held so much promise and provided so much comfort. It is difficult to forswear those early years of indoctrination, the lessons of the venerated. "This [belief in God] I have a big fight in my soul," Ben Kass told me. "I would say . . . I don't know how to express myself . . . I would say I don't really believe there is something like God. If there would be a God, if God is supposed to be so merciful, how could He let children be murdered? My six-year-old brother was killed. One and a half million Jewish children were killed. How could He? Or God is deaf. People pray and pray and pray and He doesn't hear them. Maybe He needs a hearing aid." For some of those whose faith was weakened, a belief in a very personal God was supplanted by a belief in an impersonal idea of God. The powerful human needs which embrace the Divine in the face of seeming contradiction reach a compromise which enables a continued link with the past.

Other survivors remain too agitated to settle for a midcourse. They dialogue with God, they badger Him. But to challenge God is still to preserve Him. It is significant that this form of debate is steeped in Jewish tradition. The survivor, therefore, remains within the framework of his ancestors. For the survivor who is most intensely immersed in this struggle, the structure may provide a purpose, an organizing principle to his post-Holocaust existence.

It is all I think about. . . . My life is a running, nagging dialogue with God. . . . He is always on my mind. Why? Why? I sometimes find I have been walking the lonely, crowded streets of Tel Aviv, wandering aimlessly, conducting a question and answer session with Him – with no satisfactory answers forthcoming. I believe in Him with the same certainty as ever. The Holocaust couldn't change that. But I find I want very much to keep after Him and try to the best of my ability to overcome the obscurity of His ways and I can't escape Him, however much He may have wished to escape us. I will do this to my last breath. I know it. More than this, I believe this is precisely what a Jew must do, to keep after Him for answers.[18]

The argument may also allow for the release of anger. Martin Schiff, a survivor of several concentration camps, obsesses about the question Why? "I am *Shomer Shabbos* (Sabbath observant). But I smoke on *Shabbos*. I don't care." Martin Schiff taunts God.

In the face of the evidence, many survivors lost their faith entirely. They felt abandoned by Him and chose to abandon Him in kind. Solomon Goldstein had been brought up as a deeply religious Jew. "When you sit in the barracks of Auschwitz and you look on the burning chimneys, and you see that the transports that just arrived are burning now . . . you ask God on Rosh Hashanah when we pray to You and ask for forgiveness and You should give us a good year. One prayer you have there, who should die by fire, who shall die by water, who shall die by other means. Now, let me ask You, God, Did all those people commit the same sins that they should have to die by fire?

"Sitting there, many times I asked God, What am I better than those people who supposedly committed a crime, they should die by fire? Am I a better Jew than my mother and father? Am I one of the Lamed Vovniks? [A Talmudic teaching, amplified in the Kabbalah, which asserts that there are at least 36 anonymous men in every generation who have been privileged to experience the Divine Presence. As a reward for their merit, God allows the world to exist.] I don't think so. Anyway, waiting for an answer, the Kapo screamed, 'Everybody, *raus!*' "

For the following survivor who emigrated to Palestine after liberation, his love for his previous home and family no longer allowed him to reach for God.

I began to understand what happened to my faith and my belief after liberation. This was the summer of 1945. It was at Buchenwald and Sabbath services were being conducted. Before, I would have automatically and unthinkingly attended, with little or no reflection. And I would have joined in the prayers with pleasure.

In fact had it been previous times I, having been away from prayers for a long period of time, would have returned and raced to services to sing the songs and chant the prayers with much pleasure and much enthusiasm.

This time I stood like a Golem and couldn't budge an inch toward the dining hall used for the services where the Sabbath was being welcomed. Everyone was dressed in their best new clothing and singing together familiar melodies, holding the small United States Army prayer books and swaying to

155

the melody. I felt as though they were from a different period in the distant past, before the Ice Ages or maybe from a different planet altogether.

My eyes filled with tears but my lips wouldn't quiver with prayer. It was as if I had lockjaw or a paralysis of the mouth. My mind began racing toward past times of joy in the synagogue with my father and my grandfather and the other Jews of our town; happier times and happier places.

How could they conduct services, resuming their prayers as if nothing had happened. I certainly couldn't. Too much pain. Too many recollections of the distant past. It felt like centuries ago, not just six years . . . all those holidays and tunes leading me deeper into the past, recalling an atmosphere of holiness and beauty now utterly destroyed. I couldn't even hum along with the congregation. It was impossible for me to set foot in that place. Impossible to pick up the prayer books again although part of me wanted to. Impossible for me to pray to God again. Impossible to be what I was once and am no longer. It was dead for me like everything else. Now Palestine meant everything. The past meant nothing. And I virtually never set foot in a synagogue again.[19]

Approximately three-fourths of the survivors who were nonbelievers before the Holocaust have retained that stance.[20] For some, it was not only the behavior of their persecutors which obliterated any potential faith in God. They also saw the evil which resided within. The notion of man being made in the image of God was not a tenable one. And clearly man, not God, rules.

To tell the truth I was not much of a Jew in Europe. More than this, I'm ashamed to admit I wasn't a very nice or moral person either. During the time I spent in the camps I was even worse. I behaved like an animal, but I also must point out that is why I was able to survive. I'll admit it to you confidentially, but I'd rather not admit it to others openly, that I played along and cooperated with our enemy and haters in the camps. I felt I had no choice. I was a kapo. I had to be in order to live. And eventually, through much guile, rose to a prominent and influential position in the camp which enabled me to eat relatively well and keep myself better than the other Jews. I'm not particularly proud of the way I behaved and how I treated some of my fellow Jews. And yet I believe I learned a sense of humanity. I often hoped during those years that I'd survive and then try to be a decent person and live a good life and make up for some of the things I did. But as for being an observant or religious Jew, I began to feel the opposite, whenever I gave the matter some thought, that I'd never do any of those foolish things that we Jews do. The rituals, I mean. I'd never have any part of that, which is meaningless nonsense. How anyone can live through the concentration camps and still be an observant religious Jew is beyond me. I just do not understand it. The camps convinced me that all the good Jewish practices in the world are of no value. Man is not going to be changed and made good by them and God doesn't seem to care. This is what I learned in the camps.[21]

It is clear to me that for many survivors, observance does not necessarily imply belief. Some go through the motions because they are familiar, because they help retain a closeness to murdered parents and grandparents. *They observe God's commandments, but they no longer love God.* The high percentage of survivors in America who attend Conservative synagogues,[22] despite the fact that a Conservative tradition was completely foreign to them before the war, may attest to this peculiarity, for the Conservative approach is one which maintains tradition, but nonetheless does not assert the absolute Divine authorship of all Jewish law. Thus, a compromise is struck between the survivor's need for continuity and his doubt about a perfect Creator.

In the years immediately after the war, there was a pause in the grappling with theological questions, and a diminished religious observance by many survivors as they focused on their physical and psychological rejuvenation. Theoretical questions would have been a luxury. However, as life normalized over the subsequent decades, survivors harkened back to their traditions. Craving familiarity, a significant number reverted to the fold, at least in practice.[23] As their agony and anger diminished, the reflex of rejection lost its force. Perhaps their material improvement freed time and energy for religious devotion. Perhaps the desire to infuse their children with a Jewish identity also prompted their return.

It is remarkable that despite their persecution and losses as Jews, Holocaust survivors have not forsaken a Jewish identity. It would be a mistake, however, to believe that survivors feel safe, or that survivors believe antisemites have finally learned their lesson. Moreover, survivors do not see the world as having diminished its antipathy for the Jew. For example, they are much more likely than American-born Jews to view antisemitism as "a very serious problem" and to believe that another Holocaust is possible.[24]

While their religious faith may have faltered or disappeared entirely, survivors have fervently embraced their Jewish identity. And while a need for continuity provides some explanation for their commitment, it is apparent that the survivor's torturous experiences during the Holocaust have provided the defining impetus. Having suffered as Jews, they have already invested enormously in that identity. To walk away would imply that the investment had no meaning. To walk away would also imply that Hitler had won.

"How do you feel about being Jewish?" I asked survivors.

"I'm very proud I'm Jewish. I wouldn't change for anything. Even if I had to go through it again, I would still be a Jew."

"If Hitler was like the Inquisition in Spain, I would probably be one of those who would have converted. I wouldn't dare risk my life to go to a gas chamber if I had a choice. But after the war, someone in my group had a baby boy and he didn't want to circumcise him because he didn't want his son to have to go through life as a Jew. Gee, was I mad. I screamed at him!"

"I feel more Jewish now than before. I'm not ashamed I'm a Jew. I'm proud I'm a Jew. Before, if I would see Jews in the street going with their 'Jewish uniform' – yarmulkes, and *tzitzit* in the front and back, I didn't like it. Today, if I see a Jew with the *tzitzit*, I'm proud. Today I don't believe in God, but I believe in Jews."

"Before the Holocaust, I always felt different. You didn't want to be Jewish. We were told we were the cause of everything bad. The Holocaust made me feel good about being Jewish. Now, whenever I can, I make it a point to let people who deal with me know that I am Jewish."

Of course, not all survivors are assertive of their Jewishness. While the imprint of the Holocaust has propelled many survivors forward, it has held Ethel Janov back. "I'm so Jewish. I am nothing but Jewish. But I'm not just a proud Jew. In some ways I don't feel that I am as acceptable as other people, that I'm equal. I stay in the background when I'm with non-Jews. . . . For years when I took off Rosh Hashanah and Yom Kippur, I made up lies about why I wouldn't be at work. . . . I'm not proud of all this. I'm angry at myself for being this way."

Clearly, Holocaust survivors are fiercely committed to the future of the Jewish people. Very few have married outside the faith. And survivors seem far more concerned about intermarriage than their

American-born Jewish counterparts.[25] For most survivors, their devotion and fidelity to the State of Israel has become their religious duty. Ninety percent of survivors living in America who were queried in a recent study had visited Israel compared to only one-third of American-born Jews. Almost sixty percent of these survivors had been to Israel two or more times as compared to only fifteen percent of American-born Jews. Although they constitute only a little less than two percent of the American Jewish population, survivors have bought ten percent of Israel Bonds sold in the United States.[26]

Only Israel can protect the perennially vulnerable Jew, Holocaust survivors believe. The Arabs are our present-day Nazis. They wish to extinguish us by extinguishing Israel. Survivors are angered by "naive" American Jews who criticize, who undermine the resolute stance which must be taken by the Israeli government.

"The whole world is against the Jewish people. The whole world. Every time they are busy with Israel. Any other country what does something bad, they don't care. But as soon as Israel does something, everybody criticizes. . . . Find me one person in the world who loves us. Only now will they respect us because Israel is so strong. That little guy, Yitzhak Shamir, said to Bush, 'Kish mir in tuchus' [Kiss my ass]. That's the only way to talk, so no one will push us around anymore.

"Israel is the only thing standing in the way of another Holocaust. Jews must work with all their might for Israel. Don't sit here and criticize Israel. Many of them [who criticize] are just ashamed for the goyim, that Israel doesn't do exactly what America thinks they should do."

Only Jews will protect each other, survivors believe. "We need a Jewish country," David Himmelstein emphasized. "Every Jew in the world must help Israel. Because there is no God, we sure need a country." Most of those survivors who were more universalistic in their identification before the war have also narrowed their perspective. "Before the war, I was a Polish patriot of Jewish religion. I was very Polish, very intellectually Polish," Channa Lee, a resident of Kraków until 1940, told me. "Now I feel Jewish as a nation. Maybe the war taught us a lesson – to realize we are Jews first and foremost."

Survivors have never expressed their rage to their former tormentors, nor have they exacted their revenge upon them. However, they can and have expressed their feelings toward God by shouting His nonexistence to His face. And by denying God's existence, they punish Him. "Nothing can excuse God for not having saved us," many survivors insist. But the more they shout, the more the boundary between belief and nonbelief is blurred. Why shout if He is not there? So God provides a punching bag enabling the ventilation of so much hurt, so much anger. "When the topic comes up in conversation of religion or God, I have difficulty with it," explained Jerry Singer, who is a very active participant in his synagogue. "I'm always the rebel by bringing up the Holocaust or bringing up the murder of children. I witnessed a Hungarian bayonet through an infant and mother in one thrust. I saw deeply religious people praying and being killed anyway. I'm talking about *good* people, innocent people . . . children."

The survivor who turned his back completely is relieved of the struggle and the agony of His desertion. But he also loses the continuity and comfort which faith brings. For many survivors, a belief in the power of Goodness was supplanted by the recognition of the superior power of Evil. If God is absent, Goodness is absent (or rendered relatively impotent).

A belief system asserting the dependable protection of God was replaced by an ideology of self-protection. For survivors, the God of the People of Israel has given way to the State of Israel. Ironically, while faith has often proved untenable, the Holocaust nonetheless fortified the group identity of Jews.

Rose Friedland had been a devoutly assimilated citizen of Czechoslovakia: "I might not have been a Jew at all if not for the Holocaust. I would have distanced myself more and more under normal circumstances. The first time I heard those Polish girls sing "My Yiddishe Momma" and "Belz, Mein Shtetele Belz" in Auschwitz, it had a tremendous impact on my soul. It was painful. It was something I felt I'd been deprived of. I knew something had been missing. Every time I heard those songs, I cried, and I didn't cry in Auschwitz from pain or any other reason . . . I suffered too much. I want to stay Jewish. Now, we *must* stay Jewish."

10
Revenge

Throughout the Nazi reign of terror, most Jews deluded themselves. They wanted to believe the euphemisms of their persecutors. They adopted a survival-through-work strategy. They interpreted each succeeding blow as the ultimate which would be imposed upon them. They waited for a military triumph of the Allies. And by the time the contours of the Final Solution could no longer be denied, they were too physically and psychologically enfeebled to resist.

Murderers were often known, their acts witnessed by those who were supposed to die as well. A son observed his father beaten to death, a daughter looked on as her mother was executed. A child was stripped from a parent and chosen by a person who deemed himself most worthy to condemn another to a gas chamber. The powerless watched as their loved ones were humiliated, starved, tortured, and robbed of their dignity.

But when survivors were free, when their previously seeming invincible oppressors had been humbled, why did they not exact revenge for their mother, their father, their brothers, their sisters, their children, their friends? Where was their rage? Where was the human need for retribution, for balance?

Even God exhorts us to justice:

> But if any man hate his neighbour, and lie in wait for him, and rise up against him, and smite him mortally that he die, and fleeth into one of these cities: Then the elders of his city shall send and fetch him thence, and deliver him into the hand of the avenger of blood, that he may die. Thine eye shalt not pity him, but thou shalt put away the guilt of innocent blood from Israel, that it may go well with thee. (Deuteronomy 19:11–13)

161

The first opportunities to wreak havoc on their oppressors coincided with the survivor's exhaustion, bewilderment, and disorientation at liberation. Many had long been preoccupied with the hope of finding others alive, and soon focused their depleted energies on that discovery process. "You were a beaten-down human being," Saul Garber explained. "The indignation came later."

When you are so hurt, when the sense of injustice is overwhelming, it requires some time for the anger to emerge. And when so much of you has been extinguished, and so much of your underpinnings have been removed, you must invent a new sense of direction and identity. "You don't know what was in your heart. You were so hurt. Everything in your body was hurting. You were born after the war. . . . You can't understand."

Most survivors regained their strength and equilibrium while living in Germany for a period of one to seven years after liberation. They were therefore in close proximity to many of their former, *personal* tormentors. But as their vitality returned, their gaze immediately focused forward. Enough of their life had been ruined. Stamina was to be directed to building anew. Anger, and its expression toward his enemies, would have only held the survivor back, kept him mired in the past. The survivor's rage, repressed in order for him to subsist as prisoner, would continue to be locked away as part of a different life. Prolonging the mayhem would have prolonged that life. And with the Allies in command, the rules of law and order reasserted themselves. After a season of chaos, murder was, once again, considered a crime.

Instead of "identifying with the aggressor," as some have posited,[1] the survivor was repulsed by his methods. Perhaps his distancing reflected a newfound knowledge of where man's nature can lead him. Where would *his* rage-driven impulses take him? Where would it end? What, indeed, were the choices? "The most amazing thing to me . . . and I'm pondering, I'm pondering myself and the people I knew . . . particularly the young who didn't have a base yet. What is it that after being exposed to such cruelty and such butchery, that when they were given the chance, they got out from this pit, from the bottom pit of humanity, raised themselves up, went forward, created for themselves, for their next fellow man, became decent people. They didn't rob or commit banditry because this was the easiest thing to do. They didn't. What is it?"

Survivors felt fortunate to be alive. At the same time, they understandably felt that the world owed them. However, they did not act on this conviction. William Helmreich points out that "one of the more striking aspects of the postwar generation is the almost complete absence of criminal behavior of the sort which accompanied the arrival of earlier waves of immigration. If the need to survive reduces people to animal-like behavior and if, as some have argued, the best did not make it, how are we to account for the fact that there was relatively little crime or juvenile delinquency among both the newcomers and their children?"[2]

While restraining themselves from acting, survivors nonetheless were gratified when others struck back for them. Anna Maline was liberated from Theresienstadt by the Russians. "I felt like I wanted to . . . I would do to them what they did to us. . . . But I couldn't. . . . But I was very happy when some of the other prisoners beat up the German guards." For many survivors, the fantasy of personal vengeance persisted long after liberation. "Afterward, you were too busy trying to come to yourself," Herschel Kaplan, whose parents, sisters, brother, and wife were shot at Ponar, explained. "But many times I thought if I would meet someone in the street, I would quietly kill him." Fantasy allows us at least a semblance of gratification for our unattainable desires.

David Himmelstein's inaction only exacerbates his feelings of inadequacy and survivor guilt. "Many times I'm thinking. Mostly for one person. When the two Germans wanted to let my wife go because they believed she was a Gentile, but the French gestapo guy said, No, let's check further . . . I think about going there and finding him. But then I think, okay, I go there and kill him. What is so better for me? And he had children who will miss him. I'm thinking, thinking, thinking nonstop on this . . . but I'm not doing it. I still think about it. . . . Perhaps I'm wrong that I'm not doing it. Still you are not a murderer. . . . But I wish . . . I wish . . . I have to do it . . . But I'm not doing it." David *owes* his wife and children who were murdered. But his empathy for the murderer's children and his projection of his own feelings of loss for his family get in the way. *I have to do it. . . . But I'm not doing it*. David also understands that while revenge may be momentarily satisfying, it does not provide replacement. It is ultimately futile. *But then I think, okay, I go there and kill him. What is so better for me?*

A similar sense of futility and powerlessness infects sixty-seven-year-old Barbara Lowenstein. She is disappointed in herself and others. "I always thought about revenge. Unfortunately, it's only thoughts. When I came to this country, I used to walk in the street and think that a Kapo was walking behind me and I could apprehend him and take him to a police station. The war is over doesn't mean the enemy isn't there. . . . One of the terrible guys in the Vilna ghetto was named Murer. Several survivors went from here to testify [at his trial]. Of course, it was a mockery. The survivors who went were threatened. They acquitted him. I know that a group of people from Vilna who live in Israel and were in the underground approached the Israeli government to send an agent and kill him in Austria, but the government refused. They then talked about doing it themselves, but nothing came of it." The murderers lurk and still nothing is done to them, Barbara laments.

When the perception of the other as invincible is repeatedly reinforced, that perception will not immediately change, despite a transformation of the reality of circumstances. Solomon Goldstein spoke with self-loathing and regret. "[After liberation] I saw Russians go into a German house and kill everyone inside and burn the house. We didn't have the guts to do that. The Americans gathered the Germans who were guarding our transport. They said, 'Here. Here is my rifle. You can kill them.' But we didn't."

It is difficult to erase mortal fear. Holocaust survivors (and their children) will forever feel too vulnerable. For Ethel Janov, the discrepancy of power between the Superman and the *Untermensch* remains unmitigated. "I've never felt anger at Germans . . . perhaps because I'm still afraid of them. I've felt anxiety, and I've felt hurt, but not anger. When I get depressed I feel they have won. My revenge is when I go on and survive." Ethel Janov's revenge is a revenge of sorts. It is symbolic, but it is not direct. Almost fifty years after, confrontation, looking the bogeyman in the eye, would still be too frightening.

For the most part, survivors have been left to feed on their fears and anxiety. They have nightmares. They are periodically brought to a trembling by stimuli in their present environment which elicit alarming scenes of their past. However, a survivor's rage is much more encumbered. For anger *demands* action. Anger demands a response to the insult.

Revenge

For the Holocaust survivor, revenge would have been more easily acted out immediately after freedom had been regained; that is, before a sense of normalcy was reestablished. But he was too tired, too weak, too bewildered, and too frightened at the beginning. A later burgeoning sense of equilibrium coincided with a desire to move forward, away from mayhem, death, and reminders of vulnerability. Survivors were intent on continuing their already begun investment in life.

Perhaps another impediment to vengeance was an understanding of the inevitable lack of satisfaction it would bring. How does one avenge all that? It is far easier to repay a slight. But an entire family, a people, a world taken away forever? Furthermore, killing a few of the perpetrators must not allow anyone to say that retribution has been enacted, for that would, in a way, trivialize the extent of the destruction.

Yet, the survivor craves correction, not only as a means of punishing the wrongdoer, but as a way to undo his having been singled out. "The experience of persecution was, at the very bottom, that of an extreme *loneliness*. At stake for me is the release from the abandonment that has persisted from that time until today. When SS-man Wajs stood before the firing squad, he experienced the moral truth of his crimes. At that moment, he was with *me*."[3]

And so, as Solomon Goldstein told me, "While in the DP camp, I heard bragging by a few survivors about what they had done to this German or that German. But it wasn't true." Nevertheless, upon liberation, concentration camp inmates felt completely justified in barging into German homes and taking food and clothes. Some fell upon their warders and beat them. The day after liberation from Buchenwald, nineteen-year-old Jerry Singer and two other inmates pounced on one of the guards. "We took him up to the third floor of the SS building, blindfolded him, made him walk a plank, and pushed him to his death out the window."

Many freed prisoners were given permission by their Allied and particularly Russian liberators to do what they wanted with their former tormentors. Several of the survivors I interviewed who were liberated by the Russians mentioned soldiers offering guns to the inmates and pointing to their former keepers. None remembered an inmate accepting the offer.

There are accounts of Allied soldiers themselves acting out their fury. On April 29, 1945, the 42nd and 45th Divisions liberated Dachau.

165

One American squad was unable to contain its horror and peremptorily executed 122 SS troops they were guarding. Some of the American soldiers deliberately wounded concentration camp guards in the leg and then let the Jewish inmates exact their revenge. One soldier gave an ex-prisoner his bayonet and watched him behead a guard.[4]

Seventy-four-year-old Otis Moyer was an American soldier with the 42nd Rainbow Division on April 30, 1945, when he came upon Dachau. He clearly remembers entering the camp and seeing the railroad tracks and forty to fifty boxcars filled with Jews, the majority of whom had died of starvation. "Some of the concentration camp survivors came up to us and asked if they could have some of the guards. The Colonel in charge told us to hand over four of the guards to the survivors, and we were told not to interfere. They beat the four guards to death."[5]

At the end of May 1945, volunteers from Palestine who constituted the Jewish Brigade of the British Army were poised to enter Germany from Italy. On the morning before they were to proceed, a corporal read out the "Commandments of the Jewish Soldier on German Soil":

"Remember thy six million brethren killed.

"Thou shalt always hate thy people's oppressors.

"Remember that thou are entrusted with a mission by a combatant people.

"Remember that the Jewish Brigade is a Jewish force of occupation in Germany.

"Remember that our arrival as a Brigade, with our emblem and our flag, is in itself a vengeance.

"Remember that blood revenge is the revenge of the whole community, and that any irresponsible act is detrimental to our community.

"Behave as a Jew who is proud of his race and of his flag.

"Thou shalt not dishonor thyself by mixing with Germans.

"Thou shalt not listen to their words neither shalt thou enter their houses.

"Cursed are they, they and their wives and their children, their goods and all that is theirs; cursed are they forever.

"Remember that thy mission is to rescue Jews, the emigration to Israel, and the liberation of the homeland.

"Thy duty is in devotion, loyalty, and love toward those who have escaped death, the survivors from concentration camps."

Revenge

The Israeli novelist Hanoch Bartov, then a young man serving in the Brigade, wrote later: "The blood was coursing through our veins. Our battalions drawn up in their ranks, our trucks and combat vehicles all ready to leave, our flag flying overhead, and the words we had just heard made us feel that we were an entity. Before the 'Commandments' were read out, the commanding officer of our battalion had told us: 'In your new mission you must conduct yourselves as men with a moral code dealing with men who have destroyed all morality.' Morality! We would avenge our people. We would not take any pleasure in it or acquire a taste for it, but we would avenge them! We would become known forever as the implacable enemies of our people's torturers. And each one of us was thinking, 'Tomorrow! Tomorrow I'll be in Germany.' "[6]

But instead of moving out to Germany, the Jewish Brigade was unexpectedly deployed to the small town of Tarvisio, to be held in readiness should there be any dispute over the future of Trieste. In the mountain towns overlooking Tarvisio, a scattering of SS soldiers as well as Fascists from Belgium, Hungary, Slovakia, Italy, and Croatia attempted to blend in with the local populations. Soon after the Brigade arrived in Tarvisio, there were a number of incidents – Germans were assaulted, houses belonging to known Nazis were set on fire, and several cases of rape were reported. The culprits were never found.

The staff officers of the Jewish Brigade (all of whom were affiliated with the Haganah) became uneasy at this eruption of random violence because it might harm public opinion regarding the pressing goal of the establishment of statehood. The desire for vengeance had to be channeled in a more orderly, less disruptive fashion. Haganah leaders, therefore, allowed a handful of carefully selected individuals from the Second Battalion to shed blood on behalf of the Jewish people.

Led by Israel Carmi, Chaim Laskov (later commander in chief of the Israeli Army from 1957 to 1960), Meir Zore'a (later a general in the Israeli Army), and including Moshe Korpovitz, Marcel Tobias (later a renowned lieutenant colonel commanding Israeli paratroopers), and Dov Cohen (a member of the terrorist organization Etzel, he was killed a few years later when, disguised as a British officer, he took part in an attack on the prison at Saint-Jean-d'Acre which freed a number of Jewish prisoners), this small group clandestinely identified

167

and summarily executed perhaps as many as two hundred Nazi war criminals hiding in northern Italy, Austria, and Germany. During the last months of 1945 and early 1946, SS officers, heads of the Gestapo, and high Nazi officials mysteriously disappeared from Klagenfurt, Innsbruck, and places in the Alto Adige and the Austrian Tyrol.

Unbeknownst even to other members of the Jewish Brigade, Carmi and his men often used their official intelligence functions for the British Army as their cover. In recent interviews, Carmi has spoken of those days. "We organized small squads who set out at night in British uniforms and British jeeps to pay calls on the listed suspects. The Nazis believed that they were being interrogated by British intelligence. The interrogators took the suspects away, ostensibly to a prisoner-of-war camp – and they were never heard from again. The interrogations produced further names. The important ones we executed; some of the smaller fry, we turned over to the British authorities. . . . My [Gentile] Colonel may have suspected we were up to something that was beyond or outside the regular functions of the unit. I'm sure he sensed something. But he turned a blind eye."[7]

The Avengers ("Nokmim," as they became known later) did not view themselves as murderers. They believed they were entrusted with a national mission. Oftentimes, they would read the Jewish Agency reports on the death camps before embarking on an assignment. Carmi explained to the group that the Haganah would punish only Nazis proved to have committed crimes and who, because their crimes had been directed mainly against Jews, might later be released by the Allies. The Nokmim would kill only when certain of the facts. Nazis guilty of crimes against non-Jews would be handed over to the British.[8]

While this operation was under way, a second, intially independent, revenge campaign was launched by a band of approximately fifty former Hashomer Hatza'ir partisans, whose ideological mentor was Abba Kovner, the poet and former partisan leader. They were known as DIN (Dahm Y'Israel Nokeam) and broke away from the Jewish Fighters' Organization (the central organization of Jewish partisans), whose efforts were now being directed to the illegal immigration of survivors to Palestine. There were four units of DIN, one in each of the occupied zones. Although a unit comprised only ten men, it was assisted by contacts who were often found in the Jewish Brigade. When necessary, these contacts supplied uniforms, identification cards, and vehicles. Wearing American, British, or Polish uniforms, the members of DIN would typically arrive at a POW camp and show forged orders for various prisoners to be transferred to another POW camp. The selected never reached their supposed destination.

In early 1946, Kovner had traveled to Palestine to enlist the support of the Jewish Agency and the Haganah in a most ambitious plan. His group would poison the drinking water of several major West German cities with the goal of killing six million Germans. But the Haganah refused to approve this audacious scheme. Instead, they offered equivocal approval of the group's fallback position, which was to poison several thousand former SS men in American POW camps. Kovner later said that Chaim Weizmann, a chemist by training who would become the first president of Israel, helped him obtain the poison.[9]

When Kovner attempted to reenter Europe with the poison via the port of Toulon, he was arrested by the British. Kovner became convinced that someone in the Jewish leadership of Palestine had betrayed him in order to prevent the mission. Nevertheless, on the night of April 13, 1946, several members of his group broke into the bakery that supplied bread to the Stalag 13 POW camp outside of Nuremberg. There were differing reports of how many of the internees died. Maybe none.[10]

Only a handful of Holocaust survivors such as Simon Wiesenthal and Hermann Langbein have devoted their life to methodically tracking Nazi criminals. In their choice to keep their past at the forefront of their present, they are an anomaly. The great majority of those who still stood in the spring of 1945 simply knew the partial satisfaction of perhaps observing a guard beaten or murdered during those hours after liberation.

When I first asked Martin Bornstein if he had ever had thoughts of revenge, his face showed a puzzled reaction. Clearly, the concept of revenge seemed as deranged and as senseless as the murdering which had preceded it. After recovering from his momentary perplexity, however, Martin remembered one incident of a man who lashed out, who craved a personal revenge, a personal accounting. "I knew a man, he's dead now. He had a wife and two children who were murdered. After the war was over, he went into a German house and just shot the woman and two children."

169

Paul Lee settled for a less blatant, but nonetheless psychologically meaningful, act of reversal. "We were once in a trolley car in Munich. . . . In camp, when a German finished his cigarette, several inmates would try to get it and the German would then step on his hand. I threw my cigarette down in the trolley and when the German reached for it, I stepped on his hand." With revenge, there is, at least, some discharge of the animus, the pus.

Of those few who translated the personal affront they experienced into a public assault on their persecutors, it would appear that most had previously been partisans. Inflicting violence was, therefore, familiar. Having been unleashed earlier, their rage was not circumscribed by formal, armistice boundaries. They participated in organized efforts such as the missions of the Avengers and more spontaneous gestures of accountability as well. Ben Kass, who spent most of the war years in the forests with partisans, spoke with great relish of the wrath he exacted both during and after the official hostilities. Having fought for several years with a Russian partisan group of eighteen thousand men and women, Ben was in Poland during the closing months of the war. He arrested many Poles from the AK who had previously murdered Jews, and handed them over to the Russian authorities for imprisonment. Some Jewish members of Ukrainian partisan units temporarily joined the Soviet secret police, the NKVD, in order to exact revenge. They personally arrested and liquidated collaborators of the Nazis.[11]

An ex-partisan and member of a group of Avengers from Vienna spoke of his vengeful forays:

I killed four Nazi criminals. At Judenburg, near Graz, in Austria, there was a displaced persons camp in which a large number of Jews were living. Some of them had come from Yugoslavia. I was on good terms with the British and Americans in charge of the camp, and from them I learned that a Nazi criminal by the name of Alois Gawenda was hiding in the district. I questioned some of the Jews in the camp, to try and find out more about this Gawenda. Those from Yugoslavia remembered him only too well. Gawenda had been a member of one of Ante Pavelic's infamous gangs in the Croatian nationalist movement, Ustasha. He had operated in Zagreb for a time. There, he had "questioned" the Jewish and Communist prisoners with all the cruel refinements that his sadistic mind could conceive. The Jews were then herded together, out in the open country – for concentration camps were rare in some regions of Yugoslavia – before being packed off to the death camps.

170

Revenge

Gawenda was always present on such occasions. Dozens of people testified that they had seen him shoot children and snatch babies from their mothers' arms and hurl them on the ground to crack their heads open.

When the tide began to change, Gawenda disappeared. He had crossed the frontier and got a job with a traveling fair. And now the fair had set up its stalls and sideshows in the neighborhood of Judenburg. Gawenda's job was in line with his talents – he was in charge of a shooting gallery.

Four of us went to the fairground – three Jews from Yugoslavia and myself. Some of the Allied soldiers guarding the DP camp had lent us guns. It was about ten in the morning when we arrived at the shooting gallery. There was no one about but Gawenda. We asked if we could try our hands at shooting. He handed us rifles and we fired at the dummies as they slid past at the back of the stand. Then two of us went to keep watch, and I said to Gawenda, "I know who you are. You were with the Ustasha at Zagreb, and you massacred hundreds of innocent people."

He realized he was trapped, and like so many others he tried to gain time with the usual excuse, "It wasn't my fault – I was only carrying out orders . . ."

We shot him with his own rifles and with our guns. He collapsed and died in his shooting gallery.

He was the first. The second was killed at Bad Aussee, the town where Eichmann's divorced wife was living with their children. I had gone there, like many others, in the hope of finding a clue. I was making out that I had been a member of the SS Walloon Division.

Quite by chance, I became acquainted with an antique dealer named Gunther Halle. He took a liking to me and confided that most of the objects he had for sale had been stolen from the homes of Jews. He went on to boast of having taken part in the suppression of the rising of the Warsaw ghetto, and he described in great detail how he had hunted down the last few Jews and killed them. I listened without flinching, only by making great efforts to hide my emotions.

One night, a few comrades and I went to this man's house and captured him. We told him who we were and that he was about to die. Then we took him to the Alt Aussee, the large lake just outside of town. We bound him hand and foot, gagged him, tied a large stone to him, then threw him alive into the lake. So far as I know, none of his family ever learned what had happened to him.

The [next] execution took place in the pretty but disquieting setting of the Wienerwald, the forest outside Vienna. Some of the Jewish refugees who came to the Documentation Center, and others who were being given shelter at the Rothschild Hospital, dealt in the black market, in order to live. There

171

was a man who often came to see them about these shady affairs, and one of the refugees suddenly remembered where he had come across him before. His name was Josef Belki and he had murdered a number of Jews in Czestochowa, Poland.

When the Germans occupied that town they took over the munitions factory, and one of the men they put in charge of it was this Josef Belki. The working people in some of the factory shops were supplied with special gloves and masks as protection against acids. But when Jews were brought in as slave labor, including women and children, Belki gave orders not to issue them gloves or masks. He took great delight in seeing them writhe in pain after handling acids. And when they asked to see a doctor, well, Belki just killed them.

He was a man who would do anything for money. Under the pretext of concluding a deal with him, we took him out to the forest one dark night. And there, by the light of the torches, we read out the charges against him. He was put on trial then and there, sentenced to death, and strangled with a silk stocking. We buried the body under the trees.

No, I don't feel any remorse. Who would?[12]

Paul Handel was living in a former German army barracks in a displaced persons camp, Feldalfing, near Munich. He knew of several former Jewish Kapos who were fallen upon and beaten by other survivors during this time. In Israel, survivors reported collaborators to the police. The Nazi and Nazi Collaborators Law had passed the Knesset in 1950, and by the mid-1950s about thirty Jews suspected of collaboration were under investigation. But the authorities demonstrated little enthusiasm.[13] Judges were also reticent. "It is hard for us, the judges of Israel, to free ourselves of the feeling that, in punishing a worm of this sort, we are diminishing, even if by only a trace, the abysmal guilt of the Nazis themselves," wrote Supreme Court Justice Moshe Silberg.[14]

Holocaust survivors primarily focus their ire on their non-Jewish tormentors, both past and present (e.g., the Arab world). Most are not only reluctant to speak of Jewish collaborators, but are also disinclined to condemn behavior which was perceived by the actor to be necessary in order to keep oneself alive. Perhaps survivors had glimpsed an unseemly side of their own self-protective impulses. Perhaps, because they inhabited a universe which was seemingly bereft of morality, right and wrong could no longer be used as a simple standard of judgment. While out for a walk in Stuttgart in October 1946, Jerry Singer encountered a former Jewish Kapo. "I wanted to beat him up, to hit him. . . . But then I didn't know if I could blame him for what he did."

Peter Wyden, in his book *Stella*, which concerns a notorious Jewish "catcher" (one who hunted down fellow Jews for arrest by the Gestapo) in Berlin, notes that Jewish leaders in Europe organized "Courts of Honor" to judge those Jews accused of betraying their own. These unofficial arbiters were also careful to consider extenuating circumstances.

These self-appointed forums were not empowered to impose punishments beyond the jurisdiction of internal Jewish affairs. Their harshest verdict was equivalent to excommunication, which meant the withholding of the modest special benefits available to Holocaust survivors. . . . [The] Jewish courts went to remarkable lengths to weigh judgment fairly, and their treatment of the accused was astonishingly lenient.

In Berlin the courts sat patiently for more than a decade in the Jewish Community offices, Joachimstaler Strasse 13. A lawyer survivor acted as chairman. At least one other attorney survivor assisted, as did a minimum of two lay jurors. All available eyewitnesses were heard, pro and con. Written testimonies, pro and con, were solicited and considered.

Even a Kapo, generally considered the lowest-life of traitor, received a respectful hearing and sometimes turned out to be struggling against undeserved ostracism. One such victim of postwar justice was Harry Schwarzer, whose case was heard on January 9, 1947.

Five witnesses testified. They had been inmates with Schwarzer in one of the smaller concentration camps – Plaschow, in Poland – where, unaccountably, the accused had indeed been appointed Kapo by the Nazis. Allegedly, he had beaten fellow Jews.

As his collaborator history was pieced together by the Court of Honor, Schwarzer had been eighteen years old at the time, exceptionally fragile, and starved, suffering from edema of both feet. When he occasionally slapped a prisoner, which he admitted, it was to prevent the victim from being brutalized by the imminently threatened attack of a prisoner gang.

The main charge against Schwarzer was that he had stolen food and consumed it himself. It turned out that Plaschow was an unusual camp. A large portion of its prisoner laborers were Polish and gentile and these captives received vastly more nourishment than the Jews. The witnesses swore that the Poles had food to spare and that Schwarzer stole only from them, that in fact he deprived no one and mistreated no one, Kapo or not.

The court's decision: "It is determined that Harry Schwarzer did not abuse the interests of the Jewish community."

. . . In Austria a Jewish "Disciplinary Commission" was created and administered by a survivor of the Mauthausen camp who was about to become famous: Simon Wiesenthal. . . . Yet, even under this stalker's tutelage, the commission pronounced only thirty Austrian Jews guilty of having worked with the Nazis.[15]

Anger holds us back, keeps us locked in the time of injury. Survivors, therefore, in an attempt to renew a normal life, sit on that painful acknowledgment of loss. To keep it in the forefront would make unhampered forward movement nearly impossible. Anger poisons. "Resentment . . . nails every one of us onto the cross of his ruined past . . . for this reason the man of resentment cannot join in the unisonous peace chorus all around him, which cheerfully proposes: not backward let us look but forward, to a better, common future!"[16]

For most Holocaust survivors, anger simmers just beneath the surface. It flares in their emotional outbursts, their hyperirritability, their impatience, their aggressiveness, and their survivor guilt (anger turned against the self). However, survivors have also discovered constructive channels for their implacable indignation. After the war's end, many participated in helping to circumvent the barriers to gathering in Palestine. Survivors passionately support the growth and security of Israel. And they keep the memory of the Holocaust alive, implicitly charging the criminals (a continuing form of revenge) and sanctifying the victims. *Public* remembrance is an act of deterrence, as well as a statement of fearlessness. And by their own presence and the birth of future generations of Jews, they stubbornly insist that Hitler did not triumph.

Memory and remembrance do not have the power to punish. But the survivor's need for normalcy keeps him from more blatant forms of revenge. His tendency to the indirect is buttressed by cultural conventions which also make it unacceptable to acknowledge vengeance as motivation. As Susan Jacoby, in her wide-ranging treatise on revenge, *Wild Justice*, clarifies, a quest for revenge is prone to be seen as an indication of psychological imbalance. For twenty years after her immigration from Germany with her American serviceman husband, Hermine Ryan was an ordinary housewife living in a modest residential neighborhood of New York City. But in 1972 she found herself in a court of the U. S. Immigration and Naturalization Service answering charges that she had lied about her true identity as Aufseherin Hermine Braunsteiner, a vicious officer at the Maidanek death camp.

Most of the witnesses at the deportation hearings were Maidanek survivors. All of them were asked by Ryan's attorney whether they were "out for revenge"; all replied in controlled, dispassionate tones that they only wanted justice.
. . . "Why are you here?" the reporter asked. . . . "Why am I here?" the witness responded in an incredulous tone, suggesting that the questioner was the one in need of psychiatric help. "I am here for our dead." Later in the day, the same journalist told a colleague, "You can see the woman's become unbalanced by the quest for revenge."[17]

Cruelly, survivors are often asked to demonstrate their unique sensibilities and compassion by offering forgiveness. I have no authority to forgive in the name of the dead, they politely reply. But where were the murderers stepping forward to admit wrongdoing? Did anyone say, I am sorry? Did anyone acknowledge, I did terrible things, without immediately offering excuse, justification, rationalization, ignorance?

Ironically, the issue of forgiveness has formed the debate. Distinctions designed to assert innocence and protect the majority (those not actively involved in the killing machinery during the Nazi reign, those too young to be held accountable, those born after the war) from indictment are offered to survivors in order to enervate the accusations. Where was the remorse? survivors demand. Where was the shame? Where was the tangible evidence of retribution? Where was the considered debate about *punishment*? Because there has been no retributive justice, survivors have been denied any satisfaction, any salve. Instead, they are asked to move on, to forgive and forget, in order to make others comfortable.

So they must refuse to become partners in this subversion, this insult to the dead:

The aftermath

Whoever lazily and cheaply forgives subjugates himself to the social and biological time-sense, which is also called the "natural" one. Natural consciousness of time actually is rooted in the physiological process of wound healing and became part of the social conception of reality. But precisely for this reason it is not only extramoral, but also antimoral *in character. . . . The moral person demands annulment of time."*[18]

11
Collective guilt

"It's 1945. You are the judge and jury. What punishment would you inflict on Germans?" I asked Holocaust survivors.

"Take an atomic bomb and kill them all."

"Do the same what they did to the Jews."

"Make them crawl. Let them eat bread and water for fifty years."

Understandably enraged, Holocaust survivors wanted Germans to be punished in kind. But that was not to be. Realpolitik asserted itself as the Allies desired a strong West Germany to serve as buffer to the perceived threat from the East. "In 1945, I would have insisted that anyone who was involved either as a bureaucrat or SS or any functionary, I would have said kill them," Jack Diamond, a survivor of Auschwitz and witness at several trials of war criminals, emphasized. "I would have also insisted that they suffer for fifty years. The Marshall Plan was a mistake. I'm convinced the abolishment of the death penalty in Germany had nothing to do with morals. It was strictly to save those Nazis. It sets a bad example. If those bastards could get away with murder, it encourages others. And of course in memory of my parents, how could I tolerate this? It's the Allies' fault. . . . They [the Germans] have it too good. They don't deserve it, those bastards. This bugs me tremendously. I don't care if they worked hard for it. They don't deserve it. Although I don't believe in collective guilt, I wouldn't mind if three or four generations had to work for world good and give the fruits of their labor to humankind who they brought such misery to."

A showcase of retribution, the Nuremberg trials brought a handful of the most prominent Nazis to justice. But because it was in the Allies' interest to rejuvenate Germany, Nazi schoolteachers were simply returned to the classrooms, Nazi physicians resumed their practice of medicine, and Nazi judges donned their robes again. No one spoke of those years, life resumed. A curtain descended on the Third Reich. Furthermore, as Jean Améry wrote in 1976:

> The Germans saw themselves absolutely as victims, since, after all, they had been compelled to survive not only the winter battles of Leningrad and Stalingrad, not only the bombardments of their cities, not only the judgment of Nuremberg, but also the dismemberment of their country. Thus, as can all too easily be understood, they were not inclined to do more than to take the past of the Third Reich and, in their own way, to "overcome" it, as one said back then. . . .
> Conversations like the one I had in 1958 with a South German businessman over breakfast in the hotel were enough. Not without first politely inquiring whether I was an Israelite, the man tried to convince me that there was no longer any race hatred in his country. The German people bear no grudge against the Jewish people, he said. . . . Those of us who had believed that the victory of 1945, even if only in small part, had been ours too, were forced to relinquish it. The Germans no longer had any hard feelings towards the resistance fighters and Jews. How could these still demand atonement?[1]

The politics of victimization were instrumental in fomenting dissatisfaction with the Weimar Republic. The Versailles Treaty imposed unbearable economic hardship, stripped Germany of its possessions (colonies), and imposed an un-Germanic government, Germans were told. And it was the agitation by the Jews to unnecessarily surrender which "stabbed Germany in the back" in the first place. The culture of the Third Reich maintained this message of victimization. In the Oberammergau Passion Play of 1934, Hitler was implicitly equated with Jesus and the apostles were explicitly portrayed as Aryan guards.

Confusion of identity between victim and aggressor is perhaps best exemplified and remembered in Himmler's infamous speech to a group of SS officers, in which he commends them for their perseverance in the painful task of eliminating the Jew.

> I also want to refer before you here, in complete frankness, to a really grave matter. Among ourselves, this once, it shall be uttered quite frankly. . . .
> I am referring to the evacuation of the Jews, the annihilation of the Jewish

people. This is one of those things that are easily said. "The Jewish people is going to be annihilated," says every party member. "Sure, it's in our program, elimination of the Jews, annihilation – we'll take care of it." And then they all come trudging, eighty million worthy Germans, and each one has his one decent Jew. Sure, the others are swine, but this one is an A-1 Jew. Of all those who talk this way, not one has seen it happen, not one has been through it. Most of you must know what it means to see a hundred corpses side by side, or five hundred, or a thousand. To have stuck this out and – excepting cases of human weakness – to have kept our integrity, this is what has made us hard. In our history, this is an unwritten and never-to-be-written page of glory.[2]

Writing in the 1970s, Améry would anticipate the infamous public debate or, more accurately put, the battle for the history of the Third Reich and the honor of the German people which erupted in 1986 and is known as the *Historikerstreit*. Jürgen Habermas, a professor at the Goethe University in Frankfurt, wrote an article in *Die Zeit* entitled, "A Form of Guilt Liquidation: The Apologetic Tendencies in German Modern Historical Writing." Habermas challenged a book by Andreas Hillgruber, one of Germany's leading specialists on the politics and military affairs of the Nazi era, as well as recent articles by two respected scholars, Ernst Nolte and Michael Stürmer. Habermas objected to an emerging revisionism which argued that the Holocaust must be "contextualized." The German murder of six million Jews was not a unique event and should cease to be a determining and crippling factor in German political discourse, Hillgruber, Nolte, and Stürmer argued.

Hillgruber sympathized with the plight of German citizens mercilessly accosted by the Russian hordes as they advanced on Berlin. Hadn't Germans suffered too? Nolte argued, furthermore, that Hitler learned about mass slaughter from Stalin's example. And more rhetorical questions from Nolte: Was not the Gulag and the murder of kulaks a historical precedent? Do we not know that Stalin murdered more people than Hitler? Why the emphasis on Germany? And does not the policy of Israel toward the Palestinians suggest that Germany has no monopoly on the abuse of power in modern times? Nolte wishes to stop the "demonization of the Third Reich" and let "the past pass away," that is, to free Germans from their "pathological condition" of still living in the shadow of the Holocaust.[3]

179

Charles Maier, historian and author of *The Unmasterable Past: History, Holocaust, and German National Identity*, observes that implicit in many of the new revisionist arguments was the notion that Nazism was simply a reaction to Communism. (Nolte is notorious for his theses that Hitler's invasion of the Soviet Union was arguably a *defensive* action against perceived threats from Communism and world Jewry and that the Holocaust – or, as he puts it, "the so-called annihilation of the Jews" – was a reaction to and even an imitation of the excesses of Soviet class warfare.)[4] Thus, revisionism becomes part of the neoconservative campaign to restore Germany's national pride and cement a further contemporary allegiance to the West. The revisionists have used history writing as a means to reassert an antisocialist political agenda, to reaffirm the anticommunist position of West Germany, and to redress the politicization of the academy by the Left which occurred after 1968.[5]

Now, of course, with reunification the problem of memory for East Germans does not revolve around the subtleties of revisionist arguments but, rather, is one of complete ignorance. In their desire to erase ethnic differences under a socialist umbrella, there was never mention by the ruling authorities of the East Bloc of the unique persecution of the Jews. Moreover, until 1989, East Germans were taught that World War II was inflicted by the fascist capitalists of West Germany and they, therefore, were also victims.

The lack of punishment of the murderers contributed to the ongoing mistrust and cynical view of humanity which survivors manifest. In the immediate years subsequent to liberation, survivors were turned away when they attempted to relate the horrors they had witnessed. And it became evident in succeeding years that their torturers would never even be accused – another indication that the world did not care. A continuing sense of personal victimization ensued. There was no closure, no counterbalance, for the survivor. A crime was committed and no one was to pay – further proof that there is no moral order in the universe. And because the Holocaust was a crime committed against the Jewish people, survivors were particularly bereft of the calming notion that society would protect the Jew against any future assault.

The silence, the absence of a culpable reaction in Germany, was deafening. Until 1968. As the student protest movement swept through Western Europe, its antiestablishment form in Germany included a confrontation of the participants in the Third Reich by their children. The second generation in Germany had heard little of the recent past in their classrooms. As many have told me, "German history lessons always seemed to end in 1933." After all, their teachers had been loyal Nazis only a few years earlier. But in 1968, young German adults were asking their parents, "What did you do in the war, Daddy?" And while the answers were, in most cases, less than forthcoming, this was a personal, family affair. Societal confrontation awaited January 1979, when the American television miniseries *Holocaust* was broadcast on the West German television network, ZDF.

Many Germans were outraged at the accusation. Bomb threats against the ZDF broadcasting facility in Mainz were received. But the process of *Vergangenheitsbewältigung*, which may be best translated as "mastering the past" or "coming to terms with the past," was put into motion. *Vergangenheitsbewältigung* was partially an effort to salvage from the wreckage of that twelve-year history what Charles Maier has called a "usable past." Intermingled in the process was an attempt to determine the degree to which the postwar generations are responsible for deeds committed forty years earlier by parents and grandparents.

Holocaust survivors are split on this issue. For some, the hatred they bear for Germans and other murderers of their loved ones leaves no room for equivocation. Rational distinctions are overwhelmed by visceral reactions. "I hate them. They're poison. When I just see a German I can't control myself. I cannot understand our people who drive Mercedes or travel to Germany. Naturally, the young Germans are not responsible for the sins of their fathers." Such iniquity is incorrigible, survivors believe. It is part of their national character. The enormity of the crime offers proof. "In a way, the young people born after are not responsible for what their parents did," Sonya Weiss began. "It doesn't mean they're any better than their parents, that under certain circumstances they wouldn't do it too. Don't kid yourself. Wouldn't they be happy today if they controlled the world? I'll never trust them and I want to distance myself as much as I can." For survivors such as Sonya Weiss, distinctions may also start one on the perilous, slippery slope of *forgiveness*.

Sixty-seven-year-old Carla Granot, however, differentiates the Nazi perpetrators from those Germans who came after. "Now there are three generations already, so you can't condemn everybody. I would still take all the old guys who were in the army or SS and put them on a pile and burn them."

Germans who were too young to be held responsible for the sins of their parents and grandparents have attempted to distance themselves from the evil which was unleashed. With the passage of time, they feel more comfortable absolving themselves of blame. During a 1987 state visit to Israel, Chancellor Helmut Kohl refined the notion of German guilt when he spoke of the "Gnade der spaten Geburt," the "blessing of being born late." Kohl pointed out to the Israelis that he was born in 1930 and was not even three years old when the Nazis seized power. He therefore could not be expected to feel the requisite pangs of conscience.

While the Germans of the second generation were denied information of the Holocaust during their formative years, their children are often exposed to artifacts of those atrocities. Outraged and sometimes guilt-ridden over the transgressions of their elders, second-generation schoolteachers emphasize the moral lessons which must be derived from the barbarism of their students' grandparents and great-grandparents. Understandably, many of the third generation violently reject any implication of collective guilt. For these students, the Third Reich occurred a long, long time ago. Why must I be tainted by actions of those so far removed from me? Joining the Left's condemnation of Israeli policy may be a symptom of their resentment. Jews persecute as well, they point out. As if by some magical symmetry, their own country's ignominious past therefore can be cleansed. And by defining the Jew as an oppressor, sympathy for the Jew as (past) victim can also be abbreviated.

Those survivors most apt to distinguish German culprits from German innocents are those who, during the ordeal, were shown kindness by a particular German or other Gentile. Seventy-two years old, Abe Stark lives on a picture-postcard tree-lined street, in a new suburban development outside Los Angeles. His den serves as a personal Holocaust museum. There is an intricate, small-scaled replication of the German slave labor camp in which he was incarcerated. Diagrams and photographs of Auschwitz are posted on the walls. Stacks of Holocaust-related articles are piled on bookshelves.

"There was a German foreman, about thirty years of age," Abe began. "He mentioned he was a Social Democrat before the war. I took a chance because it was 1944 already and I was very weak. I was mixing cement by hand. I asked him if he could possibly find me some easier job because I couldn't hold out much longer. The next morning he took me to the basement of a factory. He drew a large yellow circle on a wall and told me, 'Chip away at the center until you reach the other side.' I knew they had power tools which could immediately do the job. He told me, 'Don't worry, the war will be over by the time you reach the other side.' I then understood. When he left me that day, I wept. It was the first act of kindness in so long. I stayed on the 'job' until 1945. It allowed me to regain my strength and survive."

Amidst the unrelenting barrage of maliciousness, an act of human kindness allowed a tempering of Abe Stark's darkest view of his fellow man. The Talmudic aphorism "When you save one life, it is as though you have saved the entire world" is amended. When you have saved one life, the one you have saved no longer sees the entire world as murderous. "How do you feel about Germans?" I asked Abe. "It's emotional thinking, you know. You cannot take all Germans for bad. They followed their Führer and he gave them a lot of good things. You cannot condemn all the German people. There are people like Willy Brandt and you can't put him in a category with Goering."

Conversely, I heard unmitigated hatred from those survivors who experienced *betrayal* by a German or Gentile. The very personal nature of that treachery fostered a generalized cynicism regarding humanity. Betrayal leaves one feeling exceedingly alone. The boundary between I and the Other becomes impermeable, perhaps forever.

Survivors are sensitive to any German acts which imply a revision of the history of the Third Reich or a continuation of its policies. They were outraged at Helmut Kohl's invitation to President Reagan to lay a wreath at the Bitburg cemetery where members of the SS and Wehrmacht are interred. At the commemoration ceremonies, these soldiers were eulogized as "victims" of the Nazi regime. Words are used to blur distinctions, to distort the record, to trivialize mass murder.

But perhaps survivors were most disquieted on November 9, 1988, when the Berlin Wall crumbled. Forty years before, survivors had already been disheartened by the revitalization of Germany. "I don't believe they should have the help they had from the Allies. Make them suffer," I heard repeatedly during my interviews. The division of the Fatherland was, perhaps, the only palpable, discernable punishment of Germany. The Wall served as a reminder of the events which ultimately led to its creation. And when East Germans dismembered that symbol brick by brick, reporters covering the event became caught up in the euphoria. There was no mention of the irony. Exactly fifty years earlier, on November 9, 1938, Germans had perpetrated the most extensive pogrom to date on German soil against Jewish people, their property, their religious institutions, and their culture. They called it Kristallnacht, the Night of the Broken Glass, a term which has rankled because of its Nazi imprimatur.

But survivors were well aware of the painful irony. They reacted with dismay to the pictures of jubilation transmitted around the world. "They didn't suffer enough," Ben Kass futilely objected. "They had it so fast so good. They didn't pay the price of what they did to our people. I was happy when the Wall was there. I was happy the Russians were in Poland. I was happy the Russians were in Rumania. I was happy the Russians were in Estonia, Latvia, and Lithuania. Because all those bastards helped Hitler. They killed the Jews. If the East Germans are going to be free now, at least put the West Germans under the Russians . . . I thought this [the Wall coming down] would never happen in my lifetime, that I would live to see this."

Survivors did not react to the crumbling of the Wall as a victory for democracy in the Cold War. Survivors were not enchanted by the freedoms now promised to millions who had lived under the yoke of oppression. For as the Wall had also muted the potential might of Germany, its elimination engendered anxiety in many. "I wasn't happy about the Wall coming down," Dora Levinsohn told me. "I'm still afraid of the power of Germany. Because if there aren't Jews to blame there, if things go badly, they'll invent them. They rose from the ashes too fast. You should have seen Germany in 1945, how ruined it was. My God, how they rose." Just as fifty years ago when Jews were transfixed by the straight-backed, blond-haired, blue-eyed, seemingly invincible oppressors with their polished high black boots, Dora as well as many of her peers, still anticipate that country's diabolical power. And they reflexively cringe: "My God, how they rose."

Contemporary Israelis, however, have contrasting sentiments to those of Holocaust survivors. The most widely read Israeli newspaper, *Yediot Aharonot*, conducted a survey in 1990 which was designed to assess the reactions to German unification. Thirty-six percent of those questioned saw unification as a positive event, twenty-eight percent opposed the reconciliation, and thirty-five percent *did not care*. Clearly, for most Israelis the unification of Germany elicited neither the fear, the bitterness, nor the angst explicit in the survivors' reactions. Indeed, for more than one-third of them, there was simply indifference.[6] Perhaps understandably, Israelis are more preoccupied with threats to their safety which are continuous and much closer to home.

In 1939, there were far fewer Jews in Western Europe than in Eastern or Central Europe. By 1945, forty percent of Western European Jewry and ninety percent of Eastern European Jewry had been murdered. Jews in the West were more likely to be assimilated into the society of their host country. They were therefore less readily identifiable and more difficult to separate for extinction. Their non-Jewish neighbors were more apt to hide them and facilitate entry into resistance groups.

This, of course, is not meant to imply that antisemitic sentiment was absent in Western Europe during this period. On the contrary. The notorious Vichy regime, with the support of the surrounding population, was quite zealous in its collaboration with the German authorities while rounding up Jews, particularly foreign Jews, for deportation to the eastern killing centers. Perhaps Denmark was the only occupied country in the western part of the continent which did not reflect significant antisemitic prejudice. David Himmelstein was a citizen of Belgium when war came to his country. Posing as Gentiles, he, his wife, and children escaped to the south of France. Vigorously pursued and maliciously treated by the French Milice, they were finally deported from Drancy in September 1942. Holding his feverish daughter in his arms for three days and nights, he and his family finally arrived in Auschwitz, where they were separated, never to see one another again. David was sent to an auxiliary labor camp of Auschwitz, Paiskretcham in Silesia, from which he escaped and made his way back to Belgium. Living in the small southern Belgian town of Rixensar as a Gentile, he was listening one morning to the radio in his landlord's kitchen. It broadcast the news of the Russian liberation of

Auschwitz, where two hundred thousand pairs of children's shoes were discovered. David began to weep but was cut short by his host. "What are you crying for? Those were only Jewish children."

Because most assimilated Jews of the West identified not only with their homeland but also with the democratic ideals of the Enlightenment, the betrayal by their countrymen was unexpected and stunning. For the most part, the Jews of the West felt more akin to their German or French or Dutch neighbors than they did to their "backward, bearded, caftaned cousins of the East."

Ethel Janov grew up in the small Hungarian village of Miskolc, which her grandfather practically "owned" by virtue of his lumber business. "I have a stronger reaction to Hungarians [than to Germans]," she explained. "I speak their language. It's my mother tongue. I can't trust them. They are not us. I feel closer so my disappointment in them is stronger. When I was a child we sang the national anthem every morning and I had the best voice, so I led my class. We didn't speak Yiddish at home. We spoke Hungarian. My ancestors lived in Hungary. *We were Hungarians.*"

Antisemitism was something with which the Jews of the former Austro-Hungarian Empire and countries farther east, such as Poland and Rumania, were quite familiar. Antisemitically charged fascist groups – the Hlinka Guard of Slovakia, the Ustasha of Croatia, the Arrow Cross of Hungary, the Iron Guard of Rumania, the Endc of Poland – made up of well-organized cadres sprang up years before the German invasion. Fueled by centuries of both Catholic theology's contempt and the bitterness of peasants which was skillfully directed onto the Jew by local aristocracies, antipathy toward Jews was widespread. The centripetal force of nascent national movements in these areas also promoted the populations' receptivity to viewing the Jew as the Other, one who is loyal only to clan, and therefore traitorous and untrustworthy.

"How do you feel about Poles?" I asked Martha Janusz, who had grown up in Chelm, fled to Warsaw in 1942, volunteered as a Gentile to work in Germany, and subsequently was sent to the Gera labor camp and assigned to a factory. "The Poles? Ten times worse than the Germans. They should burn with one match. I wasn't afraid all of those years in camp that the Germans would find out I was Jewish. But the *Poles* were always asking, trying to find out."

And from other survivors who lived in Poland before the war I heard: "Germans? I don't trust them. Poles? I don't trust them double. I feel worse about the Poles because the Church has such a great influence and it's so antisemitic. As a child I knew they were taught from the beginning to hate Jews because they said we killed Christ. Germany thought they were a superior race and they were against Jews but also against other minorities. There was a truer antisemitism in Poland than Germany. Germans were following orders. Poles had no orders. They wanted to finish us off. Poles? This is the worst scum in the world."

"I don't hate the Germans as much as I hate the Pollacks. You weren't there! When they rounded up people for deportation, there were three German officers and five hundred Ukrainians."

And when survivors straggled back to Poland after liberation, they found their neighbors obviously disappointed. "What? You came back? They didn't kill all of you?" Disappointed because they had not been rid of the curse of the Jews. Disappointed because they had no wish to relinquish Jewish homes and businesses which they had expropriated. And their disappointment and greed propelled them to kill many Jews who believed they had outlasted their persecutors.

Survivors from other countries were no more sympathetic to their previous compatriots.

"Hungarians? I detest them more than the Germans."

"The Austrians were all Nazis. They always were antisemitic, even more than the Germans."

"The Rumanians were savages, beasts."

"I don't trust the Belgians either."

In fact, the only two national groups against whom I did not hear epithets were Czechs (those from Bohemia and Moravia) and Italians. Kindness was rare, and therefore so precious. Berliner Saul Halpern illegally crossed the border to Belgium in January 1939. In May 1940 he was separated from the non-Jews in his village by French and Belgian police, and sent to the south of France. Running from the French and German authorities, he found Italian protectors in the Italian-occupied portion of France. After Italy capitulated to the Allies and was subsequently occupied by Germany, Italians helped move Saul and hundreds of other Jews eastward, over the mountains, deeper into their country. Tears trickled down Saul's cheeks as he told me of the Italians who provided shelter, food, and money to the hunted, the pariahs.

Seventy-nine-year-old Paul Lee, one of Oskar Schindler's Jews, was a physical education teacher in a Jewish *Gymnasium* (high school) in Kraków and an officer in the Polish Army when war erupted. Paul is clearly an anomaly. Having been saved by a non-Jew and having identified himself before the war with the more nationalistic intelligentsia, Paul voiced a very different view of his countrymen from that of other survivors whom I interviewed. "Unfortunately, the Jewish intelligentsia of Poland perished first. Those who survived were mostly from small towns, ghettoized, separated from Poles. I was from Kraków, the center of high Jewish culture. Even the religious Jews spoke a beautiful Polish. Religious antisemitism was stronger in the eastern part of Poland where Poles were less educated. It was a heaven for Jews in Poland. Why were there so many Jews in Poland? Because it was better for them than in Germany, France, Italy, Switzerland, Spain, or Holland."

There were non-Jews who, at the risk of their own and perhaps their family's lives, saved Jews during the war. Those who were motivated by a sense of morality as opposed to greed have been officially recognized and extolled by Yad Vashem, the Holocaust museum and documentation center in Jerusalem. International groups, organized by Jews, have also been in the forefront of the discovery and recognition process of these men and women. As a symbol of their gratitude, individual survivors who were hidden by Gentile neighbors have regularly sent sums of money to these saviors who, until recently, lived behind the Iron Curtain. However, there is disagreement among survivors about the entire concept of according public acknowledgment to Righteous Gentiles.

Harry Tissor, the sole survivor of a family which included nine brothers and sisters, is clear about his Polish countrymen. "They were worse than the Germans. They were the ones who helped Germany kill six million Jews. They're talking about the Righteous here, the Righteous there. But there were so few, so big deal." For survivors, the affirmation of Righteous Gentiles invokes an unwarranted symmetry – there were some bad Gentiles and there were some good Gentiles – when, in fact, the overwhelming majority of non-Jews (particularly in Central and

Eastern Europe) actively participated or passively complied in the Final Solution. In most instances, Gentiles in these areas were pleased that someone was undertaking the task.

Christians killed Jews, survivors simply assert. "To me, a Jew is a Jew," seventy-four-year-old Sarah Schneider, who was persecuted and betrayed by her Hungarian countrymen as well as the Nazis, baldly stated. "Any Jew is precious. Christians are different. Goyim? I hate them. I should forget when they killed my mother and father? I'll never forgive them and I hope my children don't either."

Indeed, as a child of survivors, I had the brutal distinction between Jews and goyim inculcated at an early age by my parents. Not only were all of my grandparents and five aunts killed by them, but my mother's first husband, attempting to pose as a Gentile, was fingered on a streetcar in Warsaw by a Pole who shouted for the Gestapo to arrest the *Zyd*.

(Lessons. The world, I learned, is divided in two. There are Jews and there are goyim. There are few of us and many of them. Goyim are different from Jews. They are brutish. We are sensitive, humane. They persecute. We study. We must stick to our own, for community and safety. Goyim are to be shunned. They are to be feared. And because Jewish survival is, and has always been, precarious, we must focus our energies on ourselves, our families, our people. We live in America, but we are Jewish and alien here. It's been like this for generations. We live in their countries and they hate us. And, sometimes, they decide to murder us.)[7]

Apprehension is engendered in survivors because the concept of Righteous Gentiles smacks of historical revisionism. *They're talking about the Righteous here, the Righteous there. But there were so few, so big deal.* For most survivors, it was not simply the Nazis who perpetrated the Holocaust. It was the goyim. For the Holocaust was the apogee of two millennia of persecution by them. They have always hated the Jews, and they *will* always hate the Jew, survivors believe.

It is also the fear of revisionism which partially motivates the survivor's unwillingness to speak of Jewish collaborators. It was Christians who killed Jews, not Jews who killed their own. There are many who have already wondered, and others who will surmise that the Jews must have done something to bring this assault upon themselves. Bad things don't happen to good people, it is human nature to believe. If Jews are seen as collaborators or murderers, than the amoral image of the Jew which the Christian has perpetrated for centuries will be vindicated. And Christians will be absolved of guilt for what they have done.

It is comforting to believe in the goodness of man. An all-embracing identification with *humanity* can also provide a protective shield from attack by a group which might be prone to define you as the Other. But Jews were separated for death and will always be disjoined, Holocaust survivors assert. Survivors are, therefore, denied comfort.

Every day anew I lose my trust in the world. The Jew without positive determinants, the Catastrophe Jew . . . must get along without the trust in the world. My neighbor greets me in a friendly fashion, Bonjour, Monsieur. *I doff my hat,* Bonjour Madame. *But Madame and Monsieur are separated by interstellar distance; for yesterday a Madame looked away when they led off a Monsieur, and through the barred windows of the departing car a Monsieur viewed a Madame as if she were a stone angel from a bright and stern heaven, which is forever closed for the Jew.*[8]

And Cain fought with Abel, and almost from the outset the forces of Evil heralded their preeminence over those of Goodness. If one could not trust in one's brother, how could one place one's faith in the neighbor? So you expect less, and you anticipate the worst. "Whoever has succumbed to torture can no longer feel at home in the world. Trust in the world . . . will not be regained. . . . It is fear that henceforth reigns over him," Jean Améry wrote a few years before he committed suicide.

I often think about, of course, how there is a sort of division, a sort of schizophrenic division, you know, a compartmentalization of what happened, and it's kept tightly separated, and yet as I said, it isn't. There is this part of daily living that one has to attend to and adhere to, and family and children and their needs and everyday needs and work and so on, and that must not interfere, the other must not become so overwhelming that it will make so-called normal life unable to function. Yet it's always there; it's more a view of the world, a total world view . . . of extreme pessimism, of sort of one feels . . . of really knowing the truth about people, human nature, about death, of really knowing the truth in a way that other people don't know it. And all of the truth is harsh, and impossible to really accept, and yet you have to go on and function.[9]

Collective guilt

The breast of nurturance, the breast of succor, the breast that brings with it a primal assurance was replaced with seething coals. Survivors learned that goodness is an aberration, malice the norm. Survivors saw the impotence of piety and the tenacity of evil. Survivors saw their fellow man. And so they anxiously await the next expected blow.

12
The legacy

While the question "Why was I allowed to survive?" does not evoke guilt in all Holocaust survivors, it nonetheless claims a sense of responsibility. Few survivors became Nazi hunters, but most fulfilled an obligation to the murdered by some other means: the support of Israel, bearing children in order to sustain the continuity of the Jewish people, commemorating the Six Million, or negating revisionists by virtue of their willingness to witness. Along the way, this assertiveness helped dispel previous feelings of powerlessness and humiliation.

There is no substitute for the sheer power of personal testimony. Survivors are people, not a phenomenon. Whenever I teach a course about the Holocaust, it becomes apparent that the most important, the most *felt* resource for the student will be neither my lectures nor the assigned readings but, rather, the ninety-seven-minute videotape of a survivor, Barry Bruk, recounting what he felt, observed, and endured.

Most of us view the Holocaust from a historical perspective. It was an event in time. But we must understand that for the survivors of any trauma, the event is an ongoing one, with ongoing consequences. Sensitization to the aftereffects of the Holocaust must promote a similar awareness of the maiming potential of other tragedies.

While Holocaust survivors provide evidence of the debilitating effects of trauma, they also reflect the tremendous resilience inherent in a human being. Some commentators emphasize the former, while others insist upon the latter. But both must be recognized. On a certain level, survivors find themselves in an ironic predicament. Acknowledging their fulminating wounds implies the further, successful reach of the oppressor. Denying those hurts might imply that the onslaught was benign.

The legacy

The Holocaust survivor perceives himself to be the epitome of the victim, a direct descendant of Job. Jews have always been admonished to remember the trauma of their people: their slavery in Egypt, the genocidal plot of Haman, the destruction of the Temple, their exile to the Diaspora. The demand to remember appears in the Bible 169 times. But to focus primarily on the trauma is ultimately self-destructive, for it fosters ongoing anxiety, ongoing feelings of vulnerability. It therefore diminishes the capacity for a full life, a life of balance. The richness of Jewish heritage must not be buried beneath the memories of anguish.

Indeed, we must also acknowledge the Righteous, those whose goodness, whose moral impulses asserted themselves during those desperate times. However, to center our attention on the kind and the altruistic is merely a self-protective wish. The Holocaust exposed the evil possibilities which reside in man. "What do you want people to remember about the Holocaust?" I asked Saul Garber, who was liberated from Mauthausen. "The sufferings of human beings in a so-called civilized period, the twentieth century. We must understand how individuals can be insensitive to children's brains being splashed on their coat. How individuals cannot respond to a mother's plea not to shoot her child. If we understand how it could happen, it might help prevent future disasters."

The Holocaust exposed the ease with which we can inure ourselves to doubt or to guilt. The Holocaust exposed the ease with which man can kill and torture and justifiably believe it is the right, even the necessary, thing to do. The Holocaust exposed the ease with which we can suppress our capacity for empathy.

To refer to the Holocaust as a "monstrous, inhuman event" is to miss the point. The Holocaust was imposed by men and women on other human beings. "It was a time when there were people, not only the Germans, but the others too, what wanted to kill all the Jewish people. After they would kill the Jewish people, they would kill the black people, the brown people, the yellow people. Only people with blond hair and blue eyes would live."

And so most Holocaust survivors believe it could happen again. For those of us who did not endure the calamity, the Holocaust is a historic incident. For survivors, the Holocaust is one more manifestation of an ongoing Jewish history, a history of the antipathy of others, with its lessons for the future. Indeed, survivors insist that the Holocaust must not be seen as an isolated episode. For there was a context, a context of a group that for almost two thousand years has denied the most fundamental beliefs of their majority hosts, a context of the human strategy of finding simplistic solutions to complex problems, a context of the tendency to point the finger at a convenient scapegoat and assuage one's anxiety by acting against that target, and the context of the all too human need to feel superior to others.

Sol Feingold finally obtained a visa to enter the United States under the guise of his desire to study rabbinics. "My experience has universal implications. My first day in America, I took a bus from Miami to New York and I had to watch black women defer to me, a bum, someone who came under false pretenses to America. If someone has to suffer indignities because of what they were born, my work is never done. The world clearly hasn't changed because Auschwitz ended."

Despite the abstractness inherent in the number "six million," survivors want us to remember that these were individuals – a mother, a father, a son, a daughter. They also want us to appreciate that an entire Jewish world was lost, never to be recovered again. "The vibrant life of Eastern European Jews . . . the tumult . . . the dynamism, the culture, the publications. It was a poor life economically, and there was anti-semitism, but the vibrancy of life was indescribable. When *Shabbos* came . . . the multitude of organizations – Zionists, Bundists, Communists. When it came to elections, the tumult among Jews. It's hard to understand. . . . It's hard to comprehend. . . . The thousands of shtieblich [small synagogues]. People don't even know what was lost in Eastern Europe."

Unseemingly, new atrocities diminish our compassion for Holocaust survivors. It is as if we can only sympathize for one group at a time. Or perhaps the sheer number of ongoing atrocities normalizes them, so that we need not respond empathically to any. "I would like people should remember not only my Holocaust, but other Holocausts," Ann Charnofsky, whose parents and three brothers were killed, emphasized. "That people should *fight* more against it and not just read about it."

Soon, too soon, survivors of the Holocaust will no longer be among us. And many who know only secondhand the gas chambers, the hunger, the fear, the humiliation, will be *relieved* at their passing.

194

Numbers on forearms will no longer prod the conscience of non-Jews who already feel angry at the tattooed accusation; and some Jews, in their quest for assimilation, acceptance, or just plain "normality," will be spared another reminder of their vulnerability. All of us will be enabled to avoid the stark recognition of our own frailty and the potential callousness and cruelty of our neighbors.

"Isn't it time we put it behind us?" I am asked after a lecture at a synagogue. All too often, it is the Jew, not the Gentile, who pleads for an unburdening. The latter is more timid, more reticent about his desires for a closure that might allow him to once again treat the Jew according to his self-interest and the demands of realpolitik. But the survivor of the Holocaust will never shed the constraints of her memory.

"I have seen too much," she told me. "You live because you must. But you never forget."

Notes

Chapter 1

1. Jean Améry, *At the Mind's Limit* (New York: Schocken, 1986).
2. William C. Niederland, "Psychiatric Disorders Among Persecution Victims: A Contribution to the Understanding of the Concentration Camp Pathology and Its Aftereffects," *Journal of Nervous and Mental Diseases* 139 (1964): 458–74.
3. Leo Eitinger, *Concentration Camp Survivors in Norway and Israel* (London: Allen & Unwin, 1964), 190. See also T. DeGraaf, "Pathological Patterns of Identification in Families of Survivors of the Holocaust," *Israel Annals of Psychiatry* 13 (1975): 335–63; William C. Niederland, "The Psychiatric Evaluation of Emotional Disorders in Survivors of Nazi Persecution," in H. Krystal, ed., *Massive Psychic Trauma* (New York: International Universities Press, 1968), 8–22; P. Chodoff, "Survivors of the Nazi Holocaust," in R. Moos, ed., *Coping with Life Crisis: An Integrated Approach* (New York: Plenum, 1986), 407–15; P. Chodoff, "Late Effects of the Concentration Camp Syndrome," *Archives of General Psychiatry* 8 (1963): 323–33; K. D. Hoppe "Chronic Reactive Aggression in Survivors of Extreme Persecution," *Comprehensive Psychiatry* 12 (1971): 230–37.
4. Robert J. Lifton, "Witnessing Survival," *Transactions* (March 1978): 40–44.
5. Henry Krystal, "Patterns of Psychological Damage," in Krystal, ed., *Massive Psychic Trauma*.
6. Robert J. Lifton, "Survivors of Hiroshima and Nazi Persecution," in Krystal, ed., *Massive Psychic Trauma*.
7. Krystal, ed., *Massive Psychic Trauma*, 3.
8. Arie Nadler and Dan Ben-Shushan, "Forty Years Later: Long Term Consequences of a Massive Traumatization as Manifested by Holocaust Survivors from the City and the Kibbutz," *Journal of Consulting and Clinical Psychology* 57 (1989): 287–93. See also J. Shanan and O. Shahar, "Cognitive and Personality Functioning of Jewish Holocaust Survivors During Midlife Transition (46–55) in Israel," *Archiv für Psychologie* 135 (1983): 275–94; Na-

omi Mor, "Holocaust Messages From the Past," *Contemporary Family Therapy* 12 (1990): 371–79.

9. Joel Shanan, "Surviving the Survivors: Late Personality Development of Jewish Holocaust Survivors," *International Journal of Mental Health* 17 (1988–89): 42–71; Zev Harel, Boaz Kahana, and Eva Kahana, "Psychological Well-Being Among Holocaust Survivors and Immigrants in Israel," *Journal of Traumatic Stress* 1 (1988): 413–29; G. Butcher et al., "Survivors of the Holocaust and Their Children: Current Status and Adjustment," *Journal of Personality and Social Psychology* 41 (1981): 503–16.

10. P. Matussek, *Internment in Concentration Camp and Its Consequences* (New York: Springer-Verlag, 1975). See also Shanan and Shahar, "Cognitive and Personality Functioning of Jewish Holocaust Survivors During Midlife Transition."

11. Judith Kestenberg, "Psychoanalytic Contributions to the Problem of Survivors from Nazi Persecution," *Israel Annals of Psychiatry and Related Disciplines* 10 (1972): 311–25; Bernard Trossman, "Adolescent Children of Concentration Camp Survivors," *Canadian Psychiatric Association Journal* 12 (1968): 121–23.

12. Harvey Barocas and Carol Barocas, "Manifestations of Concentration Camp Effects on the Second Generation," *American Journal of Psychiatry* 130 (1973): 820–21.

13. Anna Kalodner, "The Socialization of Children of Concentration Camp Survivors" (Ph.D. diss., Boston University, 1987).

14. Barocas and Barocas, "Concentration Camp Effects," 821.

15. Axel Russell, "Late Psychosocial Consequences in Concentration Camp Survivors' Families," *American Journal of Orthopsychiatry* 44 (1974): 611–19.

16. Aaron Hass, *In The Shadow of the Holocaust: The Second Generation* (Ithaca, N.Y.: Cornell University Press, 1990). See also N. Solkoff, "Children of Survivors of the Nazi Holocaust: A Critical Review of the Literature," *American Journal of Orthopsychiatry* 51 (1981): 29–42; S. L. Rustin, "The Legacy Is Lost," *Journal of Contemporary Psychotherapy* 11 (1980): 32–43.

17. Shanan, "Surviving the Survivors," 47.

18. S. Davidson, "Human Reciprocity Among Jewish Prisoners in the Camps," in *The Nazi Concentration Camps* (Jerusalem, Yad Vashem), 555–72.

19. Judith Kestenberg, "Imagining and Remembering," lecture given at the Analytic Institute, Jerusalem, 1987.

20. See Judith Kestenberg, "Children Survivors of the Holocaust – 40 years Later: Reflections and Commentary," *Journal of the American Academy of Child Psychiatry* 24 (1985): 4; Y. Gampel, "I Am a Holocaust Child, Now I Am Fifty," in A. Wilson, ed., *The Holocaust Survivor and the Family* (New York: Praeger, 1990); Judith Kestenberg and Y. Gampel, "Growing Up in the Holocaust Culture," *Israel Journal of Psychiatry and Related Sciences* 20 (1983): 1–2; Sarah Moskovitz and Robert Krell, "Children Survivors of the

Holocaust: Psychological Adaptations to Survival," *Israel Journal of Psychiatry and Related Sciences* 27 (1990): 81–91.

21. William C. Niederland, "An Interpretation of the Psychological Stresses and Defenses in Concentration Camp Life and the Late Aftereffects," in Krystal, ed., *Massive Psychic Trauma*, 63.

22. Tom Segev, *The Seventh Million* (New York: Hill & Wang, 1993), 471.

23. Dorothy Rabinowitz, *New Lives* (New York: Avon, 1976), 66.

24. Segev, *Seventh Million*, 179.

25. Ibid., 183.

26. State of Israel, Public Opinion Research Institute, "Public Opinion on the Extent of Immigration," October 1949, 12.

27. Segev, 174.

28. Segev, 176.

29. Testimony of Yoel Peles (Florsheim), Moreshet Archive, A972.

30. Ben-Gurion to Yitzhak Cohen, April 10, 1961, cited in Segev, 330.

31. Segev, 478.

32. Boaz Kahana, Zev Harel, and Eva Kahana, "Predictors of Psychological Well-Being Among Survivors of the Holocaust," in John Wilson, Zev Harel, and Boaz Kahana, eds., *Human Adaption to Extreme Stress* (New York: Plenum 1988), 171–92.

33. Erik Erikson, "Identity and Life Cycle," *Psychological Issues* 1 (1959).

Chapter 2

1. Zev Harel, Boaz Kahana, Eva Kahana, "The Effects of the Holocaust: Psychiatric, Behavioral, and Survivor Perspective," *Journal of Sociology and Social Welfare* 11 (1984): 915–29; J. Hasson, "Survivors," *Community Care* (June 7, 1984): 11–14.

2. Lawrence Langer, *Holocaust Testimonies* (New Haven: Yale University Press, 1991), 65.

3. Ibid., 98.

4. Primo Levi, *The Drowned and the Saved* (New York: Summit, 1988), 81.

5. Krystal, ed., *Massive Psychic Trauma*, 4.

6. P. Chodoff, "Survivors of the Nazi Holocaust," *Children Today* 10 (5): 2–5.

7. Levi, *The Drowned and the Saved*, 76, 78.

8. Améry, *At the Mind's Limit*, 68.

Chapter 3

1. Yael Danieli, "On the Achievement of Integration in Aging Survivors of the Nazi Holocaust," *Journal of Geriatric Psychiatry* 14 (1981): 202.

2. Contact with the former Soviet Union and access to its extensive Holocaust records prompted the American Red Cross to establish a separate Holocaust and War Victims Tracing and Information Center in September 1990.

Notes

The Baltimore-based center serves as a clearinghouse, translating queries into German before forwarding them to Arolsen and making separate contact with appropriate agencies in the Commonwealth of Independent States. Of about 11,000 cases logged in less than two years, about 10,000 are people trying to find out what happened to immediate family members in the war, according to Susie Kantt, administrative supervisor of the Baltimore facility.

3. Henry Krystal, "Integration and Self Healing in Posttraumatic States," *Journal of Geriatric Psychiatry* 14 (1981): 176.
4. Danieli, "On the Achievement of Integration," 197.

Chapter 4

1. Barocas and Barocas, "Concentration Camp Effects," 821.
2. Hass, *In the Shadow of the Holocaust*, 37.
3. Ibid., 93.
4. Deborah Berger, "Children of Nazi Holocaust Survivors: A Coming of Age" (master's thesis, Goddard College, 1980), 5.
5. J. Rosen, and C. Reynolds, et al., "Sleep Disturbances in Survivors of the Nazi Holocaust," *American Journal of Psychiatry* 148 (1991): 62–66.
6. Langer, *Holocaust Testimonies*, 12.

Chapter 5

1. Améry, *At the Mind's Limit*, 29.
2. Langer, *Holocaust Testimonies*, 140.
3. Ibid., 53.
4. Ibid., 205.
5. Art Spiegelman, *Maus II* (New York: Pantheon, 1991).
6. Langer, 147.
7. Ibid., 146.
8. Kahana, Harel, and Kahana, "Predictors of Well-Being," 171–92.
9. Rabinowitz, *New Lives*, 87.
10. Langer, 52.
11. Rabinowitz, *New Lives*, 124.
12. Ibid., 109.

Chapter 6

1. Hass, *In the Shadow of the Holocaust*.

Chapter 7

1. Améry, *At the Mind's Limit*, 48.
2. Ibid., 45.

3. Eva Kahana, Boaz Kahana, Zev Harel, and T. Rosner, "Coping with Extreme Trauma," in Wilson, Harel, and Kahana, eds., *Human Adaptation to Extreme Stress*, 55–76; Kahana, Harel, and Kahana, "Predictors of Well-Being," 171–192.

Chapter 8

1. "Philip Bernstein, the U.S. Army Advisor on Jewish Affairs in Europe after the war, reported that the DP camps had the highest birth rate of any of the Jewish communities in the world. In Zielsheim alone, he noted in a January 1948 article, a new baby was born every day." In William Helmreich, *Against All Odds* (New York: Simon & Schuster, 1992), 129.
2. Helmreich, 121. Also Kahana, Harel, and Kahana, "Predictors of Psychological Well-Being," 177.
3. Helmreich, 121. Also Kahana, Harel, and Kahana, 177.
4. Helmreich, 126.
5. Ibid., 126.
6. James Pennebaker, S. Barger, and John Tiebout, "Disclosure of Traumas and Health Among Holocaust Survivors" *Psychosomatic Medicine* 51 (1989): 577–89.
7. Helmreich, 127.
8. For a more complete discussion of survivor–child dynamics, see Hass, *In the Shadow of the Holocaust*.
9. Barocas and Barocas, "Concentration Camp Effects," 821.
10. Kalodner, "The Socialization of Children of Concentration Camp Survivors."
11. Lenore Podietz et al., "Engagement in Families of Holocaust Survivors," *Journal of Marital and Family Therapy* 10 (1984): 49.
12. Hass, *In the Shadow of the Holocaust*, 92.
13. Ibid., 63.
14. Hass, *In the Shadow of the Holocaust*.
15. Levi, *The Drowned and the Saved*, 12.
16. Sophie Kav-Venaki, Arie Nadler, and Hadas Gershoni, "Sharing the Holocaust Experience: Communication Behaviors and Their Consequences in Families of Ex-partisans and Ex-prisoners of Concentration Camps," *Family Process* 24 (1985): 273–80.
17. Bernard Trossman, "Adolescent Children of Concentration Camp Survivors," *Canadian Psychiatric Association Journal* 12 (1968): 121–23.
18. Robert Prince, *The Legacy of the Holocaust: Psychohistorical Themes in the Second Generation* (Ann Arbor, Mich.: UMI Research Press, 1985).
19. Hillel Klein, "Children of the Holocaust: Mourning and Bereavement," *International Yearbook of the Association for Child Psychiatry and Allied Professions*, vol. 2 (New York: Wiley, 1973), 393–410.

20. Martin Bergmann and Milton Jacovy, eds., *Generations of the Holocaust* (New York: Basic Books, 1982), 311.
21. Prince, *The Legacy of the Holocaust*; Shamai Davidson, "Transgenerational Transmission in the Families of Holocaust Survivors," *International Journal of Family Psychiatry* 1 (1980): 95–112.
22. David Heller, "Themes of Culture and Ancestry Among Children of Concentration Camp Survivors," *Psychiatry* 45 (1982): 247–61.

Chapter 9

1. Niddah 16b, cited by George Moore in "Fate and Free Will in the Jewish Philosophies According to Josephus," *Harvard Theological Review* (Cambridge, 1929), vol. 22, p. 371.
2. Reeve Robert Brenner, *The Faith and Doubt of Holocaust Survivors* (New York: Free Press, 1980), 129.
3. David Birnbaum, *God and Evil: A Jewish Perspective* (Hoboken, N.J.: Ktav, 1989).
4. Rabbi Immanuel Jakobovits disagrees. He believes that the doctrine of collective reward and punishment is restricted to the Jewish national experience only in the land of Israel.
5. In a letter to his brother (Rabbi Yeshiah Shapiro) in Palestine in the winter of 1943.
6. Pesach Schindler, *Hasidic Responses to the Holcaust* (Hoboken, N.J.: Ktav, 1990), 38.
7. Ibid., 38.
8. Ibid., 26, 27.
9. Perhaps the first use of "Holocaust" to describe the destruction of European Jewry was by the American Jewish historian Rufus Learsi, in *Israel: A History of the Jewish People* (1949).
10. Brenner, *Faith and Doubt*, 233.
11. His ideas were first expressed in R. L. Rubenstein, *After Auschwitz: Radical Theology and Contemporary Judaism* (Indianapolis: Bobbs-Merrill, 1966). Cf. also R. L. Rubenstein, *The Cunning of History: The Holocaust and the American Future* (New York: Harper & Row, 1975).
12. R. L. Rubenstein, "Covenant and Holocaust," in Yehuda Bauer, ed., *Remembering for the Future: Working Papers and Addenda* (Oxford: Pergamon, 1989), vol. 1, 666–71; his new position is also developed in R. L. Rubenstein and J. K. Roth, *Approaches to Auschwitz: The Holocaust and Its Legacy* (Atlanta: John Knox Press, 1987).
13. See E. Berkovits, *Faith After the Holocaust* (New York: Ktav, 1973); E. Berkovits, *God, Man, and History: A Jewish Interpretation* (New York: Jonathan David, 1959); and E. Berkovits, *With God in Hell* (New York: Sanhedrin Press, 1979).
14. See E. Fackenheim, *God's Presence in History: Jewish Affirmations and Philo-*

sophical Reflections (New York: New York University Press, 1970); E. Fackenheim, *The Jewish Return into History: Reflections in the Age of Auschwitz and a New Jerusalem* (New York: Schocken, 1978); E. Fackenheim, *To Mend the World* (New York: Schocken, 1982).

15. Brenner, *Faith and Doubt*.
16. Ibid., 71.
17. Ibid., 58.
18. Ibid., 98.
19. Ibid., 110.
20. Ibid.
21. Brenner, 57.
22. Kahana, Harel, and Kahana, "Predictors of Psychological Well-Being," 177. According to the authors, 57% of their sample of 275 survivors who attended the Washington Gathering of survivors reported religious affiliation as Conservative, 23% as Orthodox, 11% as Reform.
23. Brenner notes that by the 1970s, 14 percent of those in his Israeli survivor sample who had given up observance had returned to those practices. He hypothesizes that some of this return may be linked to the miraculous character of the Six Day War of June 1967 and the Yom Kippur War of 1973.
24. Helmreich, *Against All Odds*, 200.
25. Ibid., 259. Survivors have transmitted this commitment to their children, who also have a lower intermarriage rate than their American born Jewish contemporaries. See Hass, *In the Shadow of the Holocaust*.
26. Helmreich, 185, 186.

Chapter 10

1. Bruno Bettelheim, *The Informed Heart* (New York: Free Press, 1960).
2. Helmreich, *Against All Odds*, 84.
3. Améry, *At the Mind's Limit*, 70.
4. Robert Abzug, *Inside the Vicious Heart* (New York: Oxford University Press, 1985).
5. See also Marcus Smith, *The Harrowing of Hell Dachau* (Albuquerque: University of New Mexico Press, 1972). Smith describes scenes of inmates screaming and kicking the mutilated bodies of German soldiers lying on the ground.
6. Cited in Michael Bar-Zohar, *The Avengers* (New York: Hawthorn Books, 1967), 22.
7. Interview with Carmi, *Jerusalem Post* International Edition, July 22, 1989, 9.
8. Bar-Zohar, *The Avengers*, 24.
9. Segev, 143.

Notes

10. "Poison Bread Fells 1900 German Captives in U.S. Prison Camp Near Nuremberg," *New York Times*, April 20, 1946, p. 6.
11. Segev, *Seventh Million*, 141.
12. Bar-Zohar, 73–6.
13. Segev, 261.
14. Supreme Court Opinion, Jerusalem Ministry of Justice, 1959, XIII: 1056.
15. Peter Wyden, *Stella* (New York: Simon & Schuster, 1992), 273–76.
16. Améry, *At the Mind's Limit*, 69. Améry's anger and the lack of satisfying expression proved fatal. He committed suicide.
17. Susan Jacoby, *Wild Justice* (New York: Harper & Row, 1983), 2–3.
18. Améry, 72.

Chapter 11

1. Améry, *At the Mind's Limit*, 66.
2. Cited by Lucy Dawidowicz, *The War Against the Jews* (New York: Holt, Rinehart & Winston, 1975), 149, from "Trial of the Major War Criminals," Document 1919 RS.
3. Ernst Nolte, "Between Myth and Revisionism?" in H. W. Koch, ed., *Aspects of the Third Reich* (New York: St. Martin's, 1985), 37; and Ernst Nolte, *Die Krise des liberalen Systems und die faschistischen Bewegungen* (Munich: Piper, 1968), 442.
4. Nolte, "Between Myth and Revisionism?" 17–38; and Ernst Nolte, *Das Vergehen der Vergangenheit* (Berlin: Ullstein, 1987), 171–79.
5. Charles Maier, *The Unmasterable Past: History, Holocaust, and German National Identity* (Cambridge: Cambridge University Press, 1989).
6. "The Public's Position on the Unification of Germany," *Yediot Aharonot* 6 (July 1990): 1.
7. Hass, *In the Shadow of the Holocaust*, 106.
8. Améry, 94.
9. Langer, *Holocaust Testimonies*, 59.

Index

205

Index

Index

deportation, 12

depression, 2, 3, 4, 60, 92; in children of survivors, 8; inability to mourn and, 50; in search for loved ones, 99

determination, 84

developmental course, 22

developmental stage: and psychological adjustment, 1

difference, sense of, 40, 43, 88, 89

differential experiences: and adjustment, 9–10

DIN (Dahm Y'Israel Nokeam), 168–9

disillusionment, 61

displaced persons camps, 89, 99, 111; birthrate in, 120

Divine will (concept), 150

divorce, 123

dreams, xiii, 65–8

East Germans, 180, 184

Eichmann, Adolf, 20–1, 171

Eitinger, Leo, 2–3

election, doctrine of, 150

Em Habanim Semechah (Teichthal), 147

emotional effects of Holocaust, xv, 3–4, 84–5

emotional numbing, 35, 45–6, 52, 62, 104, 108–9

emotional strains, 82, 83

emotions, 4, 62

empathy, 84, 142, 193

Endc, 186

enjoyment, 75, 76, 77–9, 89, 92, 101

entitlement: in children of survivors, 29, 131

Eretz Yisrael, 147, 148

Erikson, Erik, 22

estrangement, 1, 73, 84–9

Etzel (militant underground movement), 36, 167

European Jews, 185–9

evil, 144, 146, 149, 153–4, 156, 160, 190, 191, 193; knowledge of, xii, triumph of, 60

facade, 73

Fackenheim, Emil, 150–1

failure to save loved ones, 26–31, 39–40, 49–50; atonement for, 27; guilt in, 127

faith, 148; crisis of, 144; effect of Holocaust experiences on, 151–6, 157, 160; Holocaust as test of, 147; in humanity, 2; loss of, 155–6; in the miraculous, 144, 149

family(ies), 2, 120–42; forming new, 3, 7, 31, 44, 92; prewar, 139, 144; reconstituted, 29, 67, 79, 104; surviving, 33, 101

fantasy(ies), 10; of parents' Holocaust life, 140; of reunion, 99; of revenge, 163

fear, 4, 9–10, 13, 58, 75; of abandonment, 15; activation of buried, 65; denial of, 83; realistic, 37–8; and revenge, 164; unwarranted, 48, 127–8

feelings: inaccessibility to, 4; repression of, 104; *see also* emotions

Feldalfing (displaced persons camp), 172

Final Solution, 34, 99, 137, 161, 189; roles of Jews in, 117

Flossenburg, xvii, 71, 99

food, 60–1, 98

forgetting, 47

forgiveness, 175–6, 181

"Form of Guilt Liquidation, A" (Habermas), 179

formative years, xi, xvi; *see also* adolescence

friends, friendship, 86–7

future orientation, xiv, 43

Gawenda, Alois, 170–1

Gentiles, 133, 146; children placed with, 15, 16; marriage to, 123, (*see also* intermarriage); posing as, 1, 9, 61, 84, 89, 97, 185; saving Jews, 188–9

German culture, 106

German people, 178; blaming, for Nazi atrocities, 181–2; honor of, 179–81; kindness of, 89, 182–3

German reunification, xviii, 89, 184–5

Germany: *Holocaust* miniseries shown in, 113; reaction to Holocaust in, 180–2; rejuvenation of, 177–8, 183–4

Geulah Shelemah (Final Redemption), 147

ghettos, 1, 12; Jewish police in, 117

giving up, 11

207

Index

Index

Index

Index

Index